English for Academic Study

Grammar for Writing

Study Book

Anne Vicary

University of
Reading

Garnet
EDUCATION

Credits

Published by

Garnet Publishing Ltd.
8 Southern Court
South Street
Reading RG1 4QS, UK

Copyright © 2014 International Study and Language Institute, The University of Reading, and the author.

The right of Anne Vicary to be identified as the author of this work has been asserted by her in accordance with the Copyright, Designs and Patents Act 1988.

University of Reading and the University shield are trade marks of The University of Reading and are not to be reproduced without authorization.

All rights reserved.

No part of this publication may be reproduced, stored in a retrieval system, or transmitted in any form or by any means, electronic, mechanical, photocopying, recording or otherwise, without the prior permission of the Publisher. Any person who does any unauthorized act in relation to this publication may be liable to criminal prosecution and civil claims for damages.

This edition first published 2014.

Reprinted 2014, 2015, 2016, 2017, 2018.

ISBN: 978-1-78260-070-1

British Library Cataloguing-in-Publication Data
A catalogue record for this book is available from the British Library.

Production

Project manager:	Martin Moore
Editorial team:	Matthew George, Chris Little, Sue Coll
Design and layout:	Simon Ellway

Printed and bound in Lebanon by International Press: interpress@int-press.com

Acknowledgements

This book would not have been written without the vision and support of my colleague, Anne Pallant. She has always been a keen advocate of the notion that the context of the academic writing process provides the optimum opportunity for students to improve their awareness of grammatical choice and its impact on the reader. Her creative feedback, encouragement and determination have been a source of inspiration throughout the course of this project.

Earlier versions of this material were created by a team of experienced teachers which included not only Anne Pallant and myself, but also Clare McCullagh and Helen Fraser. I should like to thank them for their research and invaluable contributions which were instrumental in laying the foundations for this book.

Several colleagues at the International Study and Language Institute at the University of Reading have contributed their time and energy in providing feedback following classroom trials of these materials. I would like to thank, in particular, Louise Bourguignon, Sarah Brewer, Margaret Collins, Deborah Murphy, Sarah Pachonik and Emily Salvesen for

this. Deborah Murphy has, in addition, authored two of the tasks in this book. Thanks are also due to colleagues at other Higher Education institutions who have contributed to the process of trialling and evaluating this material, and to students outside the classroom who have willingly contributed feedback while studying independently.

Special thanks are due to all those students and friends who have generously donated their writing to be used anonymously in this book. These texts have provided crucial evidence of common grammatical errors; they also show how writers make grammatical choices and how they apply this knowledge to the delicate and rewarding task of academic text construction.

Finally, I would like to thank my project manager at Garnet, Martin Moore, whose practical approach, perceptive comments and constructive suggestions have been invaluable in the preparation of these materials for publication.

Anne Vicary

Pages 55–56, gap fill text reproduced with kind permission of *The Guardian* newspaper. Copyright Guardian News & Media Ltd 2010.

Pages 98–99, Chinese way of life text, reprinted with permission from the National Academies Press, Copyright 1984, National Academy of Sciences.

Pages 124–126, Byron Review © Crown Copyright 2008. Contains public sector information licensed under the Open Government Licence v1.0, www.nationalarchives.gov.uk/doc/open-government-licence/open-government-licence.htm.

Pages 124–126, video games and aggression texts, reprinted from *Aggression and Violent behaviour*, 4 (2), Griffiths, M. Violent video games and aggression: a review of the literature, 203–212., Copyright (1999) with permission from Elsevier.

Pages 124-126, educational benefits of videogames text, Griffiths, M. (2002). The educational benefits of Videogames. *Education and Health*, 20(3), 47–51. Reproduced with kind permission of Dr Mark Griffiths.

Pages 150–151, Community service text © Crown Copyright 2008. Contains public sector information licensed under the Open Government Licence v1.0, www.nationalarchives.gov.uk/doc/open-government-licence/open-government-licence.htm.

Pages 176–177, free-trade agreement text, taken from *Why America Needs to Support Free Trade*. The Heritage Foundation (2004). Reproduced with kind permission of the author Ana Eiras and The Heritage Foundation.

Page 185, Text 1, taken from the U.S. Global Change Research Information Office, © World Meteorological Organization.

Page 190, one-person households graph, data adapted from Office for National Statistics data and licensed under the Open Government License v.1.0.

Page 230, oil production graph, sourced from Wikipedia, http://en.wikipedia.org/wiki/File:Saudi_Oil_Production.png. Image has been used under the CC-BA-SA 3.0 license, http://creativecommons.org/licenses/by-sa/3.0/legalcode.

Page 231, SSE Composite Index graph, sourced from Wikipedia, http://en.wikipedia.org/wiki/File:SSE_Composite_Index.png. Image has been used under the CC-BA-SA 3.0 license, http://creativecommons.org/licenses/by-sa/3.0/legalcode.

Contents

b Book map   4

i Introduction   6

g Glossary of grammatical terms   7

1 Starting out   11

2 Information flow within a text   40

3 Looking back   59

4 Showing logical links (1)   81

5 Showing logical links (2)   103

6 Expressing shades of meaning   130

7 Expressing condition   154

8 Avoiding person-based writing   180

9 Using relative clauses   200

a Appendix A: Using *a*, *an*, *the* or no article   220
       Appendix B: Describing data   226
       Appendix C: Referring to academic sources   232
       Appendix D: Sample student essay   236

i Index   239

Unit title		Grammar focus
1 **Starting out**	A	Formal style • Subject–verb agreement • Present simple • Plural nouns for situations in general • *There is/are*
	B	Quantity expressions • Countable/uncountable nouns • Present continuous
	C	Simple clauses: S/V/O/C • Unit review
2 **Information flow within a text**	A	Using simple noun phrases
	B	Using complex noun phrases
	C	Using present simple passive • Unit review
3 **Looking back**	A	Past simple active • Present perfect active
	B	Uses of present perfect
	C	Using the present perfect in introductions • Present perfect or past simple? • Unit review
4 **Showing logical links (1)**	A	Short linking words • Sentence-connecting words • Simple and compound sentences
	B	Paired linking words within a sentence
	C	Linking words in paragraphs • Unit review
5 **Showing logical links (2)**	A	Using subordinators to make complex sentences
	B	Using further subordinators to make complex sentences
	C	Using linking words with noun phrases • Review of Units 4 and 5
6 **Expressing shades of meaning**	A	Modal verbs • Expressing certainty/uncertainty • Using modals in passive voice
	B	Semi-modal verbs • Giving advice and making recommendations
	C	Modal and semi-modal verbs • Conveying stance and building an argument • Intensifying words • Unit review

Unit title		Grammar focus
7 **Expressing condition**	**A**	Likely events (first conditionals) • Laws of nature ('zero' conditionals) • Using *unless* to give warnings • Modal and semi-modal verbs from Unit 6 are also reviewed
	B	Unlikely events (second conditionals) • Modal and semi-modal verbs in conditionals
	C	Impossible events (third conditionals) • Unit review
8 **Avoiding person-based writing**	**A**	Abstract and concrete noun phrases • Summary nouns
	B	Impersonal sentence structure to discuss opinions and refer to data
	C	Applying impersonal style to academic writing • Unit review
9 **Using relative clauses**	**A**	Defining relative clauses: expanding a subject noun phrase • Reducing relative clauses
	B	Expanding an object noun phrase • *Whose* • *Where, when* and *why*
	C	Non-defining relative clauses • Using *which* to refer back to a previous idea • Unit review

A complete *Answer Key* is available online at www.englishforacademicstudy.com in the *Student Resources* section.

i Introduction

1 Aims of the course

This book is for you if you are a learner of English as an additional language, and you want to improve your academic writing. If you already have an IELTS score (or equivalent) of 4.0–6.5, or you are preparing for an exam to assess your level of academic English, this book will help to increase your grammatical knowledge and ensure that you understand how to *apply* it to academic writing tasks. The book uses a step-by-step approach to guide you through the logic which underlies grammatical patterns. It demonstrates how you can use your knowledge of grammar to build a well-constructed academic text.

This book will be useful for you if you are preparing to study at an English-medium university or college, or if you are already studying in an English-speaking academic environment, but you feel that your current level of grammatical understanding prevents you from expressing your ideas at a sufficient level of complexity and in a suitably academic style. Your writing will become more confident and fluent as you understand how to make the right grammatical choices to convey your message accurately to the reader.

2 Structure of the course

The book has nine units and four appendices. Each unit is divided into three stages: Stages A and B aim to expand your knowledge, and Stage C acts as an extension and review section. It shows how the grammatical points you have studied can be used within written texts and essays; this will help you to consolidate your understanding. There is also a self-check test at the end of every unit. A complete *Answer key* is available online at www.englishforacademicstudy.com in the *Student resources* section. See page 4 for a full *Book map*, listing the contents of each unit.

The units follow a common pattern: learning objectives are clearly listed at the beginning of each unit, and these are itemized for you again at the beginning of each new stage. At the core of the book are self-study tasks. You will also find regular grammar explanations to help you in blue boxes. Take notice too of the *Grammar notes* in purple. Use the *Glossary of grammatical terms* to refresh your memory of grammatical terminology as necessary.

3 How to use this book

It is advisable to work through the book at your own pace; start at Unit 1 and read all of it. Don't rush through the units; complete the tasks *before* you check the *Answer key*, to test how well you have understood and assimilated the new information. It is important to spend time on each point and check that you fully understand it; there is a strong correlation between grammatical accuracy and good academic essays. Strong academic writers display good understanding and use of grammar: it is *impossible* to produce an academic essay of a high standard if grammatical knowledge is weak. Grammar is important!

Bibliography

Biber, D., Johansson, S., Leech, G., Conrad, S., & Finegan, E. (1999). *Longman Grammar of Spoken and Written English*. Harlow: Longman.

Hinkel, E. (2003) *Teaching Academic ESL Writing*. Mahwah, NJ: Lawrence Erlbaum Associates.

Leech, G. (1971). *Meaning and the English Verb*. (2nd ed.). Harlow: Longman.ß

Glossary of grammatical terms

Note: Names of word classes (e.g., **adjective**, **noun**) are in **bold** in the left-hand column.

Term	Definition	Example(s)
abstract noun	something which does not physically exist; you cannot touch, see or feel it	hypothesis; idea; awareness
active voice	when the subject of the clause performs the action (see also *passive voice*)	S The engineers **repaired** the fault.
adjectival clause (see *relative clause*)		
adjective	describes the noun	a **difficult** problem The lecture was **interesting**.
adverb	describes how the verb is performed	Morrison (2013) **rightly** draws attention to empirical evidence.
article	*a(n)* or *the* before a noun	This is **a** report on **the** banking system in India.
auxiliary verb	a verb (*be*, *have*, *do* or modal) which precedes the main verb to 'help' it	The system **has** failed. The economy **is** growing.
clause	a group of words which contains only one subject and one verb	S V Palm oil plantations are common in this area.
complement	an adjective or noun used after some verbs (e.g., *to be*; *to seem*; *to become*) to complete the clause	He seemed **interested**. She has become **a professor**.
complex noun phrase	a simple noun phrase with extra description	determiner noun noun **The research organization** is expanding.
complex sentence	a sentence which consists of a subordinate clause and a stand-alone, main clause (see *subordinate clause*)	main clause subordinate clause They studied hard because they wanted to pass the exam.
compound sentence	two or more simple clauses joined together by *and, but, so, or*	The room was full, but everyone could hear the lecture.
concrete noun	something which physically exists	computer; bank
conditional sentence	when an *if* clause is used within a sentence to show that one thing takes place *only* if the other thing happens	If the crops fail, there is no food to eat.
countable noun	a noun which has single units that you can count; it can have a plural form	assignment – assignments; place – places; apple – apples

Term	Definition	Example(s)
determiner	a word that precedes a noun phrase (e.g., *all*; *the/a*; *several*; *some*; *my, his, this*; *one*; *two*; *many*; *a few*)	**All** the students are interested. **Some** of her ideas are useful. **One** of the students volunteered as class representative.
first-person pronoun	*I* or *we* (Do not use in beginners' academic writing.)	**I** study at the University of Reading.
impersonal	not relating to personal facts about the writer	The United Nations website is considered useful. *Not*: I think that the United Nations website is useful. ✗
infinitive zero infinitive	*to* + verb ~~to~~ + verb	It was difficult **to find** a solution. They could not **find** a solution.
irregular verb	a verb which has an unpredictable past simple or past participle form	teach – taught (*past simple*) – taught (*past participle*) swim – swam (*past simple*) – swum (*past participle*)
modal verb	a verb which expresses a shade of opinion or belief; it is an auxiliary verb, not a main verb; it is followed by the zero infinitive	The students **should** study harder.
noun	a 'name' of a person, place or thing; it can stand alone or be the headword of a noun phrase.	lecture headword the first lecture
object	a thing or a person that follows a subject and verb; it is directly affected by the subject	The lack of resources creates **a problem.**
passive voice	when the subject of the clause does not perform the action (see also *active voice*) 1. used when no one needs to know the person or thing that performs the action 2. used when the person or thing that performs the action needs to be 'new information' at the end of the sentence	1. The first printing press **was invented** in approximately 1040 CE. 2. The first printing press **was invented** in the 1040s **by Bi Sheng.**
person-based noun	a noun which refers to a person	**They** work all day. **The employee** left early.
plural	more than one thing or person	books; students
preposition	a small word which shows the relationship between two ideas	The Prime Minster **of** Great Britain lives **at** 10 Downing Street **in** London.

Term	Definition	Example(s)
prepositional phrase (PP)	a group of words including a preposition + noun	The lecture **on information systems** (*preposition* on; *noun* information)
pronoun	represents a noun or a previous idea	Zaynab gave an interesting presentation. **She** is a very good speaker. She did it without notes. **This** allowed her to maintain eye contact with the audience.
punctuation	symbols used to separate ideas when writing to make information easier for the reader to understand	**,** comma **.** full stop **;** semi-colon
quantity expression	to describe 'how many' or 'how much'	**Some** lectures are interesting. There is **much** pollution in megacities.
relative clause	a new clause which gives more information about a previous noun; use *who, whom, which, that, whose, where, when* or *why* to begin the clause	The journal article **which he recommended** was useful.
second-person pronoun	*you* (s. and pl.) (Do not use in beginners' academic writing.)	It is difficult to write when **you** are tired.
semi-modal verb	a verb which expresses a shade of opinion or belief; it differs slightly in form from a modal verb	The government **ought** to cut energy prices.
simple noun phrase	a determiner + single noun; or pronoun; or uncountable noun	the organization; he; effectiveness
simple sentence	a sentence which contains only one clause	The lecture theatre **was** full. (S = The lecture theatre; V = was)
singular	one thing or person	book; student
subject	the thing or person which comes in front of verb; it directly affects the object	**The lack of resources** creates a problem.
subject–verb agreement	the form of the verb must match the subject of the clause	The exam**s are** being marked by external lecturers. She agree**s** with the first marker.
subordinate clause	a clause which is used to add a relationship to the ideas in the main clause	They studied hard **because they wanted to pass the exam**. (main clause: They studied hard; subordinate clause: because they wanted to pass the exam)
subordinator	the word which signals the relationship between the subordinate clause and the main clause	*because; whereas; although*

Term	Definition	Example(s)
third-person pronoun	*he/she/it* (singular) *they* (plural)	**It** is difficult. **They** are from China.
uncountable noun	a noun which is considered to be made up of a single mass; it cannot be used in the plural form.	information; research; money; food
verb	shows a: 1. physical action 2. state of being 3. mental process	1. The students **read** the book. 2. The campus **is** attractive. 3. Johns (2006) **believes** that …

Note that the terms: 1 *noun*, 2 *subject*, 3 *object* and 4 *complement* are short form for: 1 *noun phrase*, 2 *subject noun phrase*, 3 *object noun phrase* and 4 *complement noun phrase*. Look at the sentences below.

a. The theatre is in the centre of London.
   'The theatre' is a *noun*, which is short for *noun phrase*. It is also the *subject*, which is short for *subject noun phrase*.

b. The lecture theatre is the largest room in the building.
   'The lecture theatre' is a *noun* (or *noun phrase*). It is also the *subject* (or *subject noun phrase*). 'The largest room in the building' is the *complement*, short for *complement noun phrase*.

c. The lecturer marked all the essays.
   'The lecturer' is a *noun* (or *noun phrase*). It is also the *subject* (or *subject noun phrase*). 'All the essays' is an *object*, short for *object noun phrase*.

1 Starting out

In this unit you will:

- examine some of the basic features of grammar for academic writing
- practise correcting common errors in student writing

Stage A

In this stage you will:

- study formal and impersonal styles of writing
- examine simple clauses: subject–verb agreement
- learn to use the present simple tense to describe permanent events
- learn to use plural nouns to describe situations in general
- learn to use *there is* and *there are* to present new information

Task 1 Formality in academic writing

1.1 Read the sentence pairs below and decide which has the more formal style, a or b. Tick (✔) the correct box.

1. a I live in Tokyo, the capital city of Japan, which is on the east coast of the country. I travel around easily. ☐

   b. Tokyo, the capital city of Japan, is located on the east coast of the country. The transport system is efficient. ☐

2. a People use their own cars instead of taking the bus, so there is more air pollution. ☐

   b. We use our own cars instead of taking the bus, so we create more air pollution. ☐

3. a In Bangkok there are traditional wooden houses along the river. ☐

   b. In Bangkok you can see traditional wooden houses along the river. ☐

1.2 Re-read the sentences and answer the following questions.

1. Which sentence:
   a. gives information about the writer? _____
   b. gives information about the writer and his friends? _____
   c. speaks to the reader as a friend? _____
2. What words does the writer use:
   a. In 2a instead of *we* and *our*? _____
   b. In 3a instead of *you can see*? _____

Grammar note: Academic writing is used for discussing **facts** and **ideas** about the world. It does not give personal details. The writer does not know the reader, and so does not address him or her as a friend. Academic writing style, therefore, is not informal and personal. It is **formal** and **impersonal**. (Impersonal means avoiding *I*, *you*, *we*.)

1.3   **Read the following paragraphs from a student essay. Rewrite them in a formal, impersonal style by changing the words in bold:**

You can see many important museums where I live in Italy.

There are many important museums in Italy.

I live in Beijing, the capital city of China, **which is** in the north-east of the country. **You can see** many new offices, factories and shops. The cities are polluted because **we** use **our** cars to go to work every day. **You cannot see** many trees, and some rivers do not have clear water. Air and water pollution is becoming more serious.

Diet is also changing. **We** are wealthier than a generation ago, and **we** now always have enough to eat. **We** also understand more about which food is healthy, which means **we** eat more fish and chicken and less red meat than before. **You can see** more supermarkets now, so food shopping is easier.

Making your writing impersonal

Academic writing is usually impersonal. Therefore, a **third-person pronoun** or a **noun** is used as the subject of a sentence, rather than a first- or second-person pronoun.

	Singular pronoun	Plural pronoun
Third person	he/she/it	they

	Singular noun	Plural noun
	a/the person	people
	a/the supermarket	supermarkets
	a/the government	governments
	a/the book	books

Subject–verb agreement

The noun or pronoun that controls the verb is called the **subject**. It is important to match the subject with the verb. This is called **subject–verb agreement**.

Singular noun Subject	Singular verb Verb	
Tokyo	has	good public transport.
This law	is	unpopular
The book	contains	useful information.

Plural noun Subject	Plural verb Verb	
These laws	are	unpopular
Books	contain	useful information.

1.4 **Circle the correct form of the verb in the table.**

Subject	Verb	
The supermarket	*is / are*	closed.
Orangutans	*is / are*	intelligent animals.
They	*walks / walk*	slowly.
She	*studies / study*	every day.

Task 2 Using the present simple to describe permanent events

The present simple tense is very important in academic writing. It is often used to discuss:
a. ideas and facts which are always true
b. habits and activities which regularly happen

These are called **permanent events**.

2.1 **Study each sentence. Is it type a (ideas and facts) or type b (habits and activities)?**
1. People use their cars to go to work every day. _b_
2. Heavily loaded aeroplanes use more fuel than empty ones. _____
3. Management style sometimes affects the employees. _____
4. The cause of earthquakes is the sudden release of energy in the Earth's crust. _____
5. This energy creates seismic waves. _____

Grammar note: Using an adverb of frequency, such as *sometimes*, *occasionally*, *every day*, *often* or *always*, helps to indicate that an activity happens regularly. Because the activity happens more than once, it is considered 'permanent' (even if it is only once a year!).

2.2 **The sentences below all refer to permanent events. Complete the sentences with the correct verb from the box.**

does not reach	do not eat	understand	are (x2)	have (x2)

1. Most cities _____ are _____ polluted.
2. Very often, food aid _____ the people who need it.
3. Not enough rivers _____ clear water.
4. People _____ generally wealthier than a generation ago.
5. Families in the UK usually _____ enough food to eat.
6. People _____ more about which foods are healthy.
7. Vegetarians _____ meat.

Task 3	Present simple tense – form

The sentences in the table below show the form of the present simple tense.

Positive statements		
Subject	**Verb**	
Student**s**	work	in the library between lectures.
The student	work**s**	in the library between lectures.

Negative statements				
Subject	**Auxiliary verb**	*not*	**Bare infinitive**	
Student**s**	do	not	work	in the library between lectures.
The student	do**es**	not	work	in the library between lectures.

Questions				
Auxiliary verb	**Subject**	**Bare infinitive**		
Do	student**s**	work	in the library between lectures?	
Do**es**	the student	work	in the library between lectures?	

Grammar note: 'Auxiliary' means 'giving help or support'. Auxiliary verbs 'help' with the construction of some verb tenses.

The auxiliary verb *do* is used with the present simple to form:

- negative sentences
- questions

3.1 Study the verb table and fill in the missing information.

Present simple of the verb *to learn*

Positive statements				
Subject			**Verb**	
Students			learn	English.
He/She			_____	English.
Negative statements				
Subject	**Auxiliary verb**	*not*	**Bare infinitive**	
Students	do	not	learn	Science.
He/She	_____	_____	_____	Science.
Questions				
Auxiliary verb	**Subject**		**Bare infinitive**	
_____	the students		_____	English?
Does	he/she		learn	English?

3.2 Write sentences using the prompts below.

(+) Positive statement **(−)** Negative statement **(?)** Question

1. students / have / classes in the evening **(−)**

   Students do not have classes in the evening.

2. the university library / open / on Sundays **(+)**

   _____

3. many students / go / home / in the holidays **(?)**

   _____

4. the government / usually / pay / for childcare **(−)**

   _____

5. the committee / discuss / new projects / every month **(+)**

   _____

6. shoppers / spend / more money / in summer **(?)**

   _____

7. international students / like / English food **(−)**

   _____

3.3 Study the verb table and complete the missing information.

Grammar note: If the main verb is *to be*, the auxiliary verb *do* is not used in negative sentences and questions.

Present simple of the verb *to be*

Positive statements			
Subject	**Verb**		
Students	are		young.
He/She	_____		young.
Negative statements			
Subject	**Verb**	*not*	
Students	_____	_____	young.
He/She	is	not	young.
Questions			
Verb	**Subject**		
_____	the students		young?
_____	he/she		young?

Grammar note: In spoken English, we often use short forms of verbs like *be*, *will*, *have*: for example: *They're students; He's not young.* In formal, academic writing, however, you should use full forms.

3.4 In these sentences from student essays, there are mistakes in the form of the present simple tense. Circle the subject of each sentence and correct the verb.

1. Depression is occurs for several reasons.

   (Depression) occurs for several reasons. _____

2. Do they interested in English?

   _____

3. Developing countries are depend on aid from charities.

   _____

4. Dubai have many universities.

   _____

5. The population of Tokyo are high.

   _____

6. Many people in Oman speaks English.

   _____

7. Students cook for themselves every day?

   _____

8. People does not seem to be interested.

    _____

9. IT skills are not only benefit children but adults too.

    _____

10. Nowadays, developing countries are need help from developed countries.

    _____

11. Accidents are happen frequently on this road.

    _____

12. Most animals are die if there is insufficient water.

    _____

Task 4   Using plural nouns to describe situations in general

It is common to use a plural noun without *the* to write in an impersonal way about people or things in general.

Study the following examples:

a. *Students usually make friends easily.*
   This means: **in general**, students make friends easily, or **most** students find it easy to make friends.

b. *Families are wealthier than before.*
   This means: **in general**, families are wealthier than before, or **most** families have more money than they had in the past.

4.1 **Read the paragraphs from student essays. Rewrite them to refer to people or things in general. Change the bold words.**

The university **professor** is not well paid.

University professors are not well paid.

A wide gap still exists between **woman and man**. For example, **the** job **opportunity** for **woman is** fewer. **The employer claims** that if **woman has** enough ability, **she** will get **a job**. However, statistics show this is not true. The government should prosecute **the employer** who **does** not follow the equal opportunities law.

There are many benefits to travel. When **the traveller visits new country, she** finds many interesting differences such as **the house, shop** and **religious building**. Travel is also good for practising **the foreign language** and understanding more about **the different culture**. It also broadens **person's mind**.

Writers often use *there is* or *there are* to present new information to the reader. After the new information is presented, more information about it is usually given in the rest of the sentence or in the next sentence.

Study the following examples:

                           introducing topic of 'Windsor'   adding more information

In the UK, there is a small town called Windsor, which has a famous castle.

This writer thinks that the reader might not have heard of *Windsor*, so begins by introducing the reader to the place and then adding more information.

                        introducing topic of 'beaches'   adding more information

In the UK there are a lot of beaches; some are sandy and others are full of rocks and pebbles.

Here again, the writer introduces a new idea (*beaches in the UK*) and then adds more information.

                       introducing topic of 'reasons'   adding more information

There are many reasons why people should learn English. The first is …

In the example sentences, a noun is used after *there is* and *there are*. There may also be an adjective before the noun.

- For **plural** nouns, we use the plural of the verb *to be*, i.e., *there are*.
- For **singular** nouns, we use the singular of the verb *to be*, i.e., *there is*.

In sentences with *there is* or *there are*, it may be helpful to think of the subject as divided into two: *there* is a half-subject and the noun which follows is a half-subject.

	Half-subject	Verb	Half-subject Singular noun		
In the UK,	there	is	a small town	called Windsor,	which has a famous castle.

	Half-subject	Verb	Half-subject Plural noun	
In the UK,	there	are	many beaches;	some are sandy and others are full of rocks and pebbles.

Half-subject	Verb	Half-subject Plural noun	
There	are	many reasons	why people should learn English. The first is …

5.1 **Rewrite these student sentences, using *there is* or *there are* to present the new information correctly to your reader. Rewrite the first sentence only.**

telling your reader about jobs in London	adding more information

1. In London, it has many jobs. Some are for skilled and others are for unskilled workers.

In London, there are many jobs.

2. In China, many different types of food. Most dishes are accompanied by rice or noodles.

3. In Qatar, it has many new buildings. Some are offices, and others are homes for people to live in.

4. At university, the problems have three. The first is …

5. In London, has a lot of pollution. Cyclists should consider wearing masks.

6. In the UK, many elderly people who live alone. This creates feelings of isolation.

7. A famous underground system called 'the Metro' in Paris. It is very fast and cheap to use.

8. In the city centre, it have an area where cars and buses cannot go. It is a popular space for shops and cafés.

9. It has many universities in China. The biggest is in Beijing.

10. They have many reasons why international students want to study in an English-speaking university. The first is …

5.2 Present the following new information to your reader.

1. _There is_ _____ a new airport in Jeddah.
2. _____ some historic mosques in Istanbul.
3. _____ a 12th-century castle in Kerak.
4. _____ many, modern high-rise buildings in Amman.
5. _____ a large port in Mumbai.

Grammar note: The discussion of ideas is one of the main purposes of academic writing. Using *there is* and *there are* is an effective way of introducing new ideas into your writing.

Stage B

In this stage you will:
- learn quantity expressions for people and things
- study uncountable / countable nouns
- practise the form and use of the present continuous to express change

Task 1 | Quantity expressions – people and things

Writers often need to describe people, things and situations to their readers, before discussing them. Look at some ways to do this effectively in your academic writing.

Using quantity expressions for people: singular or plural?

Quantity expressions can help you to write about groups of people. To use quantity expressions accurately, you need to know whether an expression takes the singular or plural form of the verb.

Look at these two common quantity expressions:

Quantity expression third person singular verb form

a. *Nearly everyone in Oman is Muslim.*

Quantity expression third person plural verb form

b. *Most people in Oman own a car.*

1.1   Correct the subject–verb agreement in the following sentences.

1. Nearly everyone in the UK own a car.

   Nearly everyone in the UK owns a car.

2. Most people in the UK has a television.

   _____

3. Most people in Europe studies English at school.

   _____

4. Nearly everyone at university are worried about money.

   _____

1.2   Quantity expressions for *large numbers* of people
In 1.1 you saw how a quantity expression with the word *everyone* takes a singular verb, and a quantity expression with the word *people* takes a plural verb. Now look at some more, useful quantity expressions for **large numbers** of people.

Circle the correct verb form to go with the underlined quantity expressions.

1. The majority of students *do not like* / *does not like* homework.
2. Most couples in China only *have* / *has* one child.
3. Nearly everyone *feel* / *feels* nervous when he or she starts a new job.
4. Many elderly people *does not like* / *do not like* going out in the evenings.
5. The majority of Chinese people *do not eat* / *does not eat* with a knife and fork; they use chopsticks.
6. Many people in Saudi Arabia *thinks* / *think* that petrol is cheap.
7. Almost all international students *are* / *is* a little homesick at first.
8. People *is* / *are* always in a hurry in big cities.

1.3   Quantity expressions for *small numbers* of people. Look at the underlined expressions and circle the correct verb form to go with each one.

1. Not many children *enjoy* / *enjoys* doing homework.
2. Some students *arrive* / *arrives* late every day.
3. Few students *have* / *has* the opportunity to speak English at home.
4. A few students always *arrive* / *arrives* late to lessons.
5. Not many English people *is* / *are* able to use chopsticks.

Grammar note:
- *Few* is used to emphasize how small the number is.
- *A few* is used to mean *a small number of*. It can have a similar meaning to *some*.

1.4 **Correct the errors in the bold quantity expressions or verb forms in these sentences.**

1. **A little** people travel to the Arctic.

   Few people travel to the Arctic.

2. **A small part of students** cook together.

   _____

3. The way of life for **great part people** in Oman is farming, the oil industry and coconut planting.

   _____

4. **Large** people in Oman are under the age of 15.

   _____

5. **Most of people** in Oman speak Arabic.

   _____

6. China has **many of** farmers.

   _____

7. People in Taiwan **is** Han Chinese.

   _____

8. Nearly everybody in the UAE **own** a mobile phone.

   _____

9. **A few** farmers in Eritrea own cars because they are so expensive.

   _____

10. **Many of people** in Qatar come from other countries.

    _____

Quantity expressions for large numbers of people	Quantity expressions for small numbers of people
(Nearly) everyone*	Not many
Most	Some
The majority of …	A few
Many	Few
Almost all	

* *(Nearly) everyone* takes a singular verb. All other expressions take a plural verb.

1.5 Using quantity expressions for things

Quantity expressions can also help you to write about things. Notice that in the examples below, the quantity expression + noun is used as the object, not the subject of the sentence.

Study the sentences below and answer the questions:

a.

Subject	Auxiliary verb + *not* + Bare infinitive	Object
Electric cars	do not use	any **petrol**.

b.

Subject	Verb	Object
Saudi Arabia	has	many **mosques**.

1. Why is the object in example a in the singular form?

   _____

2. Why is the object in example b in the plural form?

   _____

Countable and uncountable nouns

An **uncountable noun** is considered to be a mass that we cannot divide into separate elements. We cannot 'count' nouns like this. For example, we can count *cans of petrol* or *litres of petrol*, but we cannot count *petrol* itself. Therefore, an **uncountable noun** always goes with a **singular verb**.

A **countable noun**, however, such as *mosque*, has a singular and a plural form and can be used with a singular verb and a plural verb (e.g., *Mosques are places of worship*).

The following table summarizes common quantity expressions which describe things. It shows how some expressions change when you use them with countable and uncountable nouns.

Countable noun			Uncountable noun		
Subject	Verb	Object	Subject	Verb	Object
She	uses	**a** book.	It	uses	petrol.
She	uses	**a few** books.	It	uses	**a little** petrol.
She	uses	**some** books.	It	uses	**some** petrol.
She	uses	**many** books.	It	uses	**much*** petrol.
She	does not use	**many** books.	It	does not use	**much** petrol.
She	does not use	**any** books.	It	does not use	**any** petrol.

* See *Grammar note* below.

Grammar note – *much/many/a lot of*: In informal English, it is common to use *a lot of* in positive sentences: for example, *We've got a lot of homework*. In academic English, however, you should avoid using *a lot of*. In positive sentences, it is possible to use *many* with countable nouns: *The report raises many questions*. With uncountable nouns, although *much* is grammatically correct, it is more common to use an expression like *a large quantity of* or *a great deal of*: *They need a large quantity of equipment*.

1.6 **Look at some nouns used in academic writing. Are they countable (C) or uncountable (U)? Put a tick the correct column. You may need to check some of the words in a dictionary.**

Noun	C	U
accommodation		✔
advice		
air		
behaviour		
book		
computer		
damage		
equipment		
essay		
evidence		
food		
help		
homework		
information		
language		
machinery		
meat		
minute		
money		
news		
oil		
paper		
permission		
petrol		
pollution		
problem		
progress		
question		
research		
solution		
student		
time		
traffic		

1.7 **Underline the correct option in each sentence.**

1. Students write <u>some essays</u> / *some essay* every term.
2. They studied the *behaviours* / *behaviour* of lions over four years.
3. *Paper was* / *Papers were* very expensive in the 12th century.
4. University *accommodations are* / *accommodation* is very basic.
5. Marco went to the library to get more *information* / *informations* for his project.
6. This issue still *require many researches* / *requires much research*.
7. The news *was* / *were* very depressing.
8. The traffic *is* / *are* heavy in the town centre.
9. One of the students needed *some advice* / *some advices* about her essay.
10. Some students do not have *much homework* / *many homeworks* to do.

1.8 **Complete the sentences with a countable or uncountable noun from Task 1.6.**

1. The World Wide Web is useful for finding out new ___information___ .

2. In today's busy world, people do not have much _____.

3. Sometimes, students need to do some _____ to find out the answer to a question.

4. There are many _____ in the library.

5. In the town centre, _____ is often a problem.

6. Students do not need _____ to use the photocopier, but they need their student card.

7. It is important to gather as much _____ as possible to solve a crime.

1.9 **Complete the sentences with a suitable quantity expression. There is one gap for each missing word.**

1. The teacher gave the student _____*some*_____ help.

2. In parts of London, there is _____ air pollution.

3. Teenagers do not often want _____ advice from their parents.

4. When people study _____ new language, they usually have _____ questions.

5. The printer needs _____ paper.

6. The department does not have _____ audio equipment, so staff cannot record their lectures.

1.10 **Read the student's paragraph about his country. There are six errors. Underline each error and correct it. The first error has been corrected for you.**

> *has*
> Saudi Arabia <u>have</u> a population of 2 million. Nearly everyone there speak Arabic, and a few people speaks English. It is very family-oriented, and the majority of people lives with their families. Jeddah is the second city of Saudi Arabia. In Jeddah, the summer is very hot and dry, and there are much pollutions.

02 Aug Homework

...ese sentences, there are errors with uncountable nouns. Underline each error
...correct it. Note that sometimes you will need to correct the verb too, if the
...ject and verb do not agree.

Nuclear power causes <u>a</u> pollution for people and the environment.

<u>Nuclear power causes pollution for people and the environment.</u>

2. Solar power does not cause damages to the environment.

   _____

3. The students require informations about this topic.

   _____

4. Scientific researches seem to prove that poverty is an important factor.

   _____

5. The Careers Service Unit at the university gives helps to both British and international students.

   _____

6. The government should give advices to young unemployed people.

   _____

7. This essay will discuss progresses in medical science.

   _____

8. The children's behaviours are unacceptable.

   _____

9. Other types of energy, such as wind power or wave power, should replace oils in the future.

   _____

10. The department uses some very expensive equipments for the experiment.

   _____

Task 2 | Using the present continuous

2.1 **Read the following paragraphs about two villages in England and answer the questions.**

1. Which paragraph describes a *temporary* change which is happening now or around now?

   _____

2. Which paragraph describes a *permanent* situation? _____

3. Where would *you* prefer to live? Why? _____

a. At the moment, Deansfield's population is growing. The village is becoming more cosmopolitan. Many people are arriving from Eastern European countries because they want to earn money. They are making money by picking the fruit and vegetables which farmers are growing in greenhouses.

> **b.** Chalkend is a small village. Most people do not have jobs because they are retired. Many of them enjoy gardening. They grow flowers and vegetables, and in the summer they hold competitions and give prizes to the people with the biggest onions or the most beautiful roses.

Grammar note: The present continuous is used for a situation which is changing 'now' or 'around now'. The present simple describes a situation which is permanent.

2.2 **Underline the time expression in paragraph a on page 26 which shows when the change is happening.**

2.3 **Study the sentences below. Circle the three time expressions which emphasize that the changes are happening now or around now.**
1. Currently, the Hyundai company is manufacturing more cars than before.
2. People are becoming more interested in healthy eating nowadays.
3. More primary-school children are learning English in China.
4. Mobile phone sales are growing at the moment.

2.4 **Complete the table for the present continuous form of the verb *study*.**

Subject	Auxiliary verb		Bare infinitive + ~*ing* (present participle)	
Positive statements				
Students	are		studying	English.
He/She	_____		_____	English.
Negative statements				
Students	are	not	_____	Science.
He/She	is	_____	studying	Science.
Questions				
Auxiliary verb	**Subject**		**Bare infinitive + ~*ing***	
Are	the students		studying	Science?
Is	_____		_____	Science?

Grammar note: If a verb ends in a single consonant + ~*e*, you need to omit the ~*e* before adding ~*ing*: e.g., hope -> hoping; confuse -> confusing.
If a verb has one syllable and ends in a single vowel + consonant, you need to double the final consonant before adding ~*ing*: e.g., stop -> stopping; cut -> cutting.
If a verb has more than one syllable, ends in a single vowel + consonant and the final syllable is stressed, you double the final consonant before adding ~*ing*: e.g., begin -> beginning; transmit -> transmitting.
If the final syllable of a multi-syllable verb is not stressed, you do not double the final consonant: e.g., follow -> following; answer -> answering.

2.5 **Read the text, which describes changes in the fictional city of Bindeen. Underline examples of the present continuous.**

Many changes are taking place in Bindeen at the moment. The number of IT industries is growing rapidly; foreign investment and tourism are also increasing. More people are coming on holiday to Bindeen which is helping the economy. For example, Bindeen earned £2.3 billion from tourism in 2014, and 8.2% of the adults are now working the tourist industry. Local teenagers like having a job in the summer holidays.

However, there are some negative changes. The cost of housing is increasing rapidly. Also, many people are working longer hours and are spending more time travelling to work.

According to the text, how many changes are taking place in Bindeen? Write four sentences from the text which describe the changes.

1. <u>The number of IT industries is growing rapidly.</u>_____
2. _____
3. _____
4. _____

Grammar note: Look at these two sentences from the text above. The words with ~*ing* in bold are **not** part of the present continuous. How do you know?

Local teenagers like having a job in the summer holidays.

Many people are spending more time travelling to work.

We know that *having* and *travelling* are not part of the present continuous here because they are not combined with the auxiliary verb *to be* (i.e., is/are). The ~*ing* form is needed after verbs such as *like* and *spend time*, and in this case is called the **gerund**.

2.6 **Complete the sentences with the present continuous form of the verb. Choose the correct main verb from the list below.**

become	~~eat~~	go	increase	learn	teach	plan

1. People <u>are</u> _____<u>eating</u>_____ more junk food nowadays.
2. Mobile phones ____ _____ more expensive.
3. Nowadays, more people ____ _____ English.
4. Student numbers ____ _____ every year.
5. Most primary schools ____ _____ French nowadays.
6. The company ____ currently _____ a new advertising campaign.
7. More international students ____ _____ to UK universities than before.

2.7 Review: present simple or present continuous? You decide!
Complete the sentences with the present continuous or present simple form of the verb in brackets.

1. This essay discusses the reasons why pollution _____ worse nowadays. (become)

2. In Iraq, employers usually _____ people according to their qualifications. (choose)

3. Oil companies usually _____ good salaries. (pay)

4. When the sun _____ on the Earth, the land and sea _____ approximately half the sun's rays. (shine; absorb)

5. The government _____ usually _____ good roads in rural areas. (not build)

6. The current pay freeze _____ young doctors from entering the profession. (discourage)

7. Saudi Arabia _____ the biggest population in the Gulf. (have)

8. Bananas _____ in the UK. (not grow)

9. Most people agree that global warming is happening because the amount of CO_2 _____. (increase)

10. The architecture of Qatar _____ very beautiful. (be)

11. Motorists _____ fast on the motorways in Germany. (drive)

Stage C

In this stage you will:
- study simple clauses in detail
- review basic features of academic writing

Task 1 Understanding clause structures

In academic writing, it is good style to use a variety of clause structures. There are three main types of clause:

- **simple**: one subject and one matching verb
  Jogging increases the heart rate.
- **compound**: two simple clauses joined with a linking word (*and*, *but*, etc.)
  Jogging increases the heart rate, and yoga improves flexibility.
- **complex**: a simple clause with an extra subordinate clause (starting with words like *since*, *although*, *who*, *that*, etc.)
  Since jogging increases the heart rate, it improves people's fitness levels.

This stage explains more about **simple clauses**. Units 4 and 5 will discuss in more depth the use of **compound** and **complex clauses** in your writing.

A simple clause is a group of words which contains one subject and one matching verb. There is a **full stop** at the end of a simple clause.

Study the simple clauses below. (S = subject; V = verb)

      S   V
a. *Bananas grow in hot countries.*

      S   V
b. *Reptiles do not have warm blood.*

      S   V
c. *Jogging increases the heart rate.*

       S   V
d. *People on holiday usually feel relaxed.*

       S   V
e. *Fruit and vegetables contain important vitamins.*

      S   V
f. *Teachers in the UK usually have six weeks' holiday in the summer.*

Grammar note: Some simple clauses are short. Other simple clauses are longer because they contain more information, but they still only have one subject and one verb.

Two or more nouns connected with *and* make **one** subject phrase (e.g., *fruit and vegetables*). The matching verb must be **plural**.

1.1 **Circle the subject and underline the verb in the sentences below. Put a cross (✗) next to the sentences which are not simple clauses. Remember: sentences with more than one subject and verb are not simple clauses.**

1. (The report) does not include a description of the changes.

2. The economy is slowing down, so people are worried about their jobs.

3. Scientists do not completely understand why people sleep.

4. The students are studying hard for their exams.

5. Soil, air and water are all essential for daily life.

6. Running sometimes damages people's knees.

7. Some children play too many computer games, but their parents do not stop them.

Task 2 — The subject

Identifying and analyzing the subject

Sometimes the subject in a simple clause is not just one word but can contain extra information. The main noun (headword) and the extra information together make the subject. When you are reading and writing, you need to be able to identify the headword. It is the headword which matches the verb.

For example:

Headword   extra information

The temperature in July is usually over 25 degrees.

Study the examples below. The headword of each subject is highlighted in blue and the extra information is highlighted in yellow.

a. Teachers in the UK usually have six weeks' holiday in the summer.

b. People on holiday usually feel relaxed.

c. The community centre collapsed during the earthquake.

d. Young men sometimes drive badly.

If you are not sure which words in the subject give the extra information, ask the question 'Which?'

For example:

a. Teachers in the UK usually have six weeks' holiday in the summer.
   Question: Which teachers usually have six weeks' holiday? Answer: Teachers in the UK.

c. The community centre collapsed during the earthquake.
   Question: Which centre collapsed? Answer: The community centre.

2.1 **Write questions with *Which?* for examples b and d. Identify the headword and the extra information.**

b. Question: _____

   Headword: _____

   Extra information: _____

d. Question: _____

   Headword: _____

   Extra information: _____

2.2 **Study the sentences below. Underline the words for each subject and circle the verb, then ask the question *Which?* to find the extra information which belongs with the subject. Highlight the headword in blue and the extra information in yellow.**

1. The village doctor often (visits) sick people in their homes.

   Question: *Which doctor often visits sick people?*

   Answer: *The village doctor.*

2. The library resources are excellent.

   Question: _____

   Answer: _____

3. Students in the UK usually want to find a good job at the end of their course.

   Question: _____

   Answer: _____

4. The Sierra Leone government does not pay for children's education.

   Question: _____

   Answer: _____

5. Sometimes, local people are not welcoming to immigrants.

   Question: _____

   Answer: _____

6. Heavy smoking is bad for people's health.

   Question: _____

   Answer: _____

7. The people in Kang do not have hot water.

   Question: _____

   Answer: _____

Task 3 | Analyzing the object

As well as the subject and verb, a simple clause contains other elements. This section focuses on identifying the **object (O)** in a simple clause. If you ask a question about the subject of the clause (usually *What?*), you can find the object. But remember: simple clauses do not always contain an object.

Study the following examples:

   S   V   O

a. *Teachers usually have six weeks' holiday.*

   Question: *What do teachers have?* Answer: Six weeks' holiday.

              S   V   O

b. *The book and the journal article discuss statistics.*

   Question: *What do the book and article discuss?* Answer: Statistics.

3.1 Ask the question *What?* about the subject of the clauses below. Then underline the verb (V), the subject (S) and object (O) of each clause. Write *S*, *V* and *O* above them.

                S   V   O

1. This report suggests solutions.

   Question: *What does the report suggest?*   Answer: *solutions*

2. Some criminals sell drugs.

   Question: _____ Answer: _____

3. Many young people like computer games.

   Question: _____ Answer: _____

4. The hospital does not need more administrators.

   Question: _____ Answer: _____

5. Playing football improves fitness levels.

   Question: _____ Answer: _____

6. Students often download journal articles.

   Question: _____ Answer: _____

3.2 The object of the clause, like the subject, can have a headword and extra information. Underline the verb (V), the subject (S) and object (O) of each clause. Write *S*, *V* and *O* above them. Then ask the question *Which?* to find the headword and the extra information for the object. Highlight the extra information in yellow and the headword in blue.

                S   V   O

1. Occasionally, the food does not reach the people who need it

   Question: *Which people does the food not reach?* Answer: *The people who need it*

2. Many young people like computer games.

   Question: _____ Answer: _____

3. The report gives simple solutions.

   Question: _____ Answer: _____

4. Some criminals sell hard drugs.

   Question: _____ Answer: _____

5. Students always submit written homework.

   Question: _____ Answer: _____

6. Nowadays, more people are driving electric cars.

   Question: _____ Answer: _____

7. Playing football improves fitness levels.

   Question: _____ Answer: _____

Instead of an object, a simple clause sometimes contains a **complement** (C). A complement can **come after** any one of the verbs:

- to be
- to seem
- to become
- to appear

The complement often gives more information about the **subject** of the clause.

For example:

        S   V   C

a. *The lecturer is a famous politician.*

           S   V C

b. *One of the disadvantages of tourism is litter.*

       S   V   C

c. *Unemployment is becoming one of the most serious issues in the country.*

4.1 Underline the verb (V) and the subject (S) of each clause. Then circle the object (O) or complement (C) of each clause. Write *S*, *V* and *O/C* above them.

              S   V   C

1. <u>Improving public transport</u> <u>seems</u> (a good solution)

2. The company is developing new products.

3. Mr Smith is fast becoming a good leader

4. One of the reasons for climate change is human activity.

5. The charity is using the money wisely.

6. The government is changing the tax laws.

7. Internet crime is a serious problem in many countries.

8. A 'hotspot' is a small area of intense activity within a bigger area of calm.

4.2 Write the subjects, objects and complements from 4.1 that include extra information. Highlight the extra information in yellow and the headword in blue.

1. improving public transport; a good solution

2. _____

3. _____

4. _____

5. _____

6. _____

7. _____

8. _____

Task 5   Review

Checklist of grammar points from Unit 1
- Formal, impersonal style
- Subject–verb agreement
- Using plural countable nouns to describe situations in general
- Using *there is/there are* to present new information
- Present simple/present continuous tense
- Quantity expressions
- Countable/uncountable nouns
- Construction of simple clauses

The following texts, written by students, contain grammar errors relating to points in Unit 1. Study the checklist above and think carefully about what you have learnt in this unit. Then correct the texts.

5.1   Correct the errors in the bold words.

At the moment, many people **moves** from the countryside to Riyadh, the capital city of Saudi Arabia. It is generally true that people who move there never **returning** to their hometown because **he** find everything easier in the city. The reason why people move is to improve their **life**. They want better **school** for their **child** or **job** for **himself**. In addition, the government provides practical **helps** to migrants, so this **encourage** even more people to move to the city.

There **is** many **facility** in Riyadh: **university**, modern markets, ministries and embassies. However, Riyadh **become** overcrowded nowadays and the city **suffer** from **traffics** congestion and environmental **pollutions**. The government currently **try** to solve the problem by providing more **service** in other towns and cities in Saudi Arabia.

5.2 Look at the bold words in the text below and correct the errors in the subjects or verbs.

Is it better to help developing countries to help themselves than to give them money, food and machinery?

Across the world, there **is** many developing **nation** which **are depending** on developed countries. This essay will show how to help developing **country** in a better way than by simply giving them **foods**, money and machinery.

Firstly, **it have education. Many of** industrialized countries offer **scholarship** for people in developing countries. **Scholarship** in **subject** such as Engineering, Maths, Medicine and Computer Science are important as they enable **student** to improve life for themselves and for **them country. Hospital**, for example, need well-trained staff. So, if developing **country** receive help to send a few **student** abroad every year to medical college, **them** healthcare service will improve.

Secondly, there **is** also some **organization** nowadays which try to help developing countries through trade. The Fairtrade Foundation, for example, always **is work** to help farmers and workers in developing countries. It **asking** companies to pay sustainable prices which must never fall lower than the market price. Divine Chocolate Ltd **are** one company which **promote** fair trade. Cocoa farmers in Africa both **sells** their cocoa to Divine and **owns** 45% of the Divine company.

Finally, there is the question of providing advanced **machineries** to developing countries. This may not be a good idea if local people **does** not know how to repair the equipment, if it **break** down. In this case, local people **losing** a lot of money while they wait for **engineer** to come from abroad and complete the repair. A better solution is to train local **person** to make their own machines using local sustainable resources.

In conclusion, it is best to help developing countries improve **itself**. Other countries can offer help in many ways, such as by granting **scholarship**, training local people and promoting fair trade **organization**. These initiatives are more helpful than simply donating money, food or machinery.

5.3 Study sentences 1–9. Find and correct the error in each sentence.

1. At the moment, society is change fast.

2. Factories regularly releasing greenhouse gases.

3. In Saudi Arabia, it has oil companies which offer well-paid jobs.

4. Students often spend too much time surf the Internet.

5. China have the biggest population in the world.

6. Currently, the quality of education is not get improve.

7. Nearly everyone in Qatar speak Arabic.

8. The majority of shops depends on advertisements to sell their products.

9. Many teenagers do not like study hard.

5.4 **Find and correct the errors in these sentences. The number of errors is indicated in brackets.**

1. At the moment, the government encourage businesses to give money to build new universities. However, are not enough jobs for new graduates even now.
(2 errors)

2. More young people currently apply for university so that they can get a better job.
(1 error)

3. The government always setting the salary according to the level of applicants' qualification.
(2 errors)

4. A lot of pollution in China. Most air pollution come from car fumes and from factories. The majority cities has this problem.
(4 errors)

Choose the correct option to complete the sentences.

1 Some schools _____ Internet access.
   a. have not
   b. do not have
   c. not have

2 Many students _____ a computer to university.
   a. are bring
   b. bring
   c. brings

3 People always want to improve their _____.
   a. life
   b. live
   c. lives

4 _____ many financial institutions which offer micro loans in India.
   a. It have
   b. There is
   c. There are

5 Almost everyone in Hong Kong _____ a computer at home.
   a. has
   b. have
   c. are having

6 _____ students plagiarize intentionally because they know that plagiarism is a serious offence at university.
   a. Many
   b. Few
   c. A few

7 She is doing _____ on collective memory.
   a. researches
   b. some research
   c. a research

8 At the moment, computer sales _____.
   a. are increasing
   b. increase
   c. is increasing

Read sentences 9 and 10. Then choose the correct word to complete the description.

9   In Western society, <u>many people</u> want to stay young.
The underlined words are the:
a. object
b. verb
c. subject

10   Ben is <u>a difficult child</u>.
The underlined words are the:
a. object
b. complement
c. verb

2 Information flow within a text

In this unit you will:

- learn how to organize your writing so that information flows in a logical way
- practise using simple and complex noun phrases to improve information flow
- learn how subject noun phrases and the passive voice are used to achieve effective information flow

Stage A

In this stage you will:

- learn about text flow
- learn how simple noun phrases are used to achieve effective text flow

Task 1 Introduction to simple noun phrases

1.1 **In Unit 1, you learnt to identify subjects, objects and complements within a simple clause. Study the sentences below. Which word class do the highlighted words all belong to?**

    S
Bananas grow in hot countries.

           O
This report offers solutions.

                   C
One of the disadvantages of tourism is litter.

The subjects, objects and complements in the examples include a **noun**. They are called **noun phrases**. Noun phrases in writing help the reader to follow ideas from one sentence to the next. Noun phrases at the beginning of a sentence often refer back to an idea in a previous sentence. Noun phrases at the end of a sentence are used to develop 'new' information.

Beginning a sentence with 'old' information and ending a sentence with 'new' information ensures that you have a well-written text with a logical flow of ideas.

Task 2 Information flow – Patterns of 'old' information to 'new' information

When you write in academic style, the 'new idea' goes at the end of the sentence. It is often picked up again at the beginning of the next sentence. In this way, 'new information' (highlighted in yellow) at the end of a sentence becomes 'old information' (highlighted in blue) at the beginning of the next one. The 'old' information in blue is a simple noun phrase.

1. *A recent study indicates that there is a link between playing too many video games and violence. This link suggests that parents should not let their children spend too long on video gaming.*

2. *PDF format is useful for making documents available on the web. They look exactly the same as the original version.*

3. *Winters have been getting colder recently. This situation is possibly related to climate change.*

4. *There is no time to write a first draft in an exam. Tests are conducted under strict time limits.*

2.1 **Study the introduction to an essay. Draw an arrow to show which word(s) the bold noun phrases link back to.**

> **Discuss the reasons why people choose to live in Reading.**
>
> **Reading** is a large town in south-east England. **It** is located about halfway between London and Oxford, with a population of 147,300. **Most inhabitants** were born in the town, but a significant minority have relocated there for personal reasons. **One reason** is the wish to improve the quality of life. **This** includes issues such as finding a new job or moving closer to friends and family.

Analyzing subjects in more detail

There are several different patterns of **simple noun phrases** (NP) which introduce 'old information' at the beginning of a new sentence. Three of these simple noun phrase patterns are:

- single noun
- determiner + noun
- pronoun

Study the sentences below:

a. **single noun**

A noun is a word which names people, places, things or ideas.

NP
⌐ S ⌐ V
Reading is a large town.

b. **determiner + noun**

A determiner is a word used in front of a noun when:

1. you know which person or thing you are referring to:

   the **dog**; their **ideas**; these **pages**; this **essay**

2. you want to refer to people or things without saying exactly who or what they are, or you do not want to state an exact quantity:

   a **student**; many **people**; several **countries**; not much **rice**; other **people**

NP
⌐ S ⌐
*This **essay** will discuss the reasons why people choose to live in Reading.*

NP
⌐ S ⌐
*Most **inhabitants** were born in the town.*

c. pronoun

A pronoun is a word which is used *instead of* a noun.

NP
⌐S⌐
They have relocated for personal reasons.

NP
⌐S⌐
It is about halfway between London and Oxford.

NP
⌐S⌐
This includes issues such as finding a job.

2.2 **Read the following short paragraph. The simple noun phrases which introduce old information are in bold. Draw an arrow to show which word(s) the noun phrases link back to. Then complete the table below with the noun phrases.**

There are good leisure facilities in Reading. **It** has a library, many places of worship, a theatre, a concert hall, an art gallery, a museum, two cinemas, a football stadium, and many restaurants. **These facilities** mean that local people of all ages have places to go. **Another attraction** is the Oracle shopping centre. **Its development** has boosted the local economy.

Single noun	Determiner + noun	Pronoun

There are other important patterns of information flow. Information at the start of a sentence often links back to the end of the previous sentence. But it can also link further back, to information at the *start* of the previous sentence or earlier in a paragraph.

a. *International donors have made an important contribution to development in Nepal. They have enabled the building of new schools in many areas.*

b. *In 2010, the government announced three popular reforms. These plans involved imposing higher tax rates on the rich*, increasing benefits for the poor*, and improving the quality of health care for the elderly*. As a result, the party was re-elected in democratic elections in 2012.*

*'the rich' means 'rich people', 'the poor' means 'poor people' and 'the elderly' means 'older people'

2.3 You have seen how information in academic writing flows from old to new. In the following paragraphs, the simple noun phrases which introduce old information are in bold. Draw an arrow to show which word(s) the bold noun phrases link back to. Then complete the table below with the noun phrases.

> **Discuss the reasons why people choose to live in Reading.**
>
> Reading is a large town in south-east England. It is located about halfway between London and Oxford, with a population of 147,300. Most inhabitants were born in the town, but a significant minority have relocated there for personal reasons. The most common reason is the wish to improve the quality of life. This includes issues such as finding a new job or moving closer to friends and family.
>
> Since **Reading** is only 25 minutes away from central London by train, many residents travel to and from their work in the capital city from Mondays to Fridays. **These commuters** choose Reading because house prices are cheaper than in London, and there are better leisure opportunities for families. There are **parks and pools** in the town and the countryside is only a short car drive away. **Shopping** is also a growing attraction. The number of retail outlets has increased by one third since the opening of the 'Oracle', a new shopping complex, in 1999. **The town** also has a library, many places of worship, a theatre, a concert hall, an art gallery, a museum, two cinemas, a football stadium and many restaurants. **These facilities** mean that local people of all ages have places to go.
>
> Many people also come to Reading to study at a language school or at the university. **They** may choose Reading because their course has a particularly good reputation. Alternatively, **the reasons** may be more practical. **Transport** is efficient; there is easy access to London and Heathrow Airport. Accommodation is fairly easy to find and cheaper than London. Job opportunities are also good. **Many students** take up part-time work, even if English is not their first language.

Single noun	Determiner + noun	Pronoun

> The noun phrase at the beginning of a sentence can link back to 'old' information in different ways:
>
> **a.** It represents a previous word.
> *PDF format is useful for making documents available on the web. They look exactly the same as the original version.*
>
> **b.** It is a synonym for a previous word.
> *There is no time to write a first draft in an exam. Tests are conducted under strict time limits.*

c. It summarizes an idea in a previous sentence.
Winters have been getting colder recently. This situation *is possibly related to climate change.*

d. It repeats a previous word.
A recent study indicates that there is a link between playing too many video games and violence. This link *suggests that parents should not let their children spend too long in front of video games.*

2.4 **Look again at the text in 2.3 and study the noun phrases in bold. Identify the type of link (a–d) for each noun phrase. Complete the table.**

Reminder: simple noun phrases

- single noun
- determiner + noun
- pronoun

Type of link	Noun phrase
a.	
b.	
c.	
d.	Reading

Task 3   Connected vocabulary

Sometimes, the noun phrase at the start of a sentence does not directly repeat 'old information', as in the examples above. Instead, it gives further **detail** or **evidence** about the old information. In this case, the noun phrase is linked by **connected vocabulary** – it uses words that are related to the vocabulary of the previous topic. The bold noun phrases in the two paragraphs below are examples of connected vocabulary. They are 'old information' because they give more detail about a previous topic.

> **International students' attitude towards British food**
>
> **British cooking** generally has a bad reputation among students **from Asia**. They tend not to eat in the student canteen but prefer to **cook dishes from their own countries**.
>
> Fortunately, **ingredients from countries such as China, India and Japan** are on sale in the local supermarkets.

3.1 **Draw an arrow to show which word(s) the bold simple noun phrases link back to. Which type of noun phrases are they?**
- single noun
- determiner + noun
- pronoun

> ### Learning English in China
>
> Many people in China want to learn English because of its status as the international language. It is the *lingua franca* of business, politics, science, arts and even education. **Children** absorb new languages more easily than adults, and many schools offer English lessons at kindergarten. **Many adults** too try to learn English, or improve their level, through classes with a private teacher or in their workplace.

1. children _____

2. many adults _____

Stage B

In this stage you will:
- learn how complex noun phrases are used to achieve effective text flow

> ### Introduction to complex noun phrases
>
> In Stage A of this unit, you studied simple noun phrases:
> - **single noun**
>   *Control* is important.
> - **determiner + noun**
>   *The shareholders* are only interested in profits.
> - **pronoun**
>   *They* may not understand the purpose of the task.
>
> In Unit 1, you learnt that subjects, objects or complements can be expanded to give extra information. When they have extra information, they are called **complex noun phrases**.
>
> Complex noun phrases are often used in academic writing to link old to new information. They enable the writer to tightly pack old information into the beginning of a new sentence. In this stage, you will study in more detail how to 'unpack' these complex noun phrases in your reading – isolating the headword from the extra information. You will also learn how to add more detail to your writing by using complex noun phrases yourself.

| Task 1 | **Adding an adjective or noun to form complex phrases** |

You can add an adjective or a noun in front of the headword of a subject, object or complement to give extra information.

Study the following examples:

a. simple noun phrase

determiner + headword

The countryside is only a short car drive away.

complex noun phrase

determiner adjective headword

The open countryside is only a short car drive away.

One way of finding the headword in a complex noun phrase is to ask yourself a question:
Question: What is only a short drive away?
Answer: The countryside. (You can't answer the question with 'open'. 'Open' is an adjective that describes the countryside.)

b. simple noun phrase

headword

Prices are going down.

complex noun phrase

noun + headword

House prices are going down.

Question: What is going down?
Answer: Prices. (You can't answer the question with 'house'. The noun 'house' shows that the writer is referring to 'house prices' not 'food prices', for example.)

1.1 **Add an adjective or a noun in front of the headword to make a complex noun phrase where you see a gap. Choose from the words in the box below.**

multi-screen	international	convenient	public
young	open	daily	~~local~~	rented	swimming

Since Reading is only 25 minutes away from central London by train, **many** (1) _____local_____ **residents** travel to and from their work in the capital city from Mondays to Fridays. **These** (2) _____ **commuters** choose Reading because house prices are cheaper than in London, and there are better leisure opportunities for families. There are **parks and** (3) _____ **pools** in the town and **the** (4) _____ **countryside** is only a short car drive away. Shopping is also a growing attraction. The number of retail outlets has increased by one third since the opening of the 'Oracle', a new shopping complex, in 1999.

The town also has a library, many places of worship, a theatre, a concert hall, an art gallery, a museum, **two** (5) _____ **cinemas,** a football stadium, and many restaurants. These (6) _____ facilities mean that local people of all ages have places to go.

Many (7) _____ **people** also come to Reading to study at a language school or at the university. They may choose Reading because their course has a particularly good reputation. Alternatively, the reasons may be more practical. (8) _____ **transport** is efficient; there is easy access to London and Heathrow Airport. (9) _____ **accommodation** is fairly easy to find and cheaper than London. Job opportunities are also good. **Many** (10) _____ students take up part-time work, even if English is not their first language.

Task 2	**Adding a prepositional phrase or relative clause to form complex noun phrases**

Adding prepositional phrases

A **prepositional phrase** (PP) is a phrase which is made up of a preposition and a noun phrase. Prepositions are words like *in, on, by, with, from, at, with.*

For example:

preposition + NP

in the library

preposition + NP

on holiday

You can add a prepositional phrase *after* the headword to make a complex noun phrase.

a. **simple noun phrase**

determiner + headword

Many people *want to learn English.*

complex noun phrase

determiner + headword + PP

Many people *in China want to learn English.*

b. **simple noun phrase**

determiner + headword

Some students *look for part-time work.*

complex noun phrase

determiner + headword + PP

Some students *with money problems look for part-time work.*

Adding adjectival clauses

An **adjectival clause** is a new clause beginning with *who, which* or *that* and containing a verb. It is also called a **relative clause**. The *relative* clause comes after a headword and gives more information about it.

Look at the examples. The relative clause is in bold. The other words are the main clause.

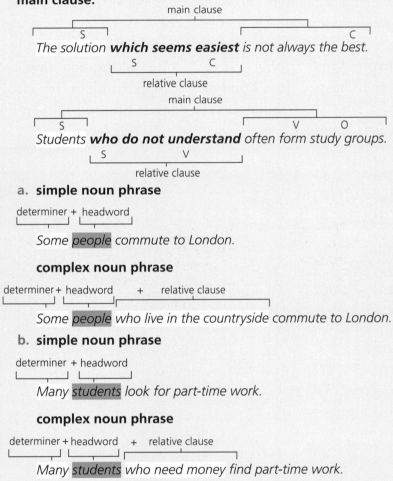

a. simple noun phrase

determiner + headword

Some people commute to London.

complex noun phrase

determiner + headword + relative clause

Some people who live in the countryside commute to London.

b. simple noun phrase

determiner + headword

Many students look for part-time work.

complex noun phrase

determiner + headword + relative clause

Many students who need money find part-time work.

2.1 **Add a PP or a relative clause after the simple noun phrases (in bold) to make complex noun phrases thus improving the text flow. Use the words in the box below.**

who have money problems	which interests them	in the town
who have well-paid jobs	~~for relocation~~	from other countries

Reading is a large town in south-east England. It is located about halfway between London and Oxford, with a population of 147,300. Most inhabitants were born in the town, but a significant minority have relocated there for personal reasons. **One reason** (1) __*for relocation*__ is the wish to improve the quality of life. This includes issues such as finding a new job or moving closer to friends and family.

Since Reading is only 25 minutes away from central London by train, **many residents (2)** _____ travel to and from their work in the capital city from Mondays to Fridays. These commuters choose Reading because house prices are cheaper than in London, and there are better leisure opportunities for families. There are parks and swimming pools and the countryside is only a short car drive away. Shopping is also a growing attraction. The number of retail outlets has increased by one third since the opening of the 'Oracle', a new shopping complex, in 1999. The town also has a library, many places of worship, a theatre, a concert hall, an art gallery, a museum, two cinemas, a football stadium and many restaurants. **These facilities (3)** _____ mean that local people of all ages have places to go.

Many people (4) _____ come to Reading to study at a language school or at the university. They may choose Reading because the course **(5)** _____ has a particularly good reputation. Alternatively, the reasons may be more practical. Transport is efficient; there is easy access to London and Heathrow Airport. Accommodation is fairly easy to find and cheaper than London. Job opportunities are also good. Many students **(6)** _____ take up part-time work, even if English is not their first language.

Task 3   Review

3.1 **Study the sentences below which all contain complex noun phrases as subjects. Underline the subject of the clause, and label the headword. Then label any other words in the noun phrase: e.g., determiner, adjective, noun, prepositional phrase or relative clause. Finally, circle the correct verb form.**

determiner + noun + headword

1. The research team *want /* (*wants*) to develop new drugs.

2. Development projects *helps / help* to combat illiteracy.

3. The equipment in the building *is / are* insufficient.

4. The price of bread *is / are* forcing people to protest on the streets.

5. Bank loans *seem / seems* to be effective in some parts of India.

6. The group participants *agree / agrees* with the result.

7. The farmers who own the fields *do / does* not allow people to walk through them.

8. Their technical knowledge *is / are* often better than the lecturer's.

3.2 Underline the headword and correct the subject–verb agreement if necessary.

1. One of the colleges are conducting unique research into socio-economic status and health.
2. This useful research show that there are several reasons for her success.
3. One of the most harmful habits of modern life are smoking.
4. Debt in the developing world forces countries to borrow more money from the World Bank.
5. The origins of public health education lies in the 19th century.
6. One of the solutions are to raise the price.
7. The number of tourists are increasing every year.
8. Unemployment are one of the most serious issues in the UK.

3.3 Complex noun phrases can be made with noun + noun combinations and are very common in academic writing. The nouns in the box are often placed *before* another noun to make a complex noun phrase. Notice how they are used to achieve good text flow.

> class community computer family government group information labour language
> library research school state surface system test time work

Complete the sentences with the correct noun to make a complex noun phrase that links to the previous sentence. Choose words from the list above,

1. The law states that prisoners cannot vote. This _____ policy is likely to change.
2. Some children achieve more than others at school. Their _____ background can determine success or failure.
3. Books are a useful resource in any society. The _____ library must not close down.
4. Many people study English for professional reasons. _____ skills are very important in the job market.
5. The government is trying to improve the quality of food served to children in educational establishments. However, _____ meals are still not popular in the UK.
6. The Master's students have submitted their proposal, but their _____ plans are not detailed enough.
7. Many people are unemployed. The _____ market is currently in decline.
8. People have instant access to knowledge via the World Wide Web. This _____ age is shaping modern society.

3.4 Complete the sentences with the correct adjective from the box below, to make a complex noun phrase that links to the previous sentence, improving text flow.

> deep cultural developing intensive fast-growing hard-working low-cost

1. Some poor countries do not have good health care systems. Such _____ countries must share resources.
2. Farmers have used chemicals in these fields to try and improve crop yields. _____ farming often damages the environment.
3. Many babies were born in Uganda last year. The _____ population needs more reliable food sources.

4. In Taiwan, the unemployment rate among young people is increasing. Many _____ students will not be able to find jobs.

5. Japanese knotweed is a tough plant. Its _____ root system means that it is difficult to eradicate.

6. There is not much money for building new schools. More _____ classrooms are necessary.

7. International students often cope well with language problems. However, _____ differences can sometimes be more difficult to overcome.

Grammar note: Adding information to a simple noun phrase to form a complex noun phrase at the beginning of a sentence enables you to create a strong link back to a previous idea. This helps the reader to follow the development of your ideas.

In this stage you will:

■ learn how subject noun phrases and passive voice are used to achieve effective text flow

Task 1   The present simple – passive voice

1.1   Read the sentences (1a, 1b, 2a and 2b) below and answer the questions.

1. Which two sentences in bold create a tighter link with the previous sentence?
2. Which two sentences in bold use the present simple active?
3. Which two sentences in bold use the present simple passive?
4. Why might the words highlighted yellow in sentences 1b and 2a be labelled 'empty'?

1. a. Students move to different classrooms for their lessons. **They are taught** once a week in the computer room, and twice a week in S27.

   b. Students move to different classrooms for their lessons. **Teachers teach them** once a week in the computer room, and twice a week in S27.

2. a. There is no time to write a first draft in an exam. **Testers conduct tests** under strict time limits.

   b. There is no time to write a first draft in an exam. **Tests are conducted** under strict time limits.

Grammar note: The present simple passive is useful for two reasons: it creates a tight link back to the information in the previous clause or sentence, and it avoids the use of 'empty' words – that is, words that are not necessary or useful.

2.1 **Study the table for the verb *to teach* and complete the missing words.**

Positive statements				
Subject	**Auxiliary verb**		**Past participle**	
Students	are		taught	in the computer room.
He/She	_____		taught	in the computer room.
Negative statements				
Subject	**Auxiliary verb**	***not***	**Past participle**	
Students	_____	not	_____	in the classroom.
He/She	is	_____	taught	in the classroom.
Questions				
Auxiliary verb	**Subject**		**Past participle**	
Are	students		taught	in the classroom?
Is	_____		taught	in the classroom?

2.2 **Read the following sentences. Are they written in the present simple active (A) or passive (P)? Write *A* or *P* in the gap. Then choose the correct verb form for each sentence.**

1. Apples __*are*__ / *is* grown in England. __P__
2. Cars *is* / *are* not produced in this city now. _____
3. Omani people *speak* / *speaks* Arabic. _____
4. Rain *help* / *helps* plants to grow. _____
5. New software *is* / *are* required to run this program. _____
6. Most of these products *is* / *are* manufactured in Vietnam. _____
7. Poorer people *has* / *have* shorter life expectancy. _____
8. Trainee teachers *do* / *does* a one-year training course. _____
9. Cultures *is* / *are* preserved by ceremony and ritual. _____
10. Most students *live* / *lives* within two miles of the university. _____

2.3 **Write three sentences in present simple passive voice, using the prompts. Remember to use the correct form of the auxiliary verb *is/are* and the past participle.**

1. Positive statement: (Chinese food / sell / here)

   _____

2. Negative statement: (this river / not / pollute)

   _____

3. Question: (these flowers / import?)

   _____

2.4 Look at the sentences. Which rules do you follow to change a sentence with 'empty words' into a sentence with a tight link to the sentence before? ('Empty' means words that are not necessary or useful.)

$\qquad\qquad\qquad\qquad\qquad$ S $\qquad$ V $\qquad$ O

Students do not have many English lessons. Teachers teach them once a week.

$\qquad\qquad\qquad\qquad\qquad$ S $\qquad$ V

Students do not have many English lessons. They are taught once a week.

2.5 Label the verb (V) and object (O) of the second sentence of each pair. Then rewrite the second sentence (or part of the sentence) to make a tight link with the first sentence. Use the passive and delete the 'empty' words in bold.

$\qquad\qquad\qquad\qquad\qquad\qquad\qquad\qquad\qquad\qquad\quad$ V $\qquad$ O

1. Bad weather sometimes delays flights. **Staff** book passengers onto new flights as soon as possible.

   <u>Passengers are booked onto new flights as soon as possible.</u>

2. Price is an important factor in food shopping. **Shoppers** find the best prices in discount stores.

   _____

3. Winter weather often causes traffic problems. Sometimes, **the snow** blocks the roads for several days.

   _____

4. The machinery works well because **someone** checks it regularly.

   _____

5. People put their paper cups in recycling bins. **Waste-disposal operators** recycle the rubbish.

   _____

6. The climate in England is good for fruit. **Farmers** grow apples in the south-east.

   _____

7. Consumers in Europe want to eat green beans in winter. **People** import beans from Africa.

   _____

8. The statistics are not always accurate. However, **people** correct errors quickly.

   _____

9. Changes to the tax system take a long time. **The government** does not make new laws quickly.

   _____

10. It is expensive to manufacture shoes in factories in the UK. **Workers** make them more cheaply in developing countries.

    _____

2.6 Read the paragraph below. The subjects in bold are 'empty'. Label the verb (*V*) and object (*O*) for each of the clauses with a bold subject.

> **Governments** force some countries to accept imported goods, while
> **governments** protect domestic markets by tariffs and subsidies. In some
> countries, **the government** imposes tariffs on foreign goods which are
> therefore more expensive to buy. In this way, **the government** protects local
> industries because they do not have to compete against cheaper foreign
> imports. **The government** also protects local industry by the use of subsidies
> for producers. Because of these subsidies, production costs are lower and
> **people** sell products more cheaply.

2.7 Complete the paragraph from 2.6 in a better academic style. Use the passive voice to replace the 'empty' words and improve the text flow.

> (1) *Some countries are forced* to accept imported goods, while (2) _____
> _____ by tariffs and subsidies. In some countries, (3) _____
> _____ on foreign goods which are therefore more expensive to buy.
> In this way, (4) _____ because they do not have to
> compete against cheaper foreign imports. (5) _____
> the use of subsidies for producers. Because of these subsidies, production
> costs are lower and (6) _____ more cheaply.

2.8 Rewrite the second sentence (or part of the sentence) to improve the links between the two. Remove the empty words and use the passive.

1. Developing countries receive help in different ways. In some cases, people give direct aid.

   In some cases, direct aid is given. _____

2. Businesses cannot grow if other people do not give them loans.

   _____

3. In some countries, the electricity supply is unreliable. The government provides hospitals with emergency generators.

   _____

4. Developing countries have many natural resources. However, people usually exploit them for the benefit of foreign companies.

   _____

5. If no spare parts are available, people do not repair the machinery for a long time.

   _____

6. The market for eBooks is growing. Booksellers sell more eBooks than printed books in the US.

   _____

Task 3   Review

3.1   **Read the essay and complete the paragraphs with the subject noun phrases. Write the correct number. Then choose the correct form for the verbs in italics.**

Paragraph 1

a.   33% of people in Africa

b.   new developments in mobile phone technology

c.   many of them

d.   many people in Africa

e.   mobile phone use

f.   this situation

g.   they

> **Discuss the impact of mobile phone use in Africa.**
>
> **(1)** _____ *suffer / suffers* because of poor infrastructure; for example, **(2)** _____ *do / does* not have good roads, hospitals or education facilities. **(3)** _____ *struggle / struggles* to find a job and feed their families. However, **(4)** _____ *is / are* making it easier for some of them to earn money. Over the last five years, **(5)** _____ has increased fivefold in Africa. **(6)** _____ can now make or receive mobile phone calls. **(7)** _____ has benefited the lives of African people in several different ways.

Paragraph 2

h.   a further use of the mobile phone

i.   another interesting new development

j.   stall holders with produce to sell

k.   fishermen in villages who in the past just had to guess which fish were the most profitable to catch on a particular day

l.   a client

m.   the recipient

> **(8)** _____ can now find out through a simple call on a mobile phone. **(9)** _____ can also find out instantly which market is selling at the best prices. **(10)** _____ has been the development of a quick and reliable money transfer system. **(11)** _____ can deposit money into a bank for another person, such as a business associate. **(12)** _____ can then go to a bank with a code transferred by mobile phone and collect the money instantly. **(13)** _____ *is / are* a texting service which allows people in remote villages to get help and advice with, for example, healthcare procedures in hospitals.

Paragraph 3

n. the government

o. these new innovations in mobile phone use

p. global telecommunications companies

q. high government taxes on mobile phone use

---

(14) Although _____ *is / are* successful on a local scale, there are certain issues to consider for the future. (15) _____ now need to set up more extensive schemes to help local people earn money across country borders. The (16) _____ *make / makes* the costs of even part-owning and using a handset too high for the poorest people in Africa. If (17) _____ *pass / passes* new tax laws, the standard of living of more people will improve.

Adapted from: Perkins, A. (2010) 'Are mobile phones Africa's silver bullet?' The *Guardian* Online available at: http://www.guardian.co.uk/katine/katine-chronicles-blog/2010/jan/14/ mobile-phones-africa. (Retrieved 7ᵗʰ March, 2011)

3.2 **Look at the noun phrases above the paragraphs in 3.1. Are they simple (S) or complex (C)? Write *S* or *C* next to them.**
Which type of noun phrase (simple or complex) is more common in academic writing, do you think?

3.3 **There is one sentence in paragraph 3 of the essay which contains an empty subject noun phrase. Rewrite it to improve the link with the previous sentence, using the passive voice.**

Unit 2 Self-check

Choose the correct option to complete the sentences.

1 When a village expands, _____ risks losing its local traditions.
   a. the local people
   b. it
   c. the village

2 Maddison (2008) analyzes 75 developing countries in terms of their economic integration. _____ are categorized into several groups.
   a. These nations
   b. Developing countries
   c. Nations

3 **Read the sentences. What does *this situation* in the second sentence refer back to? Choose the correct option.**

Import growth increased by 6% per annum and export growth by only 2%. <u>This situation</u> shows that the effects of trade liberalization are not always straightforward.
   a. The 6% increase of import growth and the 2% increase of export growth
   b. The 2% increase of export growth
   c. Import and export growth

4 **Match the 'old information' underlined in sentences 1, 2 and 3 to their corresponding noun phrase pattern.**

a. Single noun	1. <u>These rates</u> are obstacles to investment.
b. Determiner + noun	2. <u>Ricardo</u> (1997) has played a fundamental part in the development of free trade.
c. Pronoun	3. <u>They</u> show a modest increase in real terms.

Underline the complex noun phrase in sentence 5 and 6 below. Label the headword. What is the class of the word before the headword (noun or adjective)?

5 When interest rates are high, people want to save money.

6 Small classes are helpful when students are learning to write.

7 **Underline the complex noun phrase in this sentence. Label the headword and the prepositional phrase (*PP*).**

Many aspects of traditional culture are worth saving.

8 **Underline the complex noun phrase in this sentence. Label the headword and the relative clause.**

Students who could only study in the evenings were interested in the course.

9   **Underline all the complex noun phrases in this paragraph and label the headwords.**

The restricted diet of the British population during the Second World War resulted in a nation that was generally healthier than nowadays. The shortage of sugar, chocolate and sweets meant that childhood obesity was not the problem which it is today. An everyday diet consisted of home-grown organic vegetables, small portions of meat, butter and cheese, apples in season and occasional desserts.

10   **Rewrite the following sentence, removing the 'empty' words.**

People import 45,000 tonnes of Jamaican bananas into the UK every day.

3 Looking back

In this unit you will:

- learn how to use past simple tense (active voice)
- learn how to use present perfect aspect (active voice)
- learn how you can include the present perfect in essay introductions
- practise choosing between the present perfect and past simple in an essay

In this stage you will:

- study the difference in use and form between the **past simple** and **present perfect**

Task 1   Introduction to past simple and present perfect

There are several ways in which a writer can describe actions which have taken place. These include:

a. present perfect

Use the present perfect to describe a result/situation now which has occurred because of something which happened over a period of time looking back from now.

Many changes have taken place in the school this year. (Result: now the school is different).

b. past simple

Use the past simple to describe an event which started and finished at a particular time in the past.

The head teacher introduced the first change in September.

1.1   Study sentences a–d and complete the questions.

a. Computers have become more common in primary schools over the last ten years.

b. At the beginning of the 19th century, only boys from rich families went to school.

c. Marconi invented the radio in 1901.

d. The students have completed much research this term.

1. Which two sentences describe an event which started and finished at a particular time in the past? _____ _____
2. Underline the time words which are used in these two sentences.
3. Which two sentences describe a result/situation now which occurred because of something which happened over a period of time looking back from now? _____ _____
4. Underline the time words which are used in these two sentences.
5. What is the situation or result now that is described in these two sentences?

_____

Past simple: active voice form

Study some more sentences in the past simple (active voice). The sentences give examples of a regular verb *to test* and the verb *to be*.

a. **Positive statements**
   The security staff tested the fire alarm three weeks ago.
   In the autumn term, the students were interested in the lecture.

b. **Negative statements**
   The security staff did not test the fire alarm three weeks ago.
   In the autumn term, the students were not interested in the lecture.

c. **Questions**
   Did the security staff test the alarm three weeks ago?
   Were the students interested in the lecture in the autumn term?

1.2 **Complete the tables below.**

Past simple: regular verb *to protest*

Positive statements		
Subject	**Main verb**	
Students	_____protested_____	at the economic cuts.
Negative statements		

Subject	**Auxiliary verb**	***not***	**Bare infinitive**	
Students	_____	not	_____	at the economic cuts.

Questions			
Auxiliary verb	**Subject**	**Bare infinitive**	
_____	students	_____	at the economic cuts?

Past simple: *to be*

Positive statements		
Subject	**Main verb**	
Students	were	unhappy about the economic cuts.
Pollution	_____	unacceptable in the city centre.

Negative statements			
Subject	**Main verb**	***not***	
Students	_____	not	happy about the economic cuts.
Pollution	_____	_____	acceptable in the city centre.

Questions		
Main verb	**Subject**	
_____	students	happy about the economic cuts?
_____	pollution	a problem in the city centre?

1.3 **Write sentences in the past simple, using the prompts to help you.**

1. Traffic / move / fast / this morning **(−)**

    Traffic did not move fast this morning.

2. Mobile phones / be / more expensive / in the past **(+)**

    _____

3. The university library / open / on time / last week **(?)**

    _____

4. The office / be / open plan **(?)**

    _____

5. Many students / delay / their departure / at the end of term **(+)**

    _____

6. The government / pass / any business legislation / last year **(−)**

    _____

7. The workers / discuss / their strike plans / yesterday **(+)**

    _____

8. The luggage / arrive / on time **(?)**

    _____

9. Electric cars / be / in use / 20 years ago **(−)**

    _____

Present perfect: active voice form

Study some more examples of sentences in the present perfect (active voice). The sentences give examples of a regular verb _to test_ and the verb _to be_.

a. **Positive statements**

    The security staff have tested the fire alarm recently.
    The students have been ill over the weekend.

b. **Negative statements**

    The security staff have not tested the fire alarm recently.
    The students have not been ill over the weekend.

c. **Questions**

    Have the security staff tested the alarm recently?
    Have the students been ill over the weekend?

1.4 Complete the tables below.

Present perfect: regular verb *to provide*

Positive statements			
Subject	**Auxiliary verb**	**Past participle**	
These companies	*have*	*provided*	profit figures.
The government			cycle lanes.

Negative statements				
Subject	**Auxiliary verb**	***not***	**Past participle**	
These companies		not		profit figures.
The government		not		cycle lanes.

Questions			
Auxiliary verb	**Subject**	**Past participle**	
	these companies		profit figures?
	the government		cycle lanes?

Present perfect: *to be*

Positive statements			
Subject	**Auxiliary verb**	**Past participle**	
These companies	*have*	*been*	successful.
This research			useful.

Negative statements				
Subject	**Auxiliary verb**	***not***	**Past participle**	
These companies		not		successful.
This research				useful.

Questions			
Auxiliary verb	**Subject**	**Past participle**	
	these companies		successful?
	this research		useful?

Grammar note: There are many common **irregular** verbs (apart from the verb *to be*). These verbs may have irregular past simple forms and past participles. You will study these in 2.2 in the next task.

Task 2 — The UK education system in the past

You will now read an essay to help you to understand how the past simple and present perfect are used together in an academic text.

2.1 To prepare yourself for the new vocabulary you will meet, match the words in Column A with their meanings in Column B. The first one has been done for you.

	A			B
1.	compulsory (adjective)		a.	soft white rock which you can write with, and hard stone which you can write on
2.	state school (noun phrase)		b.	a soft shoe which you wear at home
3.	entertain (verb)		c.	to help
4.	the '3 Rs' (noun phrase)		d.	government school
5.	corporal punishment (noun phrase)		e.	the money your parents earn
6.	slipper (noun)		f.	obligatory, you *must* do it
7.	chalk and slate (noun phrase)		g.	computer software which gives feedback to the user
8.	support (verb)		h.	physical punishment (e.g., hitting someone)
9.	interactive resources (noun phrase)		i.	to invite people to your house and give them dinner
10.	parental income (noun phrase)		j.	reading, writing and arithmetic

2.2 Read the essay below. All the bold verbs are either past simple (PS) or present perfect (PP) active voice only. Write *PS* or *PP* for each number.

> **Describe some of the changes which have taken place in the school system in the UK in the last 200 years.**
>
> School attendance is now compulsory in the UK for children between the ages of 5 and 16. Children attend primary school from 5 to 11 years of age, and then secondary school until they are at least 16 years old. The modern state school system aims to treat all children in the same way and to give them all equal opportunities. However, the school system (1) **has not** always been like this. Some of the changes which (2) **have taken place** over the last 200 years are outlined below.
>
> At the beginning of the 19th century, only boys from rich families (3) **went** to school. Girls from rich backgrounds were

1.   *PP*
2.   _____
3.   _____

taught at home. Boys were taught Physical Education, English, Philosophy, Maths, Latin and Greek, whereas girls' education (4) **focused** on reading, writing, sewing, singing, dancing and French. This was because girls' education (5) **involved** preparation for marriage, running a home and entertaining whereas boys' education (6) **aimed** at preparing them for work: the army, perhaps, or a political life. Gradually, free state schools (7) **began** to be provided for all children, and when the 19th century (8) **ended**, school had become compulsory for all until the age of 13. This meant that all children (9) **had** the opportunity to read and write.

4. _____

5. _____

6. _____

7. _____

8. _____

9. _____

Throughout the first half of the 20th century, schools (10) **were** traditional and disciplinarian in their approach to learning. Children (11) **learnt** the '3Rs' (reading, 'riting and 'rithmetic) and the Christian religion. Pupils (12) **sat** in rows, they were not allowed to talk to each other during lessons, and girls and boys were not allowed to sit together. Many schools (13) **were** single-sex. Corporal punishment was allowed; children were hit with slippers, rulers or canes by the teachers for not knowing the answers to questions, and they were encouraged to learn facts, stories and poems by memorizing and by copying from the board or from dictation. Chalk and slates were used as they were cheaper than pen, books and paper. Only the most academic and the richest children (14) **were** able to go to university; most children (15) **left** school as soon as they could to find jobs to help support their families.

10. _____

11. _____

12. _____

13. _____

14. _____

15. _____

Gradually, such old-fashioned ways were replaced by more modern ideas. Schools (16) **became** more inclusive. In the 1970s, comprehensive schools became common for 11 to 16-year-olds. Girls and boys (17) **began** to be treated more fairly; they could study the same subjects within the same classroom, and in 1986 the government (18) **banned** corporal punishment and (19) **changed** the exam system. All children everywhere then (20) **had** the right to take the same exams. Teachers began to change the way they (21) **taught** so that learning would be more enjoyable and interesting for everyone. Modern teaching methods are likely to include pair and group work, with the emphasis on encouraging children to learn by discovering answers for themselves rather than constantly relying on the teacher. Modern technology is widely used in classrooms. Computers are available for children to use even

16. _____

17. _____

18. _____

19. _____

20. _____

21. _____

in primary schools, and most schools now have fast access to the Internet and use interactive resources and whiteboards in the classrooms.

The school system **(22) has clearly improved** in many ways since the 19th century. Most importantly, children's right to education no longer depends on parental income, and greater educational opportunities are offered more widely to all. It is important that education continues to keeps pace with developments in society throughout the 21st century

22. _____

2.3 **It is important to learn irregular verb forms. Complete the table with the three forms of all the numbered verbs from 2.2 (some are regular; others are irregular). Use a dictionary if necessary.**

Grammar note: Irregular verbs have irregular forms for the past simple and/or past participle. You should always check in a dictionary that you have used the correct form of these verbs in your writing.

Infinitive	Past simple	Past participle
1. *be*	*was/were*	*been*
2.		
3.		
4.		
5.		
6.		
7.		
8.		
9.		
10.		
11.		
12.		
13.		
14.		
15.		
16.		
17.		
18.		
19.		
20.		
21.		
22.		

Task 3	Time phrases used with the past simple

3.1 **Find and underline these four time expressions in the essay in 2.2. Match them with the sentence endings.**

Time expressions	Sentence endings
1. At the beginning of the 19th century	a. schools were traditional and disciplinarian in their approach to learning.
2. Throughout the first half of the 20th century	b. comprehensive schools became common for 11 to 16-year-olds.
3. In the 1970s	c. only boys from rich families went to school.
4. In 1986	d. the government banned corporal punishment and changed the exam system.

3.2 **As you have seen in 1.1, time phrases used with the past simple describe an event which started and finished at a particular time in the past. Write PS (past simple) next to the time phrases which indicate this.**

1. At the beginning of the 19th century _PS_	11. In the last few years _____
2. Frequently _____	12. In November 1983 _____
3. Several years ago _____	13. In the 1990s _____
4. Recently _____	14. Over this decade _____
5. One year ago _____	15. Between 1914 and 1918 _____
6. Always _____	16. For ten years _____
7. Two days later _____	17. Already _____
8. Since then _____	18. Between 1990 and 1995 _____
9. Since the year 2000 _____	19. Never _____
10. In the 20th century _____	20. This year _____

3.3 **Complete the sentences below using the prompts in brackets. Use the correct tense. Some of them need the negative form of the verb.**

1. At the beginning of the 19th century (there / be / no / mobile phones)
   There were no mobile phones.

2. (The First World War / take place) between 1914 and 1918.

   _____

3. In the 20th century (cars / become / very popular)

   _____

4. In July 2010, (the football World Cup / take place / in South Africa)

_____

5. In November 1983, (Bill Gates / launch / Microsoft Windows)

_____

6. Many years ago, (women / traditionally / work / inside the home)

_____

7. (Mitt Romney / not win) US Presidential election in 2012.

_____

8. (There / be / an economic crisis) several years ago.

_____

3.4 **Read the paragraph about Chompy. Find the four sentences which use the past simple (active voice only). Write the numbers.**

(1) Chompy, a global multinational, is the world's biggest food and drink company. (2) It began trading at the end of the 19th century. (3) It manufactures brands such as *Choccy* biscuits, *Cool* lemonade and *Trendy* ice cream and is popular in 125 countries worldwide. (4) Unlike some other corporations, Chompy is successful because it has adapted its products to local market conditions. (5) For example, 15 years ago, it introduced very small packets of *Flexo* cooking oil and *Bing* crackers in some of the poorest countries simply because most consumers in those countries did not have much money. (6) It is now clear that Chompy has invested wisely; (7) in 2001, it ventured into new markets in Central America, (8) and this year has recorded profits of €14 billion. (9) Over the last ten years, Chompy has built many schools, hospitals and community centres for the poor in small villages in Central America. (10) Two years ago, the company spent €17 million on schools in Belize.

1. _____   2. _____   3. _____   4. _____

3.5 **Look again at the four past simple sentences from 3.4. Write questions about them, using the words below.**

When … ? *When did it introduce small packets of Bing crackers?* _____

What … ? _____

Why … ? _____

How much … ? _____

Stage B

In this stage you will:
- learn how to use the present perfect aspect (active voice)
- practise using the present perfect aspect

Task 1 — Using the present perfect aspect

There are several ways in which you can use the present perfect in your writing:
- to give a reason for a current situation
- to show how events from the past affect a current situation
- to describe the duration of time of a current situation

Notice how the present perfect always refers in some way to the current situation. The present perfect gives a new perspective (or aspect) concerning the situation now.

1.1 **Study three sentences from the text about Chompy referred to in Stage A, 3.4 and answer the questions.**

a. Unlike some other corporations, Chompy is successful because it has adapted its products to local market conditions.

b. It is now clear that Chompy has invested wisely.

c. Over the last ten years, Chompy has built many schools, hospitals and community centres for the poor in small villages in Central America.

1. Which sentence gives a reason for a current situation? _____
2. Which sentence shows how events from the past affect a current situation? _____
3. Which sentence describes the duration of time of a current situation? _____

Task 2 — Giving a reason for a current situation

You can use the present perfect to give a reason for a current situation.

For example:

       Current situation   Reason

a. *Chompy is very successful because it has adapted its products to local market conditions.*

  ← ← ← (period of time) ← ← ← ↓

PAST: it has adapted its products   **NOW:** Chompy is successful

       Current situation   Reason

b. *There is a high number of refugees because many people have escaped the conflict.*

  ← ← ← (period of time) ← ← ↓

PAST: many people have escaped   **NOW:** there is a high number of refugees

2.1 **Read the sentences below and study the diagrams. Complete the blanks (a, b, c and d) with the necessary words from the sentences.**

1. Banga is a poor country because foreign companies have not invested in the economy.

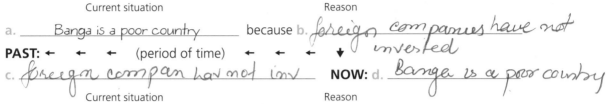

Current situation   Reason

a. _____Banga is a poor country_____ because b. *foreign companies have not invested*

PAST: ← ← ← (period of time) ← ← ← ↓

c. *foreign compan hav not inv*   NOW: d. _*Banga is a poor country*_

Current situation   Reason

2. The workers are on strike because conditions in the factory have not improved.

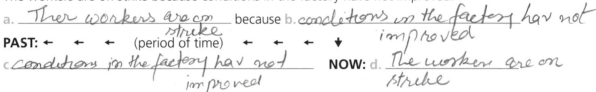

a. _*Ther workers are on strike*_ because b. *conditions in the factory hav not improved*

PAST: ← ← ← (period of time) ← ← ← ↓

c. *conditions in the factory hav not improved*   NOW: d. _*The worker are on strike*_

2.2 **Read the sentences which describe a *current situation now*. Use the present perfect to add a reason to each sentence.**

1. There are few computers in schools (government / not / invest / money / in them)
   There are few computers in schools because the government has not invested money in them.

2. The number of unemployed people is high (there / be / deep recession) in recent years.
   b'cau there has been a deep recussion in recently years.

3. Many people now live in cities (opportunities / in the countryside / decline) over the last few years.
   b'caus opportu in the countrysd have declned over the last five years

4. The economic situation is critical (banks / make / bad loans) over the last decade.
   b'se banks have made bad loans

5. Student applications are now low (tuition fees / rise) this year.
   b'cause tuition fees have risen this year

6. The sewer system cannot cope with current demand (the government) never (upgrade it).
   b'c govt has never

7. Healthcare and education in the developing world are improving (awareness of human rights issues / increase).
   _____

8. People on low incomes pay less tax (the law / change) recently.
   _____

9. Many young people in villages want to leave (the standard of living / not rise) over the last twenty years.
   _____

10. Foreign goods are often expensive (the government / impose / heavy taxes / on imports).
    _____

Grammar note: Time phrases used with the present perfect are different from those used with the past simple. In Stage A of this unit, you have seen that with the past simple, you should use time phrases which indicate a finished time in the past. However, with the present perfect, the period of time which they indicate began in the past, but the result of the activity is relevant now. Revisit the time phrases in A 3.2. The time phrases which are not used with the past simple in this exercise can all be used with the present perfect.

2.3 Look back at 2.2 and write out the time phrases used. Notice that you do not always need to use one when you use the present perfect.
Time phrases used with the present perfect aspect.

1. _____no time phrase used_____   6. _____

2. _____   7. _____

3. _____   8. _____

4. _____   9. _____

5. _____   10. _____

Task 3	**Showing how events from the past affect a current situation**

You can use the present perfect to show how past events affect a current situation.

Study the sentence below:

event over a period of time in the past   current situation

In the last few years, the situation has become clearer, and the problem must now be resolved.

3.1 Complete the sentences with the present perfect.

Grammar note: The time phrases: *always*; *frequently*; *already*; *never*; *recently* are all placed **in between** the auxiliary verb and the main verb.

1. Scholars / always / disagree / on this topic, and the controversy continues today.

   Scholars have always disagreed on this topic, and the controversy continues today.

2. The situation is not ideal, but the company / already / take action / to resolve it.

   _____

3. It is now clear that the government / frequently / compromise / its policies.

   _____

4. Since then, research / continue /, and there appears to be a direct link between obesity and diabetes.

   _____

5. Over the last five years, there / be / a banking crisis; it is more difficult to take out a loan in the current economic climate.

   _____

6. Scholars / frequently / debate / the accuracy of Taylor's (2008) decision-making process model. They suggest that it does not fully apply to real-life situations.

   _____

7. Smith (1987) / never / agree / that the two planning approaches are distinct from each other.

   _____

You can use the present perfect to show how the results of past research affect current knowledge. The reporting verbs (for example, *show*; *discover*; *find*; *prove*) go in the present perfect; the results go in the present tense.

  a. *Research has shown that criminal behaviour is often the result of poor upbringing (Mieter, 2001; Stevens and Yang, 2010).*

  b. *Green (2002) has found that parental failure to use baby talk with their babies may be a mistake.*

3.2 Rewrite the sentences according to the prompts.

1. A leading speech therapist / discover / that nurture can speed language development (Bizet, 2009).

   A leading speech therapist has discovered that nurture can speed language development (Bizet, 2009).

2. Dongwoo (2012) / prove / the theory / that there is a relationship between the two variables.

   _____

3. Behaviourists in Denmark / find / new evidence, which may dramatically change current thinking (Zachman et al., 2012).

   _____

4. Johns (2010) / publish / her research into the life expectancy of professional sports men and women. Her findings are surprising.

   _____

5. Research / over this decade / show / that stopping smoking increases life expectancy (Alan and Paige, 2003; Shen et al., 2013).

   _____

6. Scientists / recently / discover / that the complex structure of butterflies' wings enables the insects to regulate their level of heat absorption (Kovins, 2012; Marc et al., 2013).

   _____

| Task 4 | Describing the duration of time of a current situation |

4.1 Read the sentences below and answer the questions.

> Edward Crisp set up Chompy in 1890 near Manchester. It is now a multinational company with offices in major cities around the world. Its UK head office has been in London since 1915.

1. Where is Chompy's head office in the UK? _____

2. How long has it been in London? _____

3. Which verb form is used to describe 'how long' it has been there? _____

In Unit 1, Stage A, you learnt to use the present simple to describe a permanent fact or situation.

For example:

Chompy has offices around the world.

It sells food and drink.

If you want to say how long the situation has existed, you use the present perfect *instead of* the present simple. The present perfect refers to the present (the situation is true now), and also to the past (it has existed for a period of time).

Chompy's head office has been in London since 1915. (= Its London head office opened in 1915 and it is still there now.)

4.2 **Imagine that you want to write about a school which is in the centre of a town. The school opened in the year 1651 CE and is still there now. 1651 was also the year that the English Civil War ended.**

Look at the three ways to complete the sentence to describe how long a situation has existed. Complete the sentences with *for* or *since*.

The school has been in the town centre …

1. _____ the Civil War ended.

2. _____ over 350 years.

3. _____ 1651 CE.

There are three ways to write about *how long* with the present perfect:

a. *for + length of time*
   The school has been in the town centre *for over 350 years*.
   PAST: 1651 – The school opened   **NOW:** the school is still in the town centre
      in the town centre.

b. *since + date*
   The school has been in the town centre *since 1651 CE*.
   PAST: 1651 – The school opened in the   **NOW:** the school is still in the town centre
      town centre.

c. *since + event in the past*
   The school has been in the town centre *since the Civil War ended*.
   PAST: 1651 – The school opened in the   **NOW:** the school is still in the town centre
      town centre. The civil war ended.

Grammar note: Remember that if you want to say that a situation has existed for ever, you use *always* (without *since* or *for*). *Always* goes between *have/has* and the past participle: *The school has always been in the town centre.*

4.3 **Complete the present perfect sentences that describe how long a situation has existed. Use the phrases in the boxes below.**

1. Situation *now*: The computers in the classrooms do not work.

many weeks	the technician left	January

The computers in the classrooms have not worked for _____.

The computers in the classrooms have not worked since _____.

The computers in the classrooms have not worked since _____.

2. Situation *now*: Colombia is an independent country.

1819	Bolívar defeated the Spanish	about 200 years

Colombia has been an independent country for _____.

Colombia has been an independent country since _____.

Colombia has been an independent country since _____.

4.4 **Rewrite the sentences to show how long the situations have existed, using *since* or *for*, and the words in brackets.**

1. Barchester is an important place. (1700 CE)

   Barchester has been an important place since 1700 CE.

2. The equipment in this school does not improve. (a long time)

   _____

3. Farmers cultivate sugar here. (invaders / colonized the country)

   _____

4. Students at this school do not learn Latin. (ten years)

   _____

5. Local people use this plant to make indigo. (the 4th century BCE)

   _____

6. Dr Macgregor teaches English. (the 1980s)

   _____

7. Ms Sweet works for Chompy. (she finished her MBA)

   _____

8. The education system does not change. (1952)

   _____

9. The school has computers. (over 15 years)

   _____

10. Foreign languages are an important part of the curriculum. (always)

   _____

4.5 Correct the mistakes in the sentences below.

1. The organization is the same since three years.

   The organization has been the same for three years.

2. Korea has universities during 1500 years.

   _____

3. The UK school system is multicultural since 60 years ago.

   _____

4. There is free health care in the UK since the 1940s.

   _____

5. The new laws on copyright existed since 2001.

   _____

6. Farmers grow bananas fairly successfully since 600 years.

   _____

7. Bankers are under attack since five years ago.

   _____

4.6 Review: How do you use the present perfect tense (active voice)? How do you form it? Complete the sentences below. There is one gap for each missing word. Choose from the words below.

reason	current situation	_to have_	past participle	events

1. You can use the present perfect to give a _____ for a current situation.

2. You can use it to show how _____ from the past affect a current situation.

3. You can use the present perfect to describe the duration of time of a

   _____ _____.

4. In order to form the present perfect, you use the present tense of the verb

   _____ _____ plus the _____ _____

   of the main verb.

Stage C

In this stage you will:

- learn how you can include the present perfect in introductions to essays
- practise choosing between the present perfect and past simple in an essay

| Task 1 | **Using the present perfect in introductions to essays** |

1.1 **Read the following introduction and answer the questions.**

> **Discuss the advantages and disadvantages of mobile phone technology**
>
> (1) Mobile phone technology has developed rapidly over the last ten years and is now a global phenomenon. (2) It is a convenient means of communication and a popular form of entertainment for many people. (3) However, many people are concerned about the health issues surrounding its widespread use. (4) This essay will discuss the advantages and disadvantages of mobile phone technology.

1. Which sentence shows how an event from the past has affected a current situation? _____

2. Which time phrase shows the length of time of this current situation? _____

3. Which sentences gives further detail about the current situation? _____

The present perfect has been used in this introduction to set the scene for the discussion surrounding the benefits and drawbacks of mobile phone technology. Read the text and answer the questions.

> **Discuss the advantages and disadvantages of studying in another country.**
>
> (1) Over the last 20 years, students have frequently travelled abroad to study in a foreign country. (2) They benefit by improving their additional languages and experiencing a different educational culture. (3) However, studying abroad can be very expensive. (4) This essay will discuss both the advantages and disadvantages of studying in another country.

4. Which sentence shows how an event from the past has affected a current situation? _____

5. Which time phrase shows the length of time of this current situation? _____

6. Which sentence(s) give(s) further detail about the current situation? _____

> **Discuss the causes of poverty and suggest some solutions.**
>
> (1) Poverty has been a global problem for many years. (2) Nowadays 80% of the population are living on less than $10 per day (Chen and Ravallion, 2008). (3) Research teams know that lack of education is one of the main causes of poverty and that government and families can play a crucial role in developing the education system. (4) This essay will discuss the main cause of poverty and evaluate some solutions.

7. Which sentence(s) show(s) how an event from the past has affected a current situation? _____

8. Which time phrase shows the length of time of this current situation? _____

9. Which sentence(s) give(s) further detail about the current situation? _____

Grammar note: An introduction can begin with a general statement about the **topic** of the essay. It then gives background information about the key points in the essay title and describes the essay structure. It moves from general (topic) to more specific (essay structure).

1.2 **Read the following extracts from four student essays, and where phrases are in bold, correct the present perfect verb form and/or time word used.**

> 1. The use of mobile phones **rapidly increased in 15 years**.
>   _The use of mobile phones has rapidly increased over the last 15 years._
> 2. Over the last 10 years, the study advice service **improves**.
>   _____
> 3. Obesity **becomes** a very serious problem in recent years.
>   _____
> 4. Poverty exists in many parts of the world, and in the last four decades many aid organizations **raised** funds for poor nations.
>   _____

1.3 **The extracts from introductions below come from the essay *Discuss the advantages and disadvantages of mobile phone technology*. Improve them according to the instructions.**

Introduction 1

> Mobile phones are used by millions of people today. **They are the first means of communication** because it is quicker to chat on a mobile than to meet up.

Show the duration of time for this current situation (several years).

_____

Introduction 2

> Mobile phones are widely used **because they give speedy access to social networking sites.** In Saudi Arabia, many people own several mobile phones.

This is a reason for a current situation. Show how long it has continued (since / the invention of the smartphone).

Introduction 3

> Nowadays, people are keen to phone friends anytime, anywhere on their mobiles **because it becomes cheap to make calls.** For example, mobile phone cards are readily available; the price per minute is more economical than using landlines.

Show that the reason started in the past and the result is now cheap prices.

Task 2	Practise choosing between the present perfect and past simple in an essay

2.1 **Before you read the complete essay, read the introduction below and answer the questions.**

> **Nurture strongly influences early human development. Discuss.**
>
> It is a controversial issue whether nurture* strongly influences early human development or nature* decides the way a newborn baby will develop. This has been a subject of academic discussion since the 17th century, and as a result many philosophers and psychologists have carried out experiments and research, particularly over the 20th century. This essay will explain the main ideas and continue the debate as to whether it is upbringing or inherited genes which determine human behaviour.

*If you nurture a child, you give them care, attention and education. If you leave a child's upbringing to nature, you allow them to develop naturally.

1. What is the duration of time of the current nature/nurture controversy?
2. What is the duration of time of the experiments and research into this issue?

2.2 **Now read the rest of the student essay. Complete the sentences, choosing between the past simple and the present perfect.**

> Firstly, many scientists over the years **(1)** _____ (**support**) the idea that the environment which infants have been exposed to strongly influences their development. In the 17th century, the ideas of John Locke **(2)** _____ (**be**) highly influential. He **(3)** _____ (**be**) the first philosopher to support the idea that a newborn baby receives information from the environment with the five senses in order to build

his knowledge. Later, in the first half of the 20th century, the behaviourists Watson and Skinner (4) _____ (support) this idea more strongly by suggesting that they could manipulate a baby to become whatever type of adult they (5) _____(want). For example, they could 'mould' a doctor, a lawyer or a thief just by changing the upbringing of an infant.

On the other hand, the fact that children's development is determined by nature was an established position before the philosopher John Locke (6) _____ (reject) it. It was generally believed that newborn babies would grow up independently in the way nature had decided. Charles Darwin's theory of evolution in 1859 (7) _____(add) further weight to this idea by indicating the importance of the human genetic base, in comparison to the influence from the environment.

More recent research (8) _____ (suggest) that the division into two theories is not necessary. Psychologists now believe that a newborn baby is strongly influenced both by nature and nurture. The motor abilities of all babies always (9) _____ (follow) the same process. First they roll over, then they stand with their parents' support or with furniture support and then they walk without any help. However, the speed with which they develop depends on how much input they (10) _____ (receive) during these formative months. Kegan, for example, who (11) _____ (research) babies' speech development in the 1970s, (12) _____ (find) that if a baby grows up close to many people who talk to him, he speaks much faster than a baby who is alone most of the day.

Therefore, as researchers (13) _____ (show), it is evident that nurture strongly influences early human development. However, it is also clear that nature has an important role in determining human behaviour.

Unit 3 Self-check

Choose the correct option to complete the sentences.

1 The vice-president of the village committee _____ his job last year.
a. leaved
b. left
c. has left

2 In recent years, China's housing market _____.
a. expanded
b. has expanded
c. expands

3 The student did not _____ the password to access the network.
a. knew
b. know
c. known

4 _____ the toxic nature of these loans _____ directly to the financial crash?
a. Was … lead
b. Does … led
c. Did … lead

5 The stock market _____ to its lowest point in January last year.
a. fell
b. fallen
c. has fallen

6 The students _____ here _____ three years.
a. are … since
b. have been … since
c. have been … for

7 People are now living longer because medical care _____ substantially _____ over the last 50 years.
a. is … improving
b. is … improved
c. has … improved

8 The report shows that the situation _____.
a. already changes
b. already changed
c. has already changed

9 The two royal families _____ between 1939 and 1945.
   a. have not met
   b. did not meet
   c. do not meet

10 Professor Russell still gives regular lectures; she _____ in the same post for 35 years.
   a. is
   b. was
   c. has been

4 Showing logical links (1)

In this unit you will:

- learn how to link ideas logically in your writing by using linking words effectively
- practise using the words in the table below

Writer's purpose	Short linking words	Paired linking words	Sentence-connecting words
To link similar ideas	and		in addition also
To build an argument	and		furthermore moreover also
To emphasize two or more similar ideas		both … and not only … but also	
To contrast different ideas	but yet		however
To build a contrasting argument			on the other hand
To emphasize two negatives		neither … nor	
To show a result	so		therefore as a result
To give another possibility	or		alternatively
To emphasize another possibility		either … or	
To summarize			on the whole to sum up
To show time or sequence			firstly finally
To give an example			for example

In this stage you will:
- practise using short linking words to express relationships between ideas
- practise using sentence-connecting words to link to an idea in a previous sentence
- study simple and compound sentences

Writer's purpose	Short linking words	Paired linking words	Sentence-connecting words
To link similar ideas	and		in addition also
To build an argument	and		furthermore moreover also
To contrast different ideas	but yet		however
To build a contrasting argument			on the other hand
To show a result	so		therefore as a result
To give another possibility	or		alternatively

Task 1   Introduction to logical linking words

1.1   **Compare paragraphs a and b and answer the questions.**

> a. At the 10th International Health Conference, Carlos Gallo gave a paper on the link between diet and health. Elisa Jones led a seminar on heart disease. The conference fees were not cheap. Many health care workers enrolled on the conference. They paid the fees themselves.

> b. At the 10th International Health Conference, Carlos Gallo gave a paper on the link between diet and health, and Elisa Jones led a seminar on heart disease. The conference fees were not cheap. However, many health care workers enrolled on the conference, and they paid the fees themselves.

1. What is the main difference in the way that they are written?

2. Which is easier to understand: a or b? _____

Paragraph b contains logical linking words, which express relationships between ideas. In academic writing, it is important to reveal the logic behind your 'thought processes'. This shows evidence of critical thinking.

1.2 Look at paragraph b again and answer the questions.

1. Which short linking word links similar ideas between clauses? _____

2. Which sentence-connecting word expresses a contrast and shows something unexpected?

   _____

3. Why is the statement unexpected?

   _____

Task 2	Short linking words

2.1 Study the sentences. Match each linking word in bold to its function, by writing the correct letters in the table.

1. Salt is lost through perspiration during very hot weather **or** vigorous exercise.
2. The government declared a ceasefire, **but** the army did not respect it.
3. The institute needs to increase student fees, **or** they will cut the number of courses.
4. The organization is currently offering to inform, motivate, train **and** support people in rural areas.
5. The work was hard **yet** rewarding.
6. This is the beginning of a worldwide epidemic, **and** the situation is very worrying.
7. The project has received more funding, **so** the research can continue until the end of the year.

to link similar ideas	
to contrast different ideas	
to give another possibility	l.
to show a result	

Short linking words can be used in two different ways within a sentence.

Look at the examples below:

a. **to link words within one simple sentence**

   1. two words of the same class

                adjective   adjective

   *The work was hard **but** rewarding.*

   2. words of the same class in a list

                        noun   noun   noun

   *Photosynthesis requires sunlight, water **and** carbon dioxide.*

   A simple sentence contains one clause (one subject and one verb).

---

b. to link two separate clauses within a compound sentence

clause	clause
S V	S V

The government declared a ceasefire, **but** *the army did not respect it.*

A compound sentence contains two (or more) separate clauses, joined by a linking word (e.g., subject + verb, *but* subject + verb).

2.2 **Look again at the sentences in 2.1 and analyze the sentences. Do the linking words join two clauses (compound sentence), or two or more *words* (simple sentence)? Write *C* (compound) or *S* (simple).**

1. ___S___   4. _____   6. _____

2. _____   5. _____   7. _____

3. _____

2.3 **Look again at the sentences in 2.1. For the simple sentences, underline the words joined by the linking word and indicate word class (adjective, noun or verb) as in example a in the box above.**
For the compound sentences, underline and label the subject and verb as in example b above.

Grammar note: When a short linking word joins two or more words, the words must belong to the same word class: e.g., all nouns, all adjectives or all verbs.

2.4 **Study sentences 1–7 in 2.1 again.**

1. If the linking word joins two clauses, which punctuation mark is used before the second clause? (e.g., sentence 2) _____

2. If the linking word joins two words, is there a comma in between them? (e.g., sentence 5) _____

3. If the linking word *and* joins together three or more words in a list, which punctuation marks are used? (e.g., sentence 4) _____

Summary of sentence structure and punctuation using short linking words
a. simple sentence
The work was hard <u>but</u> rewarding.

word	*and* *but* *yet* *or*	word

> The organization is currently offering to inform, motivate, train <u>and</u> support people in rural areas.

word, word, word	*and*	word
	or	

b. compound sentence

The government declared a ceasefire, but the army did not respect it.

simple clause	*and*	simple clause
Subject + Verb,	*but*	Subject + Verb
	yet	
	or	

Sentences can be joined together to make one simple sentence by adding linking words and punctuation. If the subject and verb is the same in the first and second clauses, you can delete them to make just a simple clause.

After school, students can go to a university. They can go to a local college.
After school, students can go to a university or ~~they can~~ go to a local college.

2.5 **Join the sentences together to make one simple sentence by adding linking words and any necessary punctuation.**

1. They are interested in other cultures. They are interested in historic sites. They are interested in foreign languages.

   They are interested in other cultures, historic sites and foreign languages.

2. The course was excellent. It was inexpensive.

   _____

3. There is a Redwood tree in the botanic garden. There is a Redwood tree in the university gardens.

   _____

4. Arab countries are hot in summer. They are warm in winter.

   _____

5. The solar cells are non-toxic. They are non-corrosive. They are low cost.

   _____

6. Students can study independently. They can study with a partner.

   _____

2.6 **Join the sentences together to make one compound sentence by adding a short linking word and any necessary punctuation.**

1. Penguins are adapted to cold climates. They can survive in Antarctica.

    Penguins are adapted to cold climates, so can survive in Antarctica.

2. Arab people like travelling to European countries. They do not always enjoy the food.

    _____

3. Goods are delivered directly to the customer's home. They are collected from the store.

    _____

4. Many young people listen to pop music. They play video games.

    _____

5. Many people have elderly relatives with health problems. They do not want to care for them in their own homes.

    _____

6. In the past, there were not many good secondary schools. The good ones were always full.

    _____

7. Families in the UK can ask for financial help if they earn below a certain amount. They can rent out a room in their house if they have the space.

    _____

Task 3	Using sentence-connecting words

In Task 2 you looked at words which link ideas **within** a sentence. There are other linking words which connect two **separate** sentences. If, for example, you want to add to an idea, or express a contrast to an idea from the previous sentence, you use a sentence-connecting word.

3.1 **Study the sentences 1–7. Write the linking words in the table on the next page and tick (✔) the correct function.**

1. In Italy, several religious holidays fall in the middle of the week, which is inconvenient for employers. **However**, the government has no immediate plans to change these arrangements.
    OR The government, **however**, has no immediate plans to change these arrangements.

2. The government has passed a law to allow fathers to claim paternity leave, and to allow parents to ask their employers for flexible hours at work. **In addition**, it has promised free nursery places for all children over the age of three.
    OR It has, **in addition**, promised free nursery places for all children over the age of three.
    OR It has **also** promised free nursery places for all children over the age of three.

3. This job requires a good honours degree in any discipline. **Alternatively**, a degree, HND or equivalent is accepted if it is combined with experience at management level.

4. The research project has confirmed that there is a strong link between cigarette smoking and cancer. **As a result**, cigarette advertising is banned in many countries.
    OR Cigarette advertising is, **as a result**, banned in many countries.

5. Five years after the German defence minister received his PhD, Bayreuth University found evidence of plagiarism in his thesis. **Therefore**, they withdrew his degree, and he resigned from his position within the government.

6. Urban spaces are improved if users have access to sun, wind, plants, water, artworks, good night lighting and seating. Victoria Plaza has a well-designed seating area with a water fountain, which is shaded by two oak trees. **Moreover**, this area is wind protected due to the high density of buildings.

OR This area is **also** wind protected due to the high density of buildings.

7. Regular markets enhance people's quality of life; they sell local produce and residents are more likely to walk to do their shopping. **On the other hand**, the goods may not offer the best value for money nor the range of choice that big supermarkets can provide.

	To give another possibility	To show a result	To contrast different ideas (something unexpected)	To link similar ideas	To build an argument	To build a contrasting argument
1. However			✔			
2.						
3.						
4.						
5.						
6.						
7.						

3.2 **Study the sentences in 3.1 again. Write the position of the linking word or words in the sentence and punctuation.**

1. _'However' – at the beginning of a sentence followed by a comma, or after the subject and before the main verb with a comma before and after to separate it from the rest of the sentence._

2. _____

3. _____

4. _____

5. _____

6. _____
_____
_____
_____

7. _____
_____
_____
_____

Grammar note: It is not considered good academic style to begin a new sentence with *and*; *but*; *yet*; *or*; *so*. You should replace them with a suitable sentence-connecting word.

3.3 **In the sentences below, the sentence-connecting words in bold are incorrect. Replace them with a correct word.**

1. In most factories at the beginning of the 20th century, wages were low, working hours were long, and job security did not exist. **However**, sickness benefit and redundancy compensation were unknown.

   In addition, sickness benefit and redundancy compensation were unknown.
   OR _Sickness benefit and redundancy compensation were, in addition, unknown._
   OR _Sickness benefit and redundancy compensation were also unknown._

2. In 1960, the unemployment rate for the under 25s was only 2.4%. **However**, it was easy for young people to find a job.

   _____

3. Male-dominated societies are most common in countries with traditional cultures. **Therefore**, even in developed societies, some men still behave as if they have more authority than women.

   _____

4. An LCD screen consists of a thin layer of liquid crystals between two glass plates, which are illuminated in one of two ways. Behind the plates there is a small backlight. **In addition**, a mirror may be used to provide light for the screen.

   _____

5. There is a need for reliability and validity when producing statistics. **As a result**, it is often difficult to gather data in large enough samples to be considered reliable.

   _____

6. Overweight people are sometimes considered too lazy to follow a healthy diet. **Alternatively**, it can be extremely difficult not only to lose weight, but also to maintain the weight loss.

   _____

7. These studies show that children from wealthier backgrounds do better at school. **As a result**, researchers have shown that these youngsters stay physically fitter in later life.

   _____

8. There are two different definitions of cognitive development. It usually refers to the development of different cognitive skills (such as language) during childhood and adolescence. **Therefore**, it may refer in a more general sense to the overall evolution of intellectual capacity throughout the whole of a person's life.

   _____

9. Maintaining existing trade tariffs can cause problems. After signing, trade agreements cannot respond to changes in international agreements. **However**, hostility is created between trading partners.

   _____

10. This whole project will be expensive. The land acquisition costs are 0.5% of land value, and the architect and consultancy fees are 6.5% of build costs. **Therefore**, the experts' fees will increase by 1% in the coming year.

11. There are several possible consequences of the government loosening regulations concerning new housing developments on greenfield sites. There will be fewer natural places for people to enjoy leisure activities, and many animals which are already under threat, such as foxes, will have smaller hunting grounds. Pollution will extend to rural areas, increasing CO_2 emissions and encouraging climate change. **Moreover**, new buildings will attract business investment into the area, creating new jobs and a buoyant economy. There will also be a wider choice of places to live, which should make housing more affordable for many people.

Grammar note: Don't use *besides* as a linking word in academic writing; use another of the linking words in this unit instead. Don't use *eventually* instead of *finally*: *eventually* means 'after a long time', whereas *finally* is used in academic writing to show the last item in a list.

Stage B

In this stage you will:
- use paired linking words to express relationships between ideas in your writing
- learn more about compound sentences

Task 1 — both ... and

Writer's purpose	Paired linking words
To emphasize two or more similar ideas	both ... and not only ... but also
To emphasize another possibility	either ... or
To emphasize two negatives	neither ... nor

1.1 **Compare sentences a and b. Which sentence emphasizes the countries where sales have increased?**

a. Sales have increased in America and Australia. □

b. Sales have increased both in America and in Australia. □

1.2 **Study the sentences and answer the questions below.**

a. Central government controls the education system in both England and Wales.
b. Gulls both catch fish in the sea and search for rubbish left by tourists.
c. The products are both suitable and readily available.

1. Which sentence is compound? _____
2. Which sentences are simple? _____
3. Why is there no comma in sentence b?

Grammar note: To emphasize the two noun phrases, put *both … and* in front of the noun phrases. To emphasize the two verbs, put *both … and* in front of the verbs. To emphasize two adjectives, put *both … and* in front of the adjectives.

1.3 Combine the sentences below in the best way, emphasizing the nouns or verbs by adding *both … and* in the appropriate place.

Remember: If the subject is the same in both clauses, you do not need to repeat the subject or put a comma before *and* (see 1.2 b above).

1. Exercise increases serotonin levels / it helps considerably with weight loss.

   Exercise both increases serotonin levels and helps considerably with weight loss.

2. In the early modern period, European companies gained territorial power / economic power.

   _____

3. Unemployment results in loss of economic output for the country / it causes depression for individual people.

   _____

4. This essay discusses the films / the newspaper reviews from that period.

   _____

If the verb construction is auxiliary verb (AV) + main verb (MV), you place the word *both* between the auxiliary and main verb

For example:

         AV   MV   MV

a. *The government has <u>both</u> regained control of the area <u>and</u> (has) won the support of the people.*

         AV   MV   MV

b. *The government is <u>both</u> regaining control of the area <u>and</u> (is) <u>winning</u> the support of the people.*

                  AV   MV   AV

c. *the company's employees are <u>both</u> paid a good basic salary <u>and</u> (are) generously*

     MV

<u>rewarded</u> with bonuses.

1.4 Combine the sentences below into one sentence, adding *both … and* in the appropriate place.

1. Foreign companies have bought land cheaply / they have exploited its natural resources.

   Foreign companies have both bought land cheaply and exploited its natural resources.

2. Most coffee bars offer a welcoming atmosphere / they attract customers with loyalty cards.

   _____

3. These nationalized industries are badly managed / they are poorly funded.

   _____

4. The colleges are raising money / they are attracting new students.

_____

5. The classrooms are dirty / they are noisy.

_____

| Task 2 | *not only … but also* |

Not only … but also is similar to *both … and*, but allows the writer to emphasize more than two nouns, verbs or adjectives.

Study the example below:
The problems were not only racial but also religious, political and economic.

2.1 Study the sentences and answer the questions below.

a. Students use the website not only as a historical resource but also as a dictionary and an image gallery.

b. Students not only find vocabulary lists on the website, but they also create puzzles and games with new words.

1. Why is *not only … but also* placed in front of the nouns in a?

_____

2. Why is *not only … but also* placed in front of the verbs in b?

_____

3. Why is there a comma before *but* in b but not in a?

_____

2.2 Not only … but also follows the same rules for sentence position as *both … and* in 1.4 above. Study the sentences a–d, and answer the questions.

a. Sales have not only increased in America, but they have also risen slightly in Australia and New Zealand.

b. Sales are not only high in America, but they are also slightly higher in Australia and New Zealand.

c. Students not only find vocabulary lists on the website, but they also create puzzles and games with the new words.

d. Students are not only finding vocabulary lists on the website, but they are also creating puzzles and games with the new words.

1. Where do you put *not only … but also* if the verb form is auxiliary verb + main verb?

_____

2. Where do you put *not only … but also* if the main verb is *to be*?

_____

3. Where do you put *not only … but also* if there is no auxiliary verb and the main verb is not *to be*?

_____

2.3 **Draw an arrow to match the verb construction on the left with the correct position of *not only ... but also* on the right.**

Verb construction
main verb = *to be*
main verb ≠ *to be*
auxiliary + main verb

Where do not only ... but also go?
in the middle
after
before

2.4 **Rewrite the sentences, adding *not only ... but also*.**

1. In order to compete on the open market, companies consider prices / study competitors' products

   In order to compete on the open market, companies not only consider prices, but they also study competitors' products.

2. Early humans painted on cave walls / they made tools out of flint

3. The new building is used by researchers and administrative staff / it provides accommodation for 300 students.

4. The campaign is helping to tackle poverty / it is providing funds for education and healthcare.

5. Researchers have understood more about genes / they have successfully identified many thousands of genetic variants and their DNA structure.

6. Laboratory experiments are time-consuming / are often costly and unreliable.

Task 3   *either ... or*

3.1 **Study the sentences and answer the questions below.**

   a. The cells will reduce in number or disappear completely.
   b. The cells will either reduce in number or disappear completely.
   c. The cells will either reduce in number, or they may disappear completely.

   1. Which two sentences emphasize the fact that there are only two possibilities? _____
   2. Why is there a comma before *or* in sentence c, but not in sentence b?

3.2 **The position of *either* follows the same rules as *both ... and* and *not only ... but also* (see Tasks 1 and 2). Put the words in the correct order to make sentences with *either ... or*.**

1. either / air pollution / the illness / is / smoking / caused / by / or

   _____

2. written / have / either / students / paid in cash / or / a cheque / they / have

   _____

3. went to / school children / a secondary modern school / in the past / either / attended / a grammar school / or / they

   _____

4. they / in this company / employees / start at 8.00 and finish at 4.00 / start at 9.00 and finish at 5.00 / either / or

   _____

Task 4	*neither .... nor*

Study the steps you take to transform sentence a into c:

a. *The elections are not well organized, and the ballot papers are not secret.*

   neither   *nor*

b. *The elections are ~~not~~ well organized, ~~and~~ the ballot papers are ~~not~~ secret.*

c. *The elections are neither well organized, nor are the ballot papers secret.*

   You can use *neither ... nor* instead of *... not... and ... not*. The subject–verb word order is reversed when you use *nor*.

4.1 **Rewrite the following sentences using *neither* ... *nor* and the verb *to be*. Follow the procedure in a–c above.**

1. Correct procedures are not followed at regional level, and politicians are not happy with them at national level.

   Correct procedures are neither followed at regional level, nor are politicians happy with them at national level.

2. This product is not well made, and the price is not reasonable.

   _____

   _____

3. The grassland is not in good condition, and it is not well protected from development.

   _____

   _____

4. The visa application process was not easy, and it was not completed on time.

   _____

   _____

> You can use *neither … nor* instead of *…. do(es) not … and … do(es) not*. You keep the auxiliary verb in the second part of the sentence
>
> **Study the steps you take to transform sentence a into c:**
> a. *This country does not act according to international laws, and it does not cooperate with international institutions.*
> b. *This country* ~~does not~~ *neither* *act according to international laws,* ~~and~~ *nor it does* ~~not~~ *cooperate with international institutions.*
> c. *This country neither acts according to international laws, nor does it cooperate with international institutions.*

4.2 **Rewrite the following sentences using *neither … nor*. Follow the procedure in a–c above.**

1. In some countries, children do not read, and they do not have access to books.

   In some countries, children neither read, nor do they have access to books.

2. In the worst affected areas, people do not care for their animals, and they do not water their crops.

   _____

3. The company does not use harmful chemicals, and it does not allow animal testing.

   _____

4. The changes in religious custom did not occur at the same time, and they did not follow the same pattern.

   _____

4.3 **Using *neither … nor* with other auxiliary verbs. Study sentences a and b below and answer the questions.**

a. The factory has not employed more workers, and it has not increased the number of managers.
b. The factory has neither employed more workers, nor has it increased the number of managers.

1. Where does *neither* go if there is an auxiliary verb in the first clause?

   _____

2. What is the word order after *nor*? _____

4.4 **Rewrite the following sentences using *neither … nor*.**

1. Since the last meeting, factory output has not improved, and it has not worsened.

   Since the last meeting, the factory structure has neither improved, nor has it worsened.

2. Some children at the age of five have not watched television, and they have not played on the computer.

   _____

3. People are not spending money on consumer goods, and they are not taking holidays abroad.

_____

4. Outside investors are not putting money into local companies, and they are not creating work for local people.

_____

If the subject is the *same* in the second clause as in the first, the subject and auxiliary verb can be left out. This creates a less formal style.

For example:

same subject   same subject

The company does not sell its email list, and it does not ask for personal details by telephone.

a. **usual style (more formal)**
   The company neither sells its email list, nor does it ask for personal details by telephone.
b. **less formal style**
   The company neither sells its email list nor asks for personal details by telephone.

4.5 **Rewrite the sentences using *neither ... nor*. Where possible omit the subject and auxiliary in the second clause to produce a sentence with a less formal style.**

1. The school is not investing in hardware and it is not training teachers in new technology.

   The school is neither investing in hardware nor training teachers in new technology.

2. The exercises are not easy to understand, and the book does not have an answer key.

   _____

3. The strike has not improved workers' conditions, and it has not increased their salaries.

   _____

4. The rooms are not equipped with computers, and the roof is not in good condition.

   _____

5. The earthquake did not destroy any buildings and it did not damage the roads.

   _____

...will:

- ...use linking words to give supporting ideas and examples in a paragraph
- ...revise all the linking words
- lea... to use semi-colons instead of sentence-connecting words

Writer's purpose	Sentence-connecting words
To link similar ideas	in addition also
To contrast different ideas	however
To show a result	therefore as a result
To give another possibility	alternatively
To summarize	on the whole to sum up
To show time or sequence	firstly finally
To give an example	for example

Task 1   Supporting evidence – writing paragraphs

In a paragraph in an academic essay, the writer often gives supporting ideas and evidence to show that his or her ideas are valid. Giving supporting ideas and evidence means that the writer expands and develops the idea in the paragraph leader. This is an important feature of academic writing.

Look at the paragraph of an essay below. The paragraph leader (or topic sentence) contains the main idea of the paragraph (modern life in China is easier than life in the past), and the rest of the paragraph contains supporting ideas and evidence.

(1) is the paragraph leader, and is highlighted in yellow.

(2) and (3) show supporting ideas, and are highlighted in blue.

> **Compare and contrast the modern way of life in China with the way of life 50 years ago.**
>
> (1) Firstly, people's standard of living is higher than before. (2) People's lives were very difficult after the Second World War. There was no food, no electricity, and it was very hard to buy goods in shops. Because of the lack of provisions, the government had to make a rule that individuals could only buy small quantities. For example, one person could only buy five kilos of rice per month. At that

time people had to rely on the help of their neighbours more than they do now. They often knocked on each other's doors if they needed soya sauce or drinking water, for example. **(3) Nowadays, life has changed.** Almost every family has at least one TV, and most people in the towns have computers. People can buy anything they want in the shops, so they have a better diet; they eat more protein than before, such as red meat, chicken and eggs. As a result, they live longer. It used to be rare for people to live beyond the age of 70, but now longevity is common.

Each supporting idea relates to the main idea in the paragraph leader. Each supporting idea is followed by supporting evidence. The supporting evidence may include any of the following:

- details
- examples
- statistics
- new information

1.1   Study the paragraph below and answer the questions.

(1) Immigration brings economic benefits to the destination country. (2) Immigrants often accept unpleasant, low-paid jobs which are not wanted by local workers, and they pay taxes from their wages, which help everyone in society. (3) Others may be entrepreneurs who establish companies with links abroad. (4) In addition, Kanwal Rekhi, a businessman from India, moved to America and established his own company, Excelan, in 1982. (5) He is now a millionaire who supports poor university students both in India and America, and he is putting his wealth back into India's technology.

1. Draw an arrow to link the supporting ideas to the paragraph leader.
2. Underline the supporting ideas and circle any supporting evidence.
3. Label the supporting evidence, choosing from the different types noted above.
4. Identify the incorrect linking word in this paragraph. Why is it wrong? _____

_____

1.2   Study the paragraph below and answer the questions.

There are also disadvantages to migration for the receiving country. According to Rogers (2001), many migrants are unskilled workers from developing countries, which means that they do not have a work permit, and they work illegally for cash for their friends. On the other hand, governments in receiving countries may not receive any tax income from these migrants.

1. Draw an arrow to link the supporting idea to the paragraph leader.
2. Underline the supporting idea and circle the supporting evidence.
3. Label the supporting evidence, choosing from the different types noted above.
4. Identify the incorrect linking word in this paragraph. Why is it wrong? _____

_____

1.3 **Study the paragraph below and answer the questions.**

> Pupils at English secondary schools can choose the subjects they want to study at the age of 14. There are three core subjects: Maths, Science and English, and there is a wide range of non-compulsory subjects. For example, Religious Education is the study of comparative religions which also deals with philosophy; this provides useful knowledge for living in a multicultural society. However, pupils can study Citizenship to learn how to take a full part in society as adults.

1. Draw an arrow to link the supporting idea to the paragraph leader.
2. Underline the supporting idea and circle the supporting evidence.
3. Label the supporting evidence, choosing from the different types noted above.
4. Which is the incorrect linking word in this paragraph? Why is it wrong?

Task 2   Revise linking words

2.1 **Read the complete essay about China. The linking words have been removed. Replace them with correct words from each box. Try and complete paragraph 2 without checking back to Task 1.**

on the whole	both … and	so

> **Compare and contrast the modern way of life in China with the way of life 50 years ago.**
> China is developing very fast nowadays because of (1) _both_ the government's _and_ the people's hard work. Some of the changes are for the better, whereas others perhaps are not so beneficial. (2) _on the whole_, there have been more positive than negative developments, (3) _so_ life in China is generally better than before. The changes are considered below.

so	and	as a result	for example (x2)	firstly	but

> (4) _firstly_, people's standard of living is higher than before. People's lives were very difficult after the Second World War. There was no food, no electricity, and it was very hard to buy goods in shops. Because of the lack of provisions, the government had to make a rule that individuals could buy only small quantities. (5) _for example_, one person could only buy five kilos of rice per month. At that time, people had to rely on the help of their neighbours more than they do now. They always knocked on each other's doors if they needed soya sauce or drinking water, (6) _for example_. Nowadays, life has changed. Almost every family has at least one TV, (7) _and_ most people in the towns have computers. People can buy anything they want in the shops, (8) _so_ they have a better diet; they eat more protein than before, such as red meat, chicken and eggs. (9) _as a result_, they live longer. It used to be rare for people to live beyond the age of 70, (10) _but_ now longevity is common.

| neither … nor | for example | also |

Other changes have happened within the fields of technology and education. Levels of technology are increasing; the Chinese can produce a wide range of electronic equipment and household appliances, such as computers, cameras and microwaves. This was impossible 50 years ago. The education system has (11) _also_ changed. Schools now teach a new curriculum based on those in other countries. (12) _for example_, 50 years ago students spent much time learning how to speak the old Chinese language. However, they learnt (13) _neither_ Physics _nor_ any other Science subject.

| also | however | so | and (x4) | finally | but | for example |

(14) _however_, there have been changes to people's ideas (15) _and_ to some customs too. (16) _for example_, young people got married, on average, at 17 or 18 (17) _and_ it was more common to find a partner within the local community (CBASSE, 1984). Young people marry later now, partly because access to education and travel has improved, (18) _and_ they are more likely to study for longer and travel abroad before they marry. In the past, people usually got married at home (19) _and_ wore traditional red clothes, (20) _but_ now more people marry in a church and they wear Western clothes. Another example is that in the past women did not usually have jobs; they looked after the home, (21) _and_ they rarely went against their husbands' wishes. (22) _____, nowadays, most women have jobs and more independence; they (23) _____ have their own ideas too.

| however | also | and (x2) | to sum up |

(24) _____, China is now very different compared to 50 years ago. Some changes are negative, such as the increase in the number of people who smoke nowadays (25) _____ the growth in environmental pollution. (26) _____, it is certain that China is getting better and better, (27) _____ people are feeling more comfortable day by day. It is (28) _____ certain that China will continue to improve in the future.

References

Commission on Behavioral and Social Sciences and Education (CBASSE), (1984), Rapid Population Change in China, 1952–1982, National Academies Press, p.41 http://www.nap.edu/openbook.php?record_id=61&page=41. Retrieved 17th March, 2011.

2.2 **Sometimes, students overuse sentence-connecting words. Study the paragraph. Underline the three sentence-connecting words. Which one is not necessary? Why?**

Modern education has brought some obvious benefits to developing countries, but there are some problems. No one can deny the advantages of increasing literacy rates and knowledge about the rest of the world. However, a globalized education system may be based on a Western urban environment. Moreover, it teaches people to use the same global resources, ignoring those that are provided by their natural surroundings. For example, people learn about the use of chemicals and pesticides, forgetting natural, ecological methods. A new educational approach needs to be planned and absorbed carefully into its surrounding cultural and ecological context.

Task 3	Using semi-colons with sentence-connecting words

In order to vary your writing style, you can use a semi-colon instead of a full stop before a sentence-connecting word if both sentences are short.

For example:
There were many problems with the pilot phase of the project; however, the team managed to resolve them.

3.1 **Is the letter which starts a new clause after a semi-colon upper- or lower-case?**

3.2 **Complete the sentence pairs by adding the correct linking words and punctuating with a semi-colon as shown in the example above. There is one gap per missing word.**

therefore   on the whole   however (2)   ~~in addition~~   as a result   for example

1. Open-ended questions let participants answer in unexpected ways; ___in___ ___addition___, researchers have the freedom to allow participants to explain their answers more fully.

2. All these changes increased competition in the Spanish banking industry _____ they generated other problems related to solvency.

3. Until the 1960s, the Spanish banking system was regulated by the government _____ interest rates were fixed centrally.

4. Superfoods' global marketing strategy was of little practical use in Japan _____ _____ _____ Japanese consultants were employed to advise on local marketing trends.

5. The literature provides a theoretical analysis of the situation _____ _____ two management frameworks attempt to provide solutions to the problem (Morrison, 1998; Kidge, 1999).

6. The focus-group discussions lasted for 30 minutes each _____ _____ _____ the questions were used as guidelines only.

7. Participant groups were small _____ the full range of occupations was represented, from miners to landowners.

Unit 4 Self-check

Choose the correct option to complete the sentences.

1 The study aims to analyze policies _____ make recommendations.
  a. , and
  b. . And
  c. and

2 This consumer decision-making process is well known _____ there is very little literature about its application to the UK sportswear industry.
  a. , yet
  b. yet
  c. so

3 The lecture was not clear _____ no one asked questions.
  a. , and
  b. , so
  c. , but

4 The world should continue to promote free trade. _____ it is important to introduce policies that protect the poor and most vulnerable groups of society.
  a. Alternatively,
  b. Also,
  c. However,

5 In South Korea, the government announced plans to build more satellite cities. _____ investors began to buy the land, which increased in price.
  a. As a result,
  b. On the other hand,
  c. Furthermore,

6 In Kyoto, public transport is fast, efficient and convenient. _____ the carriages are clean and well-maintained.
  a. However,
  b. In addition,
  c. On the other hand,

7 The reforms are _____ sustainable.
  a. neither appropriate, nor
  b. both appropriate, and
  c. neither appropriate nor

8 These instructions _____ teach students how to download the software _____ enable them to edit the software code.
- a. not only … , but they also
- b. not only … but they also
- c. not only …, but also they

9 This area _____ suffers from pollution _____ prone to earthquakes.
- a. not …, nor is it
- b. neither …, nor is it
- c. neither … nor is it

10 In South Korea, the traditional roles of men and women are sometimes reversed. _____ husbands may stay at home to look after the children while the women go to the workplace to earn money.
- a. In addition,
- b. For example,
- c. On the whole,

5 Showing logical links (2)

In this unit you will:

- learn to link ideas logically in complex sentences by using subordinators effectively
- study the words in the shaded columns in the table below

Writer's purpose	Linking words				
	Short linking words	Paired linking words	Subordinators	Sentence-connecting words/ Signpost language	Linking words + noun phrase
To link similar ideas	and			in addition also	in addition to
To contrast different ideas	but yet		although/even though	however	in spite of despite
To compare			whereas/while		
To show time or sequence			when while	firstly finally	
To give an example				for example	such as
To give a reason			because since as		due to because of
To show purpose			so that/ in order that (so as to/ in order to)		
To show a result	so		so ... that/ such ... that	therefore/as a result	as a result of

Stage A

In this stage you will:

- learn to link ideas using the subordinators in the table below

Writer's purpose	Subordinators
To compare	whereas
	while
To give a reason	because
	since
	as

Task 1	**Overview of subordinators**

a. Artificial animal cloning is a relatively new technique. Some simple animals have always used natural cloning for asexual reproduction. Amoebas (single-cell animals) need to reproduce. The parent cell and the nucleus within the cell divide into two to form a parent and child cell. The child cell is a clone. Its genetic material is identical to that of its parent.

b. <u>Although</u> artificial animal cloning is a relatively new technique, some simple animals have always used natural cloning for asexual reproduction. <u>When</u> amoebas (single-cell animals) need to reproduce, the parent cell and the nucleus within the cell divide into two to form a parent and child cell. The child cell is a clone <u>because</u> its genetic material is identical to that of its parent.

Study the paragraphs above. Paragraph b is easier to understand because the logical links between the ideas are made clear by the use of underlined linking words.

You have already studied short linking words and sentence-connecting words in Unit 4. This unit discusses how to use subordinators in **complex sentences** and shows you how to use linking words with a noun phrase to connect back logically to a previous idea.

1.1 **Study paragraphs a and b again. Match the linking word on the left with the relationship it conveys on the right.**

Linking word		Relationship between ideas
when		gives a reason
although		shows a contrast (a surprise)
because		indicates a point in time

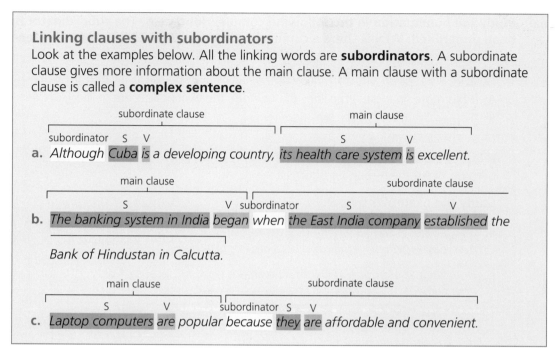

Linking clauses with subordinators
Look at the examples below. All the linking words are **subordinators**. A subordinate clause gives more information about the main clause. A main clause with a subordinate clause is called a **complex sentence**.

a. Although Cuba is a developing country, its health care system is excellent.

b. The banking system in India began when the East India company established the Bank of Hindustan in Calcutta.

c. Laptop computers are popular because they are affordable and convenient.

Grammar note: The subordinate clause is the clause which begins with the subordinator.

1.2 **Underline and label subject (S) and verb (V) of each clause in the sentence. Identify and label the subordinator, and finally label the main clause and subordinate clause of each sentence.**

1. Although plastic bags are useful, they damage the environment.

2. When a country's economy goes into a recession, exports decrease.

3. People moved from the countryside to the town because they needed to find work.

Task 2   Using *because/since/as*

2.1 **Study sentences a–c and answer the questions below.**
a. The night-time temperature fell to -2°C because there were no clouds.
b. Since they wanted to improve the area, they applied to the Development Agency for a grant.
c. As the students needed their visas urgently, they went straight to the Embassy.

1. Highlight and label the subject and verb of each clause in the sentence. Identify and label the subordinator.

2. Label the main clause and subordinate clause of each sentence.

3. Which subordinators do we use to give a reason?

2.2 **Study the links between the first and second sentences in 1–3. Which two have the tightest link, and therefore the most effective text flow?**
1. Elephant-nose fish live in dense muddy rivers and pools. They have no need to see because their surroundings are dark.

2. Elephant-nose fish live in dense muddy rivers and pools. Since their surroundings are dark, they have no need to see.

3. Elephant-nose fish live in dense muddy rivers and pools. As their surroundings are dark, they have no need to see.

2.3 Study the punctuation in the following complex sentences. The subordinator has been underlined. Why is there a comma in sentences 2 and 3 but not in sentence 1?

1. They want to stay in the area <u>because</u> Asko is offering employment.
2. <u>Since</u> oil has a lower density than water, spillages float on the surface of the sea.
3. <u>As</u> it has more financial difficulties than before, the waiting lists are getting longer.

We use *as/since* when the reason links back to a previous idea in the text. We use *because* when the reason introduces a new idea.

Study the examples below:

a. *Visual defects can be inherited or appear later in life. <u>As</u> they interfere with everyday activities, regular eye tests are important.*

b. *House prices are rising in Oxton. The area is popular <u>because</u> Asko is offering employment.*

c. *The local culture was patriarchal. <u>Since</u> only males were allowed to go to school, many older women are not well educated.*

Grammar note: *As* and *since* give the reason at the beginning of a new sentence. *Because* gives the reason in the second clause of the sentence.

2.4 Study the sentence pairs below. For each question, tick (✔) the sentence pair (a or b) which has the better link between the sentences.

1. a. Education was for boys only until the 1950s. Since only males were allowed to go to school, many older women are not well educated. ☐

   b. Education was only for boys until the 1950s. Many older women are not well educated because only males were allowed to go to school. ☐

2. a. The South Korean company Asko has the support of local people. They want to stay in the area because Asko is offering employment. ☐

   b. The South Korean company Asko has the support of local people. As it is offering employment, they want to stay in the area. ☐

3. a. The government has cut funding to the Health Service. As it has more financial difficulties than before, the waiting lists are getting longer. ☐

   b. The government has cut funding to the Health Service. The waiting lists are getting longer because it has more financial difficulties than before. ☐

2.5 Study the following sentence pairs. Is the reason in the first or the second sentence? Underline. Then join the sentences to make a complex sentence, using a reason subordinator (*as, since* or *because*). Keep the order of information, and add punctuation as necessary.

1. <u>Swimming is not weight bearing.</u> It is good for people with back problems or arthritis.

   As/Since swimming is not weight bearing, it is good for people with back problems or arthritis.

2.   There is traffic everywhere. People prefer to use public transport.

      _____

3.   Many countries suffer from lack of food. The crops fail when there is insufficient rain.

      _____

4.   Crops may not be safe to eat. Farmers are using too much insecticide.

      _____

5.   Cereal shortages are common in some countries. Over half the world's cereal harvest is
      fed to livestock instead of to people.

      _____

6.   Global warming is becoming a serious problem. People should try to use their cars less.

      _____

7.   The school needs to increase income. They are attempting to advertise the courses
      more widely.

      _____

8.   The growth in genetically modified crops is driven by companies and small-scale
      farmers. They both want to make money.

      _____

9.   Government plans for new computer systems are behind schedule. The projects are
      badly organized.

      _____

10.   This research is useful. It illustrates the importance of networking.

      _____

Task 3 *whereas/while*

You may know that *while* is often used to describe events which happened at the same time.

For example: <u>While</u> Ahmed wrote his essay, Sue prepared her presentation.

However, *while* can also have the same meaning as *whereas*. Both words can be used to make comparisons.

**3.1   Study the sentences below and answer the questions. Notice the position of
whereas/while in the sentence and the use of punctuation.**

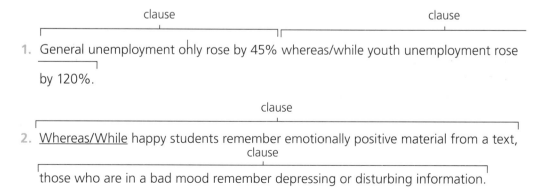

1. General unemployment only rose by 45% whereas/while youth unemployment rose by 120%.

2. <u>Whereas/While</u> happy students remember emotionally positive material from a text, those who are in a bad mood remember depressing or disturbing information.

Which two facts are compared in each sentence?

1. _____

   _____

2. _____

   _____

3.2 Follow the example of the sentences in 3.1 and punctuate the sentences below.

1. Whereas young children love doing activities with their parents teenagers often prefer to be with their peers.

   Whereas young children love doing activities with their parents, teenagers often prefer to be with their peers.

2. Lions are social animals and live in groups while tigers are usually solitary in nature.

3. While the motorway is the fastest route from A to B it is not usually the most scenic.

4. Ahmed worked hard for his exam whereas Toni spent her time playing computer games.

3.3 Read the sentences a and b, and answer the questions below.

a. The study of foreign languages is not generally popular in the UK. <u>Whereas</u> British pupils can drop foreign languages at the age of 14, they are compulsory in most other European countries until the age of 18.

b. The study of foreign languages is not generally popular in the UK. British pupils can drop foreign languages at the age of 14 <u>whereas</u> they are compulsory in most other European countries until the age of 18.

1. Which sentence catches the reader's attention more successfully? _____

2. Which sentence has the better *academic* style? _____

3.4 Read the sentences a and b. Why do you think that the writer of these sentences prefers b?

a. There is often conflict over how to make the best use of the world's limited resources. Some people are motivated by the desire to make money, and do not consider whether their actions will damage the world's ecosystem in the process, <u>while</u> others firmly believe that it is important to preserve the natural world for the sake of future generations.

b. There is often conflict over how to make the best use of the world's limited resources. <u>While</u> some people are motivated by the desire to make money, and do not consider whether their actions will damage the world's ecosystem in the process, others firmly believe that it is important to preserve the natural world for the sake of future generations.

Grammar note: *While* can also mean *at the same time as*. The reader can usually tell from the context (the rest of the words in the text) whether the subordinator refers to *time* or *comparison*. To avoid confusion, you may prefer to use *whereas* instead of *while* when you are making comparisons.

3.5 **Write sentences comparing two facts using the prompts in the table below, adding verbs as necessary. Use the best academic style. Remember to include commas.**

Fact 1	Fact 2
1. book / about religion	film / concerned with traditions
2. Rio / famous for its beaches	São Paulo / well known for its skyscrapers
3. Charlie Chaplin / known worldwide	Buster Keaton / not so widely recognized
4. red squirrels / rare in the UK	grey squirrels / very common and considered a pest
5. Bindang's per capita GDP / from $450 to $600 / over the first millennium	it / to $500 at the beginning of the 11th century

1. *Whereas/While the book is about religion, the film is concerned with traditions.*
2. _____
3. _____
4. _____
5. _____

Stage B

In this stage you will:
- study more subordinators and understand how they link ideas effectively
- practise using linking words and phrases to link clauses and sentences

Writer's purpose	Subordinators
To contrast different ideas	although/even though
To show a result	so … that/such … that
To show purpose	so that/in order that (so as to/in order to)

Task 1   *although/even though*

You studied the short linking words *but* and *yet* in Unit 4A. *Although* can also be used to contrast different ideas. It is a subordinator, so it is used to make complex sentences.

1.1 **Compare the sentences a and b, then answer the questions which follow.**
a. <u>Although</u> Amazon parrots are at risk of extinction, they are often captured and sold.
b. Amazon parrots are at risk of extinction, <u>but</u> they are often captured and sold.

1. Which word comes at the beginning of the first clause, and indicates that a contrast or surprise is coming in the second clause? _____

2. Which word comes after the first clause, and indicates that a contrast or surprise is coming in the second clause? _____

3. Which sentence emphasizes the contrast/surprise more strongly? _____

4. What do you notice about the punctuation used with these clauses? _____

1.2 **Rewrite the following sentences using *although* to emphasize the contrast and catch the reader's attention. Remember to include commas as necessary.**

1. Skiing is a dangerous sport, yet many people still enjoy it.

   Although skiing is a dangerous sport, many people still enjoy it.

2. The fire brigade arrived swiftly, but the building continued to burn.

   _____

3. Spring was a dry season, yet there was an excellent wheat harvest.

   _____

4. His name is famous, but his face is relatively unknown.

   _____

1.3 **Study and compare sentences a and b and answer the question below.**

a. Even though the doctors and nurses have not received their salary for a year, they continue to work in the hospital.

b. Although the doctors and nurses have not received their salary for a year, they continue to work in the hospital.

Which sentence indicates a stronger contrast or surprise? _____

1.4 **First, read the sentences 1–6 and match each one with two sentences from the box. Label the sentences from the box as statement and surprise. Then use them to write a second sentence with *although*, or *even though* (if you think the surprise is big!).**

It is well preserved.	They sell a wide range of goods at cheap prices.
The company had cash-flow problems.	~~He won the election~~
They prefer to watch TV or play computer games after school.	
They lost their homes in a flood.	~~He was inexperienced in politics~~
Some people never use them.	The government did not help them.
Exercise is important for future health.	It invested in a new computer system.
It dates back to 3,000 BCE.	

1. In 1998, Jesse Ventura, a wrestler, stood for election as Governor of Minnesota.

   He was inexperienced in politics. (statement) He won the election. (surprise)

   Although he was inexperienced in politics, he won the election.

2. The number of supermarkets is increasing.

_____

_____

3. Eight thousand people lived in the area.

_____

_____

4. There was no business plan.

_____

_____

5. Scientists have recently found the body of a man in an ice field.

_____

_____

6. Many children do not enjoy playing sport.

_____

_____

1.5 **Correct the following sentences.**

> **1.** Although farm workers were poor they always had enough to eat.

Although farm workers were poor, they always had enough to eat.

> **2.** Although the sea is cold in summer but people still enjoy swimming in it.

_____

> **3.** Although the economic recession, many families still have money to spend.

_____

> **4.** Production levels continued to decline. Although the company took on more people.

_____

> **5.** Although students often return their books late the fines are high.

_____

Task 2   *so ... that/such ... that*

In Unit 4A, you studied how to show a result with *so* in a compound sentence.

For example:

a. *The project was very successful,* <u>so</u> *the council extended funding for another year.*

You can also show a result in a complex sentence by using the structure: *so* + adjective + *that*, or *so* + adverb + *that*. This intensifies the adjective or adverb. Study the examples below. Note that the subordinator *so ... that* is spread over two clauses.

b. *The project was so successful* *that the council extended funding for another year.*

c. *The project was completed so successfully* *that the council extended funding for another year.*

Grammar note: You do not need a comma between the main clause and subordinating clause when you use so ... *that*.

2.1   **Match the 'results' from the box with the sentences 1–6. Then link them using the structure *so ... that*.**

the government abandoned its plans to build new power stations

banks are not lending money to entrepreneurs

they all passed the test with a high score   people have been advised to stay indoors

cars are banned on certain days of the week   ~~they started to riot for food~~

1. The people were hungry.

   The people were so hungry that they started to riot for food.

2. The students worked hard.

   _____

3. Business confidence is weak.

   _____

4. Pollution is taken seriously in some places.

   _____

5. The situation on the streets is dangerous.

   _____

6. Opposition to nuclear power was strong.

   _____

You can also show a result by intensifying a noun phrase (adjective + noun). In this case, we use *such ... that*.

For example:

a. *They had <u>such</u> a successful year <u>that</u> they paid their debts in full.*

b. *They created <u>such</u> interesting designs <u>that</u> they quickly dominated the market.*

2.2 **Match the 'results' sentences from the box with the sentences 1–6. Then link them using the structure *such … that*.**

prices are rising fast   ~~the farmers moved to a new area~~
new businesses cannot afford to operate in the town   costs are continually being cut
many companies want to move there
advertisers pay thousands of pounds to sponsor big matches

1. The area had poor quality soil.

   The area had such poor quality soil that the farmers moved to a new area.

2. There is a high demand for oil.

   _____

3. Chicago is a perfect location for business.

   _____

4. Football is a popular sport.

   _____

5. The local government demands high rents.

   _____

6. There is a pressure to be profitable.

   _____

Task 3 *so that / in order that; so as to / in order to*

You can show a purpose by using *so that/in order that* with a subordinate clause. The action in the second clause explains the purpose of the action in the main clause. The second action cannot happen if the first action has not taken place.

Study sentences a and b:

a. *The banks are making arrangements to protect deposits <u>so that</u> savers' money is secure in the event of bankruptcy.* (If the banks do not make arrangements, savers' money will not be secure).

b. *Stores try to display their goods in logical sections <u>in order that</u> shoppers can make their choices easily.* (If stores do not display their goods in logical sections, shoppers cannot make their choices easily.)

Study sentences c and d with the phrases *so as to* and *in order to*:

Notice that there is only one clause in each sentence. There is no new subject in the second half of the sentence, and the verb in the second half of the sentence is in the infinitive.

    S   V   infinitive
c. *Cameras and intercom systems are installed <u>so as to</u> observe and record all activities.*

    S   V   infinitive
d. *Society requires a change in behaviour <u>in order to</u> preserve biodiversity.*

3.1 **Study the sentences a and b. Then complete sentences 1 and 2 with the correct linking words.**

a. Companies prefer to hold prices stable <u>in order not to/so as not to</u> lose regular customers.

b. Companies prefer to hold prices stable <u>so that/in order that</u> regular customers continue to purchase their goods.

1. We use _____ when the subject of the verb is the *same* before and after the linking words.

2. We use _____ when the subject of the verb is *different* before and after the linking words.

3.2 **Combine each pair of sentences into one, using suitable linking words of purpose.**

1. Manufacturers always label products fully. **Purpose:** The consumer understands what they contain.

   <u>Manufacturers always label products fully in order that / so that the consumer</u>
   <u>understands what they contain.</u>

   (The subject of each original sentence is different, so we use *in order that* or *so that*.)

2. The government is sponsoring 'healthy eating' advertisements. **Purpose:** School children do not become obese.

   _____

3. The scientists have teamed up with another university. **Purpose:** Scientists continue the research.

   _____

4. The banks are developing new policies. **Purpose:** Banks encourage investment.

   _____

5. The management team is monitoring the budget closely. **Purpose:** The budget is not exceeded.

   _____

3.3 **Study sentences 1–3 below. Tick the sentence which shows the weakest sense of purpose.**

Grammar note: *So as to* and *in order* to can be replaced by just the infinitive (with *to*). However, the advantage of using *so as to* and *in order to* is that you make your purpose very clear.

1. Cameras and intercom systems are installed in order to observe and record all activities. ☐

2. Cameras and intercom systems are installed to observe and record all activities. ☐

3. Cameras and intercom systems are installed so as to observe and record all activities. ☐

| Task 4 | Using purpose linking words to start new sentences |

You can also begin a new sentence with **linking words of purpose** if this improves the text flow. If the purpose links back to an idea from a previous sentence, you can begin a sentence with *in order to* or *in order that*. If the purpose presents new information, you should put it in the second half of the sentence.

4.1   **In each question below, compare paragraphs a and b. In each case, tick the paragraph which demonstrates the better academic style.**

1. a. Experts believe that listening to the radio while driving causes accidents. <u>In order to</u> test this theory, they checked databases containing accident details.

☐

   b. Experts believe that listening to the radio while driving causes accidents. They checked databases containing accident details <u>in order to</u> test this theory.

☐

2. a. Student feedback is important. <u>In order that</u> the university can improve the quality of its courses, learners are asked to give their views before they leave.

☐

   b. Student feedback is important. Learners are asked give their views before they leave <u>in order that</u> the university can improve the quality of its courses.

☐

Grammar note: If you need to begin a new sentence with a strong sense of purpose, you cannot use *so as to* or *so that*; you should use *in order to* or *in order that*.

Task 5	Linking sentences of result and purpose

In Unit 4A, you practised using *as a result* and *therefore* to begin a new sentence and link back to a previous idea. (Go to this unit if you cannot remember the punctuation you use with these sentence-connecting words.) In Task 4.1 above, you have practised using *in order that* and *in order to* at the start of a new sentence to link back to a previous idea.

5.1   **Read sentences 1–8 from student essays. Add the correct linking words in the gaps, choosing between the expressions in the box below. You will need to use each expression more than once. Add a comma where necessary.**

as a result	in order that	in order to

1. In the case of Japan, it is important for students to know the result of their trial examinations. _____As a result_____ , they only choose which university to apply to after completing these examinations.

2. People in authority are sometimes corrupt. _____ stay in power, they bribe other people around them.

3. Nowadays, the population of elderly people is increasing dramatically around the world. _____ it is becoming urgent to discuss issues relating to ageing.

4. Many people in the countryside have to manage their lives without access to convenient public transport. _____ rural people have a better lifestyle, buses should be subsidized by the government.

5. It is generally agreed that travel broadens the mind. _____people should be encouraged to visit other countries _____ broaden their minds.

6. The government does not spend enough money on the education system. _____ schools cannot provide textbooks for every student.

7. Using a mobile to phone home from abroad can be expensive. _____ reduce this cost, international students should install Skype on their computers and buy a set of headphones.

8. Global warming has had a damaging effect on coral reefs around the world. _____ predict future changes, it is critical to understand more about the effect of water temperature on sea coral plants.

Task 6	**Compound–complex sentences**

You have studied simple and compound sentences in Unit 4A and complex sentences in this unit. It is also possible to form **compound–complex sentences**, by joining a simple sentence and a complex sentence.

Study the examples below:

simple   +   complex

a. *The city was formed by merging six villages, and its rural style is still so well preserved today that it is frequently visited by urban architects.*

complex   +   simple

b. *Although it was very time-consuming, the interviews were analyzed, and all the data were recorded.*

6.1 **Use subordinators (*when, although, since, because*) and linking words (*and, but*) to combine the sentences, in each case, to create a compound–complex sentence. Keep the clauses in the same order.**

1. The reference section was clear. Students frequently failed to use sources as evidence. They often forgot to write a bibliography.
   Although the reference section was clear, students frequently failed to use sources as evidence and they often forgot to write a bibliography.

2. Military rule ended in Japan in 1868. More children could learn the martial art of kendo in school. Eventually it was introduced into all schools.
   _____
   _____

3. The open sewers in Arbash are often blocked with sewage. They overflow in the rain. Diseases such as typhoid and cholera are common.
   _____
   _____

4. It is always difficult to rescue injured people from earthquakes. It is harder in the winter. Casualties cannot survive hypothermia. Ambulances may be stopped by snow and ice.

_____

_____

5. Oil tankers sometimes wash out their tanks at sea. It is cheaper than paying for this to be done in port. This practice is illegal. It pollutes the marine environment.

_____

_____

6.2 **Read the paragraph and analyze the complex–compound sentences. Identify the complex and simple sentence parts in each sentence.**

> **(1)** There is a vast quantity of data about school performance, and detailed research is needed in order to identify important trends. **(2)** Students from certain white British backgrounds are making less progress than students from ethnic minority backgrounds, and this issue must be tackled because educational success is important for future employment, pay, health and happiness. **(3)** Poor children in rural areas may be disadvantaged because their schools lack financial resources, but this situation may change with the government's promise to launch a review.

1. _____

2. _____

3. _____

Task 7	Using a semi-colon instead of a linking word

Accurate use of the semi-colon can add useful variety to your writing style. A semi-colon can be used between short sentences when the second sentence gives a reason, a result or extra detail.

For example:
The meeting finished early; several students needed to leave to take an exam.

(Here, the second sentence gives a reason.)

7.1 **Read the sentence pairs below. Does the second sentence give a *reason*, a *result* or an *extra detail*?**

1. *Extrastore's* takeover of *Superfood* will create new global competition; *Extrastore* now has full access to southern region markets. _____reason_____

2. Family members influence each other's spending habits; children's consumption patterns as adults will typically be based on those of their parents. _____

3. An oligopoly is when a few firms dominate the market; they often collude to sell goods at similar prices. _____

4. There are many different types of personal computers; laptops are currently the most popular. _____

5. Taylor rejects the closed space of the artist's studio; the freedom of the outside world is now essential to her creativity _____ .

6. There was a widespread drought in 2011; earnings from livestock production fell _____ .

Stage C

In this stage you will:
- study linking words and expressions in the table below that are used with noun phrases
- review the linking words from Units 4 and 5

Writer's purpose	Linking words + noun phrase
To link similar ideas	in addition to
To contrast different ideas	in spite of despite
To give an example	such as
To give a reason	due to because of
To show a result	as a result of

Task 1   *in spite of/despite*

In spite of and *despite* introduce a contrast or surprise, like the subordinator *although*, or the short linking words *but* and *yet*. *In spite of* and *despite* are followed by a noun phrase and a comma. Sometimes the noun phrase is a gerund. This is a noun made from a verb and is also called the *~ing* form (e.g., *reading, playing*) – see Unit 1B, Task 2.

For example:
a. *It rained hard for several weeks, and the rivers overflowed. In spite of/Despite the flood, the people chose to stay in their homes.*
b. *The airline hired experts to investigate the accident. In spite of/Despite analyzing all the information, the experts were unable to discover the cause.*

1.1 **Study the sentences. Underline the gerund.**

1. Despite losing the election, the president is still in control of foreign policy.
2. In spite of finding the data collection difficult, the students continued with their research.

1.2   **Rewrite the sentences below using *despite/in spite of* + gerund. Notice that the subject in both halves of the sentence is often the same when a gerund is used.**

1. Although the students were tired, they could not sleep.

   Despite/In spite of being tired, the students could not sleep.

2. Although many graduates have work experience, they still find it difficult to gain employment.

   _____

3. Although the children do not eat healthily, they are not overweight.

   _____

4. Although the government wants to encourage tourism, it has not approved a fifth runway at Heathrow Airport.

   _____

5. Although the weather forecast predicted rain for the morning, it said the afternoon would be hot and sunny.

   _____

6. Although she lost a lot of blood in the accident, she is in a stable condition.

   _____

1.3   **Study the following sentences. Correct the errors. Add punctuation where necessary.**

1. Despite there is public concern, the government continues to build nuclear power stations.

   Despite public concern, the government continues to build nuclear power stations.

2. Despite the weather is bad. The building work is continuing.

   _____

3. In spite of there was noise during the night no one woke up.

   _____

4. Despite only exports a few products the country is still prosperous.

   _____

5. Although in spite of there are exams, the library will close early.

   _____

6. In spite of people know the harmful effects of tobacco. They continue to smoke.

   _____

Task 2   *as a result of*

You learnt how to use the sentence-connecting expression *as a result* in Unit 4A. It shows the result of an idea in a previous sentence.

For example:

a. *In the Second World War, sugar was not readily available. As a result, people had fewer dental problems.*

As a result of + noun phrase has the same purpose. You can use it at the beginning of a sentence to link back to a previous idea, or you can use it at the end of a sentence to introduce new information.

For example:

b. *In the Second World War, sugar was not readily available. As a result of this shortage, people had fewer dental problems.*

c. *In the Second World War, there was an improvement in general health. For example, people had fewer dental problems as a result of eating less sugar.*

2.1 **Complete the sentences by adding *as a result of* + noun phrase. Choose from the phrases in the list below and pay attention to punctuation.**

exploiting cheap local labour and resources   this neglect
the worsening economic situation   this ban   ~~obesity~~   this research
climate-related natural disasters

1. In modern society, with food readily available, increasing numbers of middle-aged people are dying _____as a result of obesity_____.

2. People can no longer smoke in enclosed public spaces. _____ _____ there has been an improvement in the health of café workers.

3. Global warming is beginning to affect large numbers of people. In 2008, 20 million people had to leave their homes _____.

4. According to three independent studies, corporate fraud has risen _____ _____.

5. A government report concludes that the quality of pre-school education is important for children's future academic achievements. _____ the government plans to spend more money on early-years childcare programs.

6. Multinational companies are aware of the economic potential of developing countries. Some of them make huge profits _____.

7. Some parents do not take an interest in their children's education. _____ their children underachieve.

Task 3   *because of/due to*

In Unit 5A you learnt how to use a subordinator (*because, as, since*) to give a reason. You can also give a reason by using *because of/due to* + noun phrase.

3.1   **Study sentences a–f. Underline and label the noun phrases which follow *due to* and *because of*. Are they simple or complex noun phrases? (If necessary, look again at Unit 2A and B). Then answer questions 1–4.**

simple noun phrase

a.   In the year 2000, Mount Etna erupted. Due to this eruption, thousands of particles thickened the air, blocking the sun's rays.

b.   The success of the business was largely due to the well-qualified members of staff.

c.   Communication is changing, partly due to the growing role of social media in people's lives.

d.   Heavy snow has fallen overnight. Because of severe weather conditions, many flights are cancelled.

e.   Almost two-thirds of Jersey's natural landscape has disappeared in the past two centuries, largely because of construction and development.

f.   Attendance at the meeting was low, partly because of illness.

1.   Which position in the sentence can the phrases *due to* and *because of* go in? _____

2.   What punctuation follows *due to* and *because of* if they are at the beginning of a sentence? _____

3.   What does *largely* in sentence b mean? _____

4.   What does *partly* in sentences c and f mean? _____

Grammar note: *Due to* and *because of* have the same meaning, but *due to* is frequently used after the verb *be*.

For example: *The UK government estimates that up to 40,000 deaths a year are due to the effects of junk food.*

3.2   **Complete the following sentences with *due to/because/because of* and a phrase from the box below.**

the cost of flights has decreased	the dry weather	~~the postal strike~~
the growing unrest in the country		they do not read questions properly
high levels of unemployment in their country		the opening of a new hypermarket
their fear of street crime		oversleeping

1.   The letters are late _____ *due to the postal strike* _____ .

2.   The high price of vegetables is largely _____

3.   Many local shops have closed _____

4.   Each year several students fail to attend an exam _____

5.   Many exam candidates lose marks _____

6.   Many old people are afraid to leave their homes _____

7.   Many graduates are forced to work abroad _____

8.   The huge increase in air travel over recent years is _____

9.   The Prime Minister returned home _____

Task 4 | *such as*

Study the following extract from a paragraph you read in Unit 4C.
Notice the position of *for example* in this sentence and the punctuation that follows it.

> People's lives were very difficult after the Second World War. [...] Because of the lack of provisions, the government had to make a rule that individuals could only buy small quantities. <u>For example</u>, one person could only buy five kilos of rice per month.

You can also give examples at the beginning of a short list, by using the expression *such as*.

> People eat more protein than before, <u>such as</u> red meat, chicken and eggs. Some changes are negative, <u>such as</u> the increase in the number of people who smoke nowadays and the growth in environmental pollution.

Grammar note: Try to avoid using *like* and *etc.*, when giving a list of examples. Use *such as* instead.

4.1 Correct the sentences below.

1. Switzerland sells its expertise to other countries. ~~Such as~~ *For example,* it has helped people in Bhutan to produce cheese, apple juice and honey.

2. People need water for many reasons, drinking, watering their gardens, growing crops etc.

3. There is overuse of water in Oman, for example, there are insufficient controls on factories which use it for industrial processes, and in parks, where the grass is watered every day to keep it a vibrant colour.

4. The Internet is used both for academic research and for practical tasks, like finding books in libraries and organizing patient lists in hospitals.

Task 5 | Review of linking words (Units 4 and 5)

5.1 Rewrite the sentences using the linking words or punctuation in brackets.

1. New technologies bring opportunities to young children, but some parents' lack of awareness is leaving children vulnerable to risk. (although)

   _____

   _____

2. School children have better literacy levels than in the past, even though they read fewer books at home. (despite)

   _____

   _____

3. Plagiarism is becoming a serious problem at universities. Therefore, many institutions have introduced plagiarism detection software. (such … that)

_____

_____

4. Wi-Fi freeloading is a crime, but it is difficult for the police to track and very few arrests have been made. (however)

_____

_____

5. This international aid project was very successful because the agencies respected local culture, traditions and resources. (;)

_____

_____

6. Education is of great importance. It encourages the acquisition of knowledge. It ensures well-qualified future employees. (both … and)

_____

_____

7. There was an explosion in the oil pipeline. As a result, oil pumping has been suspended. (due to)

_____

_____

5.2 **Rewrite the sentences below using an appropriate linking word or words from the box below. In some sentences you can use more than one word. Remember to use the correct punctuation.**

Note: A complete table of linking words from Units 4 and 5 is on page 127 at the end of this unit.

whereas	for example	however	such (a) ... that	as a result
so	not only ... but also		because	but

1. Some companies are enthusiastic about GM food. Many people are very worried about its dangers.

_____

_____

2. Over-dependence on oil has several effects. It causes serious damage to the environment. It is a source of conflict.

_____

_____

3. International students often want to practise their spoken English. The English-speaking club has many members.

_____

_____

4. Japanese people live longer than most other nationalities. They have healthy diets.

_____

_____

5. Diet is one factor in determining how long people live. It is not the only issue to be taken into consideration.

    _____

    _____

6. Most universities have a balanced assessment system. There are mid-term tests, group presentations and end-of-term exams.

    _____

    _____

7. There is a serious shortage of food. The army is helping to distribute supplies.

    _____

    _____

8. The company has lost more than 3,000 customers over the past six months. It has been forced to cut back its advertising budget.

    _____

    _____

9. People do not want to give away their personal information online. They are frightened of being victims of fraud.

    _____

    _____

10. Doctors say that stress is a major cause of heart attacks. They advise patients not to take work home at the weekend.

    _____

    _____

11. Arabic is read from right to left. English is read from left to right.

    _____

    _____

5.3 **Read the student essay below. Complete the text with linking words in each box. Add punctuation as necessary.**

both	whereas	as	and	so

Discuss the extent to which video and computer gaming has a harmful effect on young people.

In the current, computer-assisted digital world, IT skills have become indispensable for undertaking many daily tasks. **(1)** _____ the older generation sometimes has difficulties with the new technology children are introduced to it at a young age **(2)** _____ at home **(3)** _____ at school **(4)** _____ they naturally interact with it easily. Video and computer games are becoming increasingly popular (Byron, 2008); **(5)** _____ these games represent an expanding area, it is important to be aware of the possible negative and positive consequences of these activities on children. This essay focuses on the advantages and disadvantages of video and computer games for young people, suggesting the best way in which the new generation can benefit from the virtual world.

such as	also	in addition

There is much evidence to show that games have educational value, aimed at increasing knowledge and skills in many different areas. Griffiths (2002) states that computer and video games help in the development of social, language, reading and maths skills. Researchers have **(6)** _____ found that games can be used to reinforce learning in children with problems **(7)** _____ autism or attention deficit disorder (Griffiths, 2002). **(8)** _____ game playing is helpful for brain development; it brings about changes in mental skills and improves attention resources, cognitive skills, concentration, spatial abilities and hand-eye co-ordination (Dye, Green & Bavelier, 2009; Gagnon, 1985).

however	despite	due to

(9) _____ all these positive aspects, one of the main concerns about gaming is the detrimental effect that it can have on children. Some children are thought to be aggressive **(10)** _____ their exposure to violent games. **(11)** _____ there is only weak evidence from the literature for a direct, causal relationship between game-playing and aggressive behaviour; all studies which conclude that there is a direct link focus largely on short-term effects, and do not take into consideration long-term influences (Griffiths, 1999).

in addition	for example	however	because of

It is often said that playing video games is dangerous for health **(12)** _____ the sedentary lifestyle that is associated with games. **(13)** _____ if children play on the computer with a few friends, they are often not seated for long periods. **(14)** _____ children's health is sometimes improved by playing games; for example, there are games for diabetes and asthma self-management which improve the level of self-care and medical compliance in children (Griffiths, 2002). In the health domain, video and computer games are used as resources for rehabilitation and prevention. **(15)** _____ some programs aim at providing children with specific information about AIDS (Griffiths, 2002).

so as to	and	as a result

This shows that the effects of video games on children are not as harmful as first thought because health problems and short-term aggressive behaviour only affect children who are excessive users of video games (Griffiths, 2002). The problems seem to stem from the way in which children play, from the games they are allowed to play, **(16)** _____ on how much time they spend playing, rather than on the fact of playing itself. **(17)** _____ parents have a fundamental role to play in taking care of their children, reducing the risks that the digital world can bring. Children need to be controlled and monitored. As Byron (2008) states in her review, parents, government, video-games businesses and schools should all collaborate **(18)** _____ reduce risks connected with computer and video games, and promote games that have educational and non-violent features.

such … that	in addition to	to sum up

(19) _____ video and computer gaming have a great positive potential, ranging from children's skill reinforcement and development to educational input. **(20)** _____ these benefits, playing represents an innovative way of learning that is more effective among children than traditional ways of teaching. The extraordinary opportunities that technology offers have to be considered. It is parents' responsibility to provide their children with adequate guidance. This can happen if games developers, the government and all society support and encourage the development of **(21)** _____ sociable and interesting games **(22)** _____ young people always benefit from the advantages that game playing undoubtedly offers.

References

Byron, T. (2008). Safer children in a digital world. *Byron Review. Children and new technology*. Retrieved March, 2008, from http://www.education.gov.uk/ukccis/userfiles/file/FinalReportBookmarked.pdf

Dye, M. W. G., Green, C. S., and Bavelier, D. (2009). The development of attention skills in action video game players. *Neuropsychologia*, 47, 1780–1789.

Gagnon, D. (1985). Videogames and Spatial Skills: An Exploratory Study. *Educational Technology Research and Development*, 33(4), 263–275.

Griffiths, M. (1999). Violent video games and aggression: a review of the literature. *Aggression and Violent Behavior*, 4(2), 203–212.

Griffiths, M. (2002). The educational benefits of Videogames. *Education and Health*, 20(3), 47–51.

Linking words: summary

Writer's purpose	Short linking words	Paired linking words	Subordinators	Sentence-connecting words / Signpost language	Linking words + noun phrase
To link similar ideas	and			in addition also	in addition to
To build an argument	and			furthermore moreover also	
To emphasize two similar ideas		both … and not only … but also			
To contrast different ideas	but yet		although/even though	however	in spite of despite
To build a contrasting argument				on the other hand	
To emphasize two negatives		neither … nor			
To show a result	so		so … that/such … that	therefore as a result	as a result of
To compare			whereas/while		
To give another possibility	or			alternatively	
To emphasize another possibility		either … or			
To summarize				on the whole to sum up	
To show time or sequence			when while	firstly finally	
To give an example				for example	such as
To give a reason			because since as		due to because of
To show purpose			so that/ in order that (so as to/ in order to)		

Choose the correct option to complete sentences 1–7.

1 Hypermarkets can buy goods cheaply in large quantities from their suppliers. _____ their overhead costs are low, their prices are extremely competitive.
a. Because
b. As
c. Although

2 In the 1970s there was only one television in the village _____ nowadays most families have one.
a. when
b. so that
c. whereas

3 _____ the banking system is well regulated, some loans are very risky.
a. when
b. since
c. although

4 The transition to a market economy has been successful _____ the number of registered credit institutions has risen dramatically over the past few years.
a. whereas
b. so that
c. ;

5 The economy grew _____ the lifting of the export ban.
a. because of
b. in addition to
c. in spite

6 The workers were _____ they agreed not to complain to the manager.
a. so worried about their jobs that
b. worried about their jobs so that

7 The researchers _____ local people could meet them.
a. so travelled to Gupa that
b. travelled to Gupa so that

8 **Read the sentence. Then rewrite it using *despite*.**

Although they analyze the costs carefully, they always exceed the budget.

_____, they always exceed the budget.

9   **Read the sentences. Then combine them into one simple sentence by using** *because of* **+ noun phrase.**

Many employees left. The working conditions were poor.

Many employees left _____.

10   **Read the sentences. Then combine them into one simple sentence. Put the examples of brands at the end of the sentence.**

There are many well-known brands of disposable nappies. There are Tinyworld, Cleanex and Tweenie.

There are many well-known brands _____.

6 Expressing shades of meaning

In this unit you will:

- learn how to use modal and semi-modal verbs to express:
  - certainty and uncertainty
  - remote possibility
  - obligation
  - advice
- practise using modal verbs in active and passive voice

Stage A

In this stage you will:

- study the correct form and sentence position of modal verbs
- practise expressing certainty/uncertainty and remote possibility
- learn to use *can* to describe typical situations
- learn to use modal verbs in active and passive voice

Task 1 Introduction to modal verbs

1.1 **Study the three pairs of sentences below. Tick the sentence in each pair that gives the more accurate meaning.**

Note that all the sentences are grammatically accurate, so you will need to study the context of each sentence.

1. a. The study was carried out in two classes only. The results of the study indicate that learning <u>is</u> more effective in small groups.

   b. The study was carried out in two classes only. The results indicate that learning <u>might</u> be more effective in small groups.

2. a. Chicken that is raised indoors <u>does</u> not have as much flavour as free-range organic chicken, but it is undoubtedly cheaper to buy.

   b. Chicken that is raised indoors does not <u>have</u> as much flavour as free-range organic chicken, but it <u>can</u> be cheaper to buy.

3. a. The government does not give enough help to retired people. Older people do not <u>have to</u> worry about paying expensive heating bills in very cold weather.

   b. The government does not give enough help to retired people. Older people <u>should</u> not have to worry about paying expensive heating bills in very cold weather.

1.2 **Look at the underlined words in the sentences in 1.1. Circle those which are modal verbs.**

1. How do modal verbs affect meaning?

2. How do they affect the grammar of the main verb?

1.3   **Find and circle the intensifying adverb in sentence 2a in 1.1. What does it mean?**

Grammar note: Modal verbs and intensifying adverbs are useful in academic writing, because they help you to express shades of meaning. This unit will help you to use modals with greater accuracy and confidence, and thus improve the quality of your writing.

Task 2	Modal verbs – form and sentence position

2.1   There are nine **primary** or **true modal verbs** in English.
Add the four missing modal verbs to the table below.

_____	*may*	_____	*shall*	*must*
could	_____	*would*	_____	

2.2   **Study the modal verb sentences in the table below and answer the questions that follow.**

Positive statement (+)	Many people <u>can</u> speak English in Bartoum.
	The government <u>should</u> help them.
Negative statement (–)	Many people <u>cannot</u> speak English in Bartoum.
	The government <u>should not</u> help them.
Question (?)	<u>Can</u> many people speak English in Bartoum?
	<u>Should</u> the government help them?

1. What type of words are underlined in the table?
2. How do you form questions with modal verbs?
3. How do you form negative sentences with modal verbs?
4. The auxiliary verb *do* is not used in any of the above sentences. Why not?

2.3   **Each sentence contains an error in the form or position of a modal verb. Write the correct sentence.**

1. Do will they make an announcement soon?

   Will they make an announcement soon?

2. Class sizes should be smaller?

   _____

3. The plants do not might grow if the rainy season fails.

   _____

4. The predictions of climate change experts will come true?

   _____

5. Women can to get access to a better education nowadays.

   _____

6. The domination of English maybe a problem in the future.

_____

7. Most people in the UK can not speak Chinese.

_____

Task 3 Expressing certainty, uncertainty and possibility

3.1 Read sentences a–d, and answer the questions.
  a. Dictionaries <u>might</u> be necessary for this assignment.
  b. Dictionaries <u>may</u> be necessary for this assignment.
  c. Dictionaries <u>will</u> be necessary for this assignment.
  d. Dictionaries <u>could</u> be necessary for this assignment.

  1. Which modal verb shows that the writer feels certain? _____
  2. Which ones show that the writer feels uncertain? _____
  3. Which one shows remote possibility? (*Remote* possibility means a *small* possibility.) _____

3.2 Study sentences a–d, which use negative forms of the modals in 3.1. In which sentence is the modal used *incorrectly*?
  a. Dictionaries <u>might not</u> be necessary for this assignment.
  b. Dictionaries <u>may not</u> be necessary for this assignment.
  c. Dictionaries <u>will not</u> be necessary for this assignment.
  d. Dictionaries <u>could not</u> be necessary for this assignment.

3.3 Complete the sentences below, using the modal verbs *will/will not*, *may/may not*, *might/might not*, or *could*. Use the text in brackets to help you.

Grammar note: The modal verbs *will/will not*, *may/may not*, *might/might not* and *could* are useful for expressing a precise level of probability and possibility in academic writing. Read the extract from the conclusion of a student's essay.

> To sum up, increasing the price of airline tickets <u>could</u> paralyze the tourist industry and damage the economies of many countries which depend on tourism. Making air travel much more expensive <u>may</u> minimize air pollution, but this is not an effective sustainable solution because travelling by plane is the main way to exchange goods and cultures.

  1. The British economy _____*will*_____ change as a result of the banking crisis. (*This is certain to happen.*)

  2. Neuroscientists _____ understand how the brain works within the next ten years. (*This is uncertain.*)

  3. Local languages _____ become more important in the future. (*This is a remote possibility.*)

4. The rise in consumer spending _____ not be good for the environment. (*This is certain.*)

5. The MERS virus _____ pass from camels to humans. (*This is a remote possibility.*)

6. The decrease in the bee population _____ slow down once the cause has been identified. (*This is certain.*)

7. The use of English on university courses _____ continue to increase for at least the next ten years. (*This is certain.*)

8. People _____ take care of the environment if they are taught about it at school. (*This is uncertain.*)

3.4 **The sentences below all use *perhaps*, *possibly* or *maybe* to express uncertainty. Rewrite each sentence using a modal verb instead. Try to vary your choice of modal verb.**

1. Perhaps men and women have a different approach to life.
   Men and woman might have a different approach to life.

2. Maybe better housing is not the only solution to the problem of overcrowding.
   _____

3. Perhaps advertising will persuade people to eat genetically modified food.
   _____

4. Different sources of energy will possibly replace oil in the future.
   _____

5. Perhaps people will stop buying physical books when electronic books become cheaper.
   _____

6. Perhaps more and more workers will move to cities to find a better job.
   _____

7. Maybe the economic downturn will not affect employment as much as people think.
   _____

Grammar note: You are probably familiar with using the words *perhaps*, *possibly* and *maybe* to express uncertainty, but using modal verbs is a way of introducing variety into your written work.

3.5 **Write four sentences, using *will/will not*, *may/may not*, *might/might not* or *could*.**

1. Write two sentences about events that you think are certain to happen/not to happen.
   Mobile phones will become cheaper.
   _____
   _____

2. Write two sentences about events that are only *remote* possibilities.
   Cars could run on solar power.
   _____
   _____

| Task 4 | **Expressing uncertainty about the past** |

Sometimes, you need to express uncertainty about an event which happened in the past. Instead of using *might/may/could* + bare infinitive, we use *might/may/could* + perfect bare infinitive. (Perfect bare infinitive = auxiliary verb *have* + past participle of main verb.)

Study the examples below:

a. *Perhaps the designs are faulty.*   ⟶   *The designs might* **be** *faulty.*

        (modal verb — bare infinitive)

   Perhaps the designs were faulty.   ⟶   *The designs might* **have been** *faulty.*

        (modal verb — perfect bare infinitive)

b. *Perhaps she does not like the question.*   ⟶   *She may not* **like** *the question.*

        (modal verb — bare infinitive)

   Perhaps she did not like the question.   ⟶   *She may not* **have liked** *the question.*

        (modal verb — perfect bare infinitive)

c. *Perhaps they will make a mistake.*   ⟶   *They may* **make** *a mistake.*

        (modal verb — bare infinitive)

   Perhaps they made a mistake.   ⟶   *They could* **have made** *a mistake.*

        (modal verb — perfect bare infinitive)

4.1 **The sentences below all use *perhaps*, *possibly* or *maybe* to express uncertainty. Rewrite each sentence using a modal verb instead. Try to vary your choice of modal verb.**

Grammar note: do not use *could* + *not* as it means *was not/were not able*. See 3.2 above.

1. Perhaps the government published the statistics on a different website.

   The government might have published the statistics on a different website.

2. Perhaps the figures were not accurate.

   _____

3. Perhaps the public did not support the high tax on fuel.

   _____

4. Perhaps they made an unpopular decision.

   _____

5. Perhaps the committee members did not understand the issue well enough.

   _____

6. Perhaps the civil servants gave the minister bad advice.

   _____

Task 5 — The uses of *can*

5.1 **Read sentences 1–3, and decide how *can* is being used in each case. Write *a*, *b* or *c* next to each sentence.**

a. to express possibility

b. to express ability

c. to express permission

1. Most students can speak English. _____

2. Students can use the drinks machine at break time. _____

3. Students can fail examinations if they don't study hard. _____

> **Additional use of *can* – describing typical situations**
> Sometimes in academic writing, we describe 'typical' situations – situations which are normally but not always true. We can use *can* to modify the certainty of a 'fact'.
> **For example:**
> a. It *is* hot in the summer in Bartoum.
>   (This means that Bartoum is *always* hot in the summer.)
> b. It *can be* hot in the summer in Bartoum.
>   (This modifies the certainty. You know that Bartoum is *normally* hot, but you are aware that sometimes it is not hot.)

5.2 **Complete the sentences below with a modal verb from the box. Use the text in brackets to help you. More than one choice may be possible.**

will	can	could	might	may

1. Lack of understanding about cultural differences, local regulations and language barriers _may/might_ block trade. (*The writer is making an uncertain prediction about the future.*)

2. Lack of understanding about cultural differences, local regulations and language barriers _____ block trade. (*The writer is confidently referring to the future.*)

3. Lack of understanding about cultural differences, local regulations and language barriers _____ block trade. (*The writer is generalizing about a typical situation.*)

4. Lack of understanding about cultural differences, local regulations and language barriers _____ block trade. (*The writer is referring to a remote possibility in the future.*)

5.3 **Read the statements, and rewrite each as a typical situation. You may add *sometimes* to the typical situation.**

1. Poor standards of hygiene cause ill health.

   Typical situation: _Poor standards of hygiene can sometimes cause ill health._

2. Tourism destroys the natural environment.

   Typical situation: _____

3. The weather is cold in the UK in the winter.

   Typical situation: _____

4. Many students have financial difficulties at university.

    Typical situation: _____

5. Exposure to direct sunshine causes skin problems.

    Typical situation: _____

| Task 6 | **Using modal verbs in the present passive voice** |

6.1 **Sometimes, you may need to express certainty, uncertainty or possibility in a passive sentence. Study the following sentences and answer the questions.**

a. Production is now expensive, so people may not produce cars here any longer. *A*
    (S ... V ... O)

b. Production is now expensive, so cars may not be produced here any longer. *P*
    (S ... V)

1. Which sentence is in the active voice ? _a_
2. Which sentence is in the passive voice? _b_
3. Which sentence contains redundant words? _____ *merely repeats the meaning*

Grammar note: You studied **redundant** or **empty words** in Unit 2C.

6.2 **How do you form the present passive with a modal verb? In the table below, number the parts of the sentence 1–5 to show their correct order.**

Past participle of main verb	Bare infinitive verb *be*	(*not*)	Subject	Modal verb
known	be	not	the results of the experiment	may
5	4	3	1	2

6.3 **In each sentence below, label the subject (S), verb (V) and object (O) of the *second clause*. Then rewrite the sentence using the passive with a modal verb, making a tight link between the clauses and omitting the redundant words in bold.**

1. China is gaining in economic power, so **people** might speak Chinese more widely in the future.
    (S ... V ... O)

    China is gaining in economic power, so Chinese might be spoken more widely in the future.

2. The government is concerned about on-screen violence, so **they** might ban this website.
    _____ *, this website might be banned.*

3. The negative effect of this price reduction is that **people** will consume more alcohol.
    _____ *, more alcohol will be consumed.*

4. As a result of this research, **the bosses** could develop a new system.
    _____ *, a new*_____

5. The government is now promoting healthy eating, so **shoppers** may buy less junk food.

    _____

6. This article is out of date, but **publishers** may publish new research on the subject before the end of the year.

_____

7. The instructions state that **gardeners** can plant these roses in the summer.

_____

6.4 **Read the question. Rewrite the answers using modal verbs with the present simple passive.**

How might social media such as Skype, Facebook and Twitter benefit or harm people?

1. People might make more friends.

   More friends might be made.

2. People may share more information.

   _____

3. People will receive information more quickly.

   _____

4. People might not maintain high levels of literacy.

   _____

5. People could ignore the problems of the real world.

   _____

Stage B

In this stage you will:
- learn to use semi-modal verb forms accurately (active and passive voice)
- pract se giving advice and making recommendations with modal and semi-modal verbs

Task 1	Semi-modal verbs – meaning, form and sentence position

1.1 **There are several semi-modal verbs in English. Three of them are underlined below. Match the semi-modal verb in each sentence (1–3) to its meaning (a–c).**

1. The students <u>need to</u> pass the exam in order to continue their studies.
2. Farmers <u>have to</u> water crops in the growing season.
3. Local people <u>ought to</u> welcome immigrants.

a. It is important or necessary to do this.
b. It is the right thing to do this.
c. It is important or necessary to do this.

These verbs are called **semi-modal verbs** because the rules for their use are not exactly the same as for primary modal verbs, which you learned about in Stage A of this unit.

1.2 **Study the semi-modal verbs in the table below and answer the questions which follow.**

Positive statement (+)	Negative statement (−)	Question (?)
The team <u>ought to</u> work together	The team <u>ought</u> not to work together.	<u>Ought</u> the team to work together?
The students <u>ought to</u> help each other.	The students <u>ought</u> not <u>to</u> help each other.	<u>Ought</u> the students to help each other?
The government <u>has to</u> offer support to poor people.	The government does not <u>have to</u> offer support to poor people.	Does the government <u>have to</u> offer support to poor people?
The teachers <u>have to</u> offer email support to students.	The teachers do not <u>have to</u> offer email support to students.	Do the teachers <u>have to</u> offer email support to students?
The team <u>needs to</u> meet once a week.	The team does not <u>need to</u> met once a week.	Does the team <u>need to</u> meet once a week?
The students <u>need to</u> learn English for their future careers.	The students do not <u>need to</u> learn English for their future careers.	Do the students <u>need to</u> learn English for their future careers?

1. A semi-modal verb is in two parts. Which word is always the **second** part? _____to_____

2. Which verb form is used **after** the second part? _____

3. Do you need the auxiliary verb *do* with *ought to* in questions and negative sentences?

    _____

4. Do you need the auxiliary verb *do* with *have to* and *need to* in questions and negative

    sentences _____

5. Modal verbs do **not** add an ~s in the third-person singular (*he can*, not *he cans*). Is this the

    same for semi-modal verbs in the third-person singular? _____

6. Of the three semi-modal verbs above, which one behaves most like a **primary modal**
    verb? Give your reasons for this.

    _____

    _____

7. Of the three semi-modal verbs above, which two behave most like **ordinary main** verbs?
    Give your reasons for this.

    _____

    _____

1.3   Read the grammatical rules and put a tick or a cross for each verb.

	Auxiliary verb *do* is used in questions and negative sentences	Verb ending changes to match the third-person singular subject
need to	✔	
ought to		
have to		

1.4   Each sentence contains an error in the use of the semi-modal verb. Write the correct sentence.

1. The students have to write essays?

   Do the students have to write essays?

2. The country not ought to take part in the war.

   _____

3. Has the swallow to migrate to Africa in the summer?

   _____

4. Needs she learn how to write a list of references?

   _____

5. She has not to write a complete essay.

   _____

6. She oughts to be careful when she goes out.

   _____

1.5   Tick the correct meaning for each verb in the table below.

The semi-modal verbs *have to* and *need to* and the modal verb *must* all mean 'it is important or necessary to do something'. The negative forms can be tricky! Don't rush this task. Take some time to think about it and get it right.

	a. It is important or necessary to do it.	b. It is important or necessary not to do it.	c. It is **not** important or necessary to do it.
1. She has to finish her essay now.	✔		
2. She does not have to finish her essay now.			
3. She must finish her essay now.			
4. She must not answer that question.			
5. She needs to finish her essay now.			
6. She does not need to finish her essay now.			

1.6 **Rewrite sentences 1–9, giving them the same meaning, but using the semi-modal verbs *have to* or *need to*. Use *must not* where necessary.**

Grammar note: There is no semi-modal verb which means 'it is important not to do something'. Use the modal verb *must not* for this.

1. It is necessary for the government to spend more money on education.
   The government <u>needs to spend more money on education.</u>

2. It is not necessary for the research team to count the birds on the river.
   The research team _____

3. It is important that students do not forget the date of the test.
   Students _____

4. It is necessary for deep-sea divers to carry oxygen in a cylinder.
   Deep-sea divers _____

5. It is important that researchers do not make mistakes when analyzing the data.
   Researchers _____

6. It is necessary that the scientists set up the experiment correctly.
   The scientists _____

7. It is not necessary for the government to intervene in this matter.
   The government _____

8. It is important for minority language speakers not to forget their mother tongue.
   Minority language speakers _____

9. It is not important for people to be rich in order to be happy.
   People _____

As you learnt in Stage A 2.2 of this unit, primary modal verbs are **not** used with the *do* auxiliary verb in negative statements and questions. This is because **primary modal verbs** are a type of **auxiliary verb**.

The students <u>might not</u> complete the survey on time. ✔
The students <u>do might not</u> complete the survey on time. ✘

The semi-modal verbs *have to* and *need to*, which are used with the auxiliary *do*, can also be used together with primary modal verbs (*may*, *might* and *will*).

a. *The birds <u>might have to</u> leave the area if they cannot find food.*
b. *Land <u>may need to</u> be purchased to prevent further development.*
c. *Because of the economic recession, there <u>will have to</u> be redundancies.*

Grammar note: It is not common to use *could* with *have to* and *need to*.

1.7   **Complete the sentences using *have to* or *need to* and the correct verb from the list below. Add *will*, *might* or *may* as appropriate. There is one gap for each missing word. Use the instructions in brackets to help you.**

retake	survive	employ	reduce	~~drop~~	act	check	consider

1. The rescue services _might_ _need_ _to_ _drop_ supplies by helicopter if the flooding continues. (*This is uncertain.*)

2. The situation is urgent. All world leaders who have signed the agreement _____ _____ _____ _____ in order to solve the problem of carbon emissions. (*This is certain.*)

3. They _____ _____ _____ _____ passengers' luggage allowance on planes in order to save fuel. (*This is uncertain.*)

4. If the drought continues, farmers _____ _____ _____ _____ planting GM seeds which are more resistant to lack of water. (*This is uncertain.*)

5. These animals _____ _____ _____ _____ long periods without food. (*This is certain.*)

6. Health experts _____ _____ _____ _____ the water quality again next year. (*This is certain.*)

7. The company _____ _____ _____ _____ more workers if sales continue to rise. (*This is uncertain.*)

8. Students on this course _____ _____ _____ _____ the exam if they fail the first time. (*This is certain.*)

Task 2   **Giving advice and making recommendations – *should, ought to, have to, must***

2.1   **Look at the pairs of sentences. Which sentence in each pair gives the *stronger* advice: a or b? Tick your answers.**

1. a. Parents <u>must</u> encourage their children to learn a foreign language. ☐

    b. Parents <u>ought to</u> encourage their children to learn a foreign language. ☐

2. a. World leaders <u>should</u> understand cultural differences. ☐

    b. World leaders <u>have to</u> understand cultural differences. ☐

2.2   **Study the sentences and read the question below. Tick the correct boxes in the table.**
Which verb (*must* or *have to*) implies an obligation which is the choice of the writer? Which verb implies an obligation for which there is no choice?

	a. **Choice of the writer**	b. **No choice**
1. Students on the pre-sessional English course <u>must</u> study in the evenings, or they will fall behind.		
2. The referee <u>has to</u> give a yellow card if a footballer deliberately touches the ball with his hands.		

2.3 **Complete sentences 1–8 with an appropriate form of *must* or *have to*. In some cases, information is provided in brackets to help you.**

1. A multinational corporation _____ has to _____ employ speakers of various different languages.

2. According to government regulations, tourists _____ apply for their visas within six months of their trip abroad.

3. Polluters _____ pay for the damage they are doing to the environment. (The writer is an environmental campaigner.)

4. Publicly funded works of art _____ gain the approval of several committees. (Student essay which summarizes information from an official website.)

5. The dissertation _____ be submitted by 5 p.m. on the day of the deadline, or there will be a 5% deduction from the final grade. (Extract from a lecturer's instructions.)

6. In conclusion, the shareholding company _____ improve the restaurant facilities for the public in the shopping centre. (Extract from report about the strengths and weaknesses of a shopping centre.)

7. Many people _____ continue living in earthquake zones as they have no means of moving to a safer place.

8. Weather forecasters _____ collect data from different instruments all over the world in order to create accurate weather maps.

Grammar note: Don't forget that *need to* can also be used to show *obligation*, in the same way that *must* and *have to* can. With *need to*, it doesn't matter whose choice the obligation is.

Task 3	**Giving advice and recommendations using the passive voice**

3.1 **Sometimes, we use a modal or semi-modal verb in a passive sentence to give advice or recommendations. Study the following sentences. Write *P* by the sentences which are in the passive voice. Write *SMP* by the sentence which uses a semi-modal verb in the passive.**

1. The government should give advice on how to start a business. _____
2. Advice should be given on how to start a business. _____
3. The government ought to give advice on how to start a business. _____
4. Advice ought to be given on how to start a business. _____

3.2 **You have already studied how to form the passive with a modal verb. How do you form the passive with a *semi-modal* verb? Number the table below to show correct sentence order.**

Past participle of main verb	Bare infinitive of verb *be*	Subject	Semi-modal verb
given _____	be _____	advice _____	ought to _____

3.3 **Label the subject (S), verb (V) and object (O) of the second clause or sentence. Then rewrite the sentence in the passive, making a tight link between the clauses and omitting the redundant words in bold.**

Grammar note: Remember that you can use *will*, *might* or *may* in front of *have to* and *need to*. (You have practised this in 1.7 of this stage.)

1. The government is concerned about on-screen violence, so **they** might have
   to ban this website.

   The government is concerned about on-screen violence, so this website might have to be banned.

2. Small film companies do not have much money, so **film-makers** have to make new films as cheaply as possible.

   _____

3. Many people have donated money for development projects. **Administrators** must use it by the end of March.

   _____

4. Students must hand their essays in on time because **the teachers** might have to show them to external moderators.

   _____

5. It is difficult to understand the changing political situation in Bakoo. **Local people** should use Twitter to give regular updates.

   _____

6. Many Britons have retired to Spain because of the Mediterranean climate. **Spanish people** need to encourage them to learn Spanish.

   _____

7. There is a serious problem with the nuclear fuel plant so **engineers** might need to close it down.

   _____

8. The UK is now in third place globally for scientific research publications. **Scientists** should publish more British scientific research studies.

   _____

9. Fish stocks are declining in local lakes due to pollution, so **the local government** may have to restrict fishing.

   _____

Task 4 — Writing conclusions

4.1 It is useful to use *should, ought to, have to, need to* and *must* when giving advice or recommendations in conclusions. Read the following extract from a student essay conclusion, and fill each gap with a suitable modal or semi-modal verb. Add *might*, *may* or *will* if there are two gaps. (The *to* is already in the text if you need a semi-modal verb.)

> In order to reduce carbon dioxide emissions, the weight of aeroplanes **(1)** _should/must_ be reduced. In Japan, some companies are inventing lighter materials for aeroplane frameworks; they are also using light tableware to decrease overall weight, so less fuel is used in flight (Nikkei Net, 2009). In addition, airline companies **(2)** _____ fund research into other sources of energy, such as hydrogen-powered fuel cells. As for the noise problem, the airports **(3)** _____ _____ to be moved away from residential areas to the coast, or to areas where people do not live.
>
> All governments worldwide **(4)** _____ to act to solve the problem of carbon dioxide emissions. They **(5)** _____ increase fuel tax in order to make their flights more expensive, which will, in turn, decrease the number of flights and encourage people either to not travel, or to use other forms of transport.
>
> In conclusion, managing flights and producing new technical materials will decrease environmental damage. Government and air travel companies **(6)** _____ act responsibly to ensure that this happens.

Task 5 — Review and practice (Stages A and B)

5.1 Think about the topic 'mobile phones and social networking' and look at the prompts below. Write your own sentences in academic style.

1. A statement which expresses certainty:

   _____

2. A statement which expresses uncertainty or remote possibility:

   _____

3. A situation which sometimes happens and sometimes does not happen:

   _____

4. A statement opinion which expresses that it is (perhaps) an obligation for people to do something:

   _____

5. An statement which expresses that it is (perhaps) not necessary for people to do something:

   _____

6. A recommendation:

   _____

7. A statement which expresses an obligation which is the personal choice of the writer:

   _____

8. A statement which expresses an obligation about which there is no choice:

   _____

Stage C

In this level you will:
- use modal and semi-modal verbs to convey your stance and to build an argument within an essay
- learn how to intensify modal verbs

| Task 1 | **Planning your stance and preparing your argument** |

1.1 **Read the essay title below.**

> **'All children should learn to play a musical instrument at state schools.'**
> **Discuss.**

1. What is the hidden question in the essay title?

_____

2. Does the title demand that you agree with the opinion, or can you make up your own mind?

_____

1.2 **What is your opinion about the essay title? Generate your own ideas and fill in the table below.**

This process will help you to decide how far you agree or disagree with the statement. There are no reading sources to help you to prepare to write this essay, so you need to use your own background experience, and draw on any knowledge you may have of research which has been carried out on this topic.

Advantages for children of learning an instrument at school	Disadvantages for children of learning an instrument at school
Advantages of the government paying for this service	**Disadvantages of the government paying for this service**

1.3 **Compare your list of advantages and disadvantages with the list of another student.**

Advantages for children of learning an instrument at school	Disadvantages for children of learning an instrument at school
They learn hand-eye coordination.	Practising an instrument can be very boring.
Research shows it helps children with Maths and English.	They might be forced by teachers to learn an instrument too early in their lives, not enjoy it, and then never play again.
They might make new friends.	Instruments can be expensive and parents and schools might not be able to afford them.
If they join an orchestra, they will learn to be part of a team – a useful life skill.	There might not be enough teachers available to teach everyone.
It is much easier to learn new things when you are young.	Children are already very busy in school, and need free time to play on their own and with friends. They should not learn all the time.
If children learn an instrument, they may start a band when they are teenagers, and have a lot of fun.	If they do not like it and do not make very much progress, children may feel that they have failed and have less confidence.
They might become more confident generally and aim higher in other areas of their life.	Some children will always be better at playing an instrument than others.
Advantages of the government paying for this service	**Disadvantages of the government paying for this service**
All children can choose the instrument they prefer without parents worrying about how to pay for it.	If the government pays for instruments and tuition, there may not be enough money to pay for other more important equipment in schools, such as computers.
The government must be seen to be promoting equality of opportunity for all.	Parents may not take the children's musical tuition seriously. They might not encourage their children to practise.

Stance

Your opinion is called your **stance**. Your stance should be expressed at the end of your introduction in your **thesis statement**. The rest of your essay should be devoted to persuading your reader that your stance is correct by using evidence in the form of factual details, statistics, examples or background knowledge. The supporting argument for your stance needs to be set out logically, with an introduction, paragraphs in a logical order and a conclusion.

1.4   **Identify your stance. Tick the box which most closely matches your opinion.**

All children should learn a musical instrument of their choice at school. The government should pay.	
All children ought to learn a musical instrument of their choice, and there should be government assistance to help poorer families buy instruments.	
All children should learn a simple, cheap musical instrument at school. The government should pay.	
All children should learn a simple, cheap musical instrument at school to see if they like it. The government should only pay for a trial period; after that, parents should pay if the children decide to continue with an instrument of their choice.	
Children ought not to be forced to learn a musical instrument. Only children who are interested ought to do it, and there should be government assistance to help the poorer families buy instruments.	
Children should not have to learn a musical instrument. Only interested children ought to do it, and the government should not have to help the poorer families to buy instruments.	
Learning a musical instrument is not a core subject such as Maths or Science, so it ought not to be offered at school. Lessons should be taken outside school by children who are interested. Parents should pay privately.	

1.5   **Read the paragraph extracts (a–d) from a student's essay. Underline the modal and semi-modal verbs, and answer the questions at the top of the next page.**

a. Children should be encouraged to learn an instrument rather than be forced to learn, and the range of musical instruments taught should be as wide as possible to cater for different personalities and tastes. Ensuring equality of opportunity is the responsibility of the government, so financial help should be available for families who need it.

b. There are many advantages of learning an instrument, but only if the children are willing to try it. Children could learn a new skill and have the opportunity to make new friends. They might also enjoy playing in an orchestra and learning to be part of a team.

c. Children ought not to be forced to learn a musical instrument. Only children who are interested ought to do it, and there should be government assistance to help the poorer families buy instruments.

d. On the other hand, if children are forced to learn when they are not interested, they may not enjoy the experience, and they may even avoid music later on in their lives. Children need to have some time in the school day to be creative, but if they prefer playing football or painting to playing music, this should be encouraged.

1. Which paragraph contains a stance from 1.4? _____
2. Which paragraph discusses why only interested children should learn a musical instrument? _____
3. Which paragraph explains the disadvantages of forcing children to learn an instrument? _____
4. Which paragraph provides a summary and a recommendation_____
5. What is the logical order of the paragraph extracts? _____ _____ _____ _____
6. Why has the writer not included the phrases *I think or in my opinion* in this essay?

_____

Task 2	Intensifying words

2.1 **Read sentences 1–7, look at the bold words, and decide how the shades of meaning differ in each case. Match them with the appropriate descriptions a–e. Note that you need to use sentences a and b twice.**

1. Research shows that learning a musical instrument **will** help to improve hand-eye coordination. ___c___
2. Research shows that learning a musical instrument **will undoubtedly** help to improve hand-eye coordination. _____
3. Research shows that learning a musical instrument **could** help to improve hand-eye coordination. _____
4. Research shows that learning a musical instrument **could easily** help to improve hand-eye coordination. _____
5. Research shows that learning a musical instrument **may** help to improve hand-eye coordination. _____
6. Research shows that learning a musical instrument **might well** help to improve hand-eye coordination. _____
7. Research shows that learning a musical instrument **can** help to improve hand-eye coordination. _____

a. Research suggests that learning a musical instrument is perhaps useful for hand-eye coordination.
b. Research strongly suggests that learning a musical instrument is useful for hand-eye coordination.
c. Research has proved that learning a musical instrument is useful for hand-eye coordination.
d. Research suggests that learning musical instrument helps to improve hand-eye coordination in a typical situation.
e. Research has proved that learning a musical instrument is useful for hand-eye coordination. The writer wants to emphasize this point.

Grammar note: Whatever your opinion, intensifying adverbs can help you to express yourself more accurately.

2.2 Complete the sentences using an intensifying adverb. Use the intensifying adverbs given in the box below.

will certainly/undoubtedly/definitely	can/could easily	may/might well

1. If children do not like playing an instrument, and do not make very much progress, they may _____*well*_____ feel that they have failed.

2. Some researchers claim that children will _____ become more confident and aim higher in other areas of life.

3. If they start a band when they are teenagers, they could _____ have a lot of fun.

4. Practising an instrument can _____ become very boring.

5. They will _____ make new friends.

6. Musical instruments can _____ cost a lot of money.

7. If all children are forced to learn an instrument, there might _____ be children who refuse to practise.

8. Children's Maths and English scores might _____ improve.

9. Some children will _____ be better at playing an instrument than others.

10. If this suggestion becomes law, many children will _____ start learning an instrument before they are ready.

Task 3   Stance and argument – further practice

3.1 Read the essay title.

> **'Imprisonment is a more appropriate punishment for offenders than community service.' Discuss.**

What is the hidden question in the essay title? _____

_____

3.2 Read the text to find out more about community service.

Many people convicted of crimes (offenders) are not sent to prison. They can be given fines or community service. Community service requires the offender to complete a set number of hours of unpaid work. Local residents can make suggestions online for appropriate projects, such as:

- cleaning up litter
- clearing public land
- repairing and redecorating community centres and other buildings
- removing graffiti from public buildings

Offenders doing community service are easy to spot, wearing bright orange jackets as they do their work.

Adapted from: Gov.uk (n.d.). Community Sentences. Gov.uk. Retrieved 15th July, 2013, from https://www.gov.uk/community-sentences/overview

3.3 **Read the essay title again. Write your own ideas in the table below. Then compare your answers with those of another writer (see completed table in the *Answer key*). What is your stance?**

Advantages of community service for offenders	Disadvantages of community service for offenders
Advantages of community service for the government and society	**Disadvantages of community service for the government and society**

3.4 **Read thesis statements 1–3 below. Which one does *not* show the writer's stance?**

1. Avoiding a jail sentence brings obvious benefits to offenders. However, if the offender is not violent, it can also be good for society as a whole, by reducing the costs of imprisonment and the rates of reoffending.

2. Although community service may be cheaper, the punishment does not deprive a criminal of their freedom and can therefore be regarded as a soft option. The government should review and improve its prison system.

3. This essay will discuss the topic of community service and the positive and negative aspects of this type of punishment.

3.5 **Read the student essay below. The thesis statement and the modal verbs have been removed. Which thesis statement from 3.4 best fits gap A? Why?**

_____

3.6 **Fill the gaps (1–15) using the modal verb phrases in the box.**

could have	can encourage	may expose	might well make	will certainly keep
should be	can remain	might have to be kept	can do	~~could have~~	might help
can learn		could be		can contribute	may avoid

> **'Imprisonment is a more appropriate punishment for offenders than community service.' Discuss.**
>
> Community service is a well-known term. It consists of doing unpaid work with the two-fold aim of benefiting society and allowing offenders to avoid imprisonment. **(A)** _____
>
> _____
>
> _____

In fact, a jail sentence **(1)** _____*could have*_____ some negative effects on the offenders as is explained below.

Some prisons are not always the best place for offenders to spend a long time. They **(2)** _____ friendships between criminals, and they **(3)** _____ minor offenders to violent behaviour and drugs (STV News, 2010).

Community service offers a chance for offenders to be given an alternative sentence to prison, depending on the type of crime. This is beneficial because offenders **(4)** _____ a job in a semi-free environment which **(5)** _____ to keep them away from harmful influences. Moreover, they **(6)** _____ to society through their work and also have the chance to learn new skills, so they **(7)** _____ as useful members of society while carrying out their punishment. (GOV.UK, n.d.)

On the other hand, there are some negative aspects of community service. First of all, there is the possibility of people on community service programmes reoffending due to not being jailed and controlled 24 hours a day. There is also the issue for offenders of wearing orange jackets in public which **(8)** _____ a little embarrassing or uncomfortable. However, this public exposure **(9)** _____ benefits for offenders in that it **(10)** _____ them feel guilty and ashamed of what they have done and make them re-evaluate their behaviour.

Imprisonment **(11)** _____ offenders off the streets and makes sure that they do not reoffend during that period. Prisons offer a tightly controlled environment where the risk of escape is very low. However, imprisonment involves a huge expense to society, and prisons are becoming overcrowded. As the number of inmates in prisons increases, so other ways of punishing offenders without shutting them in jail **(12)** _____ explored.

In conclusion, there are many different types of crimes and not all the crimes deserve the same punishment. An offender **(13)** _____ away from society because of the violence of the crime. However, in some cases, if there is no risk of violence and the offender agrees to it, doing community service **(14)** _____ the problems associated with a term in prison and also reduce costs to the taxpayer. In this way, offenders **(15)** _____ to take responsibility for their crimes and help other people.

References

GOV.UK (n.d.). Community Sentences. GOV.UK. Retrieved 15th July, 2013, from https://www.gov.uk/community-sentences/overviewSTV.tv (2008).
Barlinnie – a day in the life. STV news. Retrieved 1st February, 2010, from http://news.stv.tv/scotland/39445-barlinnie-a-day-in-the-life/

Unit 6 Self-check

Choose the correct option to complete sentences 1 and 2.

1 The increase in life expectancy _____ problems for developing economies.
   a. could cause
   b. could to cause
   c. coulds cause

2 _____ the government subsidize rail companies?
   a. Shoulds
   b. Should
   c. Does should

Read quotes 3–8. Then choose the correct answer for each question.

3 'Some international students may not be prepared for life in a different country.' Does the sentence express …?
   a. certainty
   b. uncertainty
   c. remote possibility

4 'There could be several reasons for this.' Which sentence below has the same meaning?
   a. There might have been several reasons for this.
   b. There are several reasons for this.
   c. There are perhaps several reasons for this.

5 'Perhaps the experiment did not fail.' Which sentence below has the same meaning?
   a. The experiment might not fail.
   b. The experiment might not have failed.
   c. The experiment could not have failed.

6 'Students can accidentally exceed the word limit for their assignment.' Which sentence below has the same meaning?
   a. Students have permission to exceed the word limit if they want to.
   b. Students are able to exceed the word limit if they want to.
   c. Sometimes students unintentionally exceed the word limit, but they do not always do this.

7 'The researchers might not need to visit Australia.' Which sentence below has the same meaning?
   a. Perhaps it is necessary for the researchers not to visit Australia.
   b. Perhaps it is not necessary for the researchers to visit Australia.
   c. Perhaps it is necessary for the researchers to visit Australia.

8 'The dominance of English as a global language may well endanger the creation of new literature in other languages.' Which sentence below has the same meaning?

   a. There is a possibility that English might endanger the creation of new literature in other languages.

   b. It is certain that English will endanger the creation of new literature in other languages.

   c. There is a strong possibility that English might endanger the creation of new literature in other languages.

9 **Choose the correct option to complete the sentence.**

Students _____ understand Chinese to study Chinese history.

   a. must not

   b. ought not to

   c. do not have to

10 **Read the sentence. Rewrite it, omitting the redundant word, using the present simple passive voice.**

People could easily misunderstand the instructions.

_____

Expressing condition

In this unit you will:

- learn how to use the subordinators *if* and *unless* to form conditional sentences

You use conditional sentences to:

- make a personal prediction about a likely event
- describe laws of nature
- give warnings
- give advice
- evaluate unlikely and impossible events

This unit builds on information about modal and semi-modal verbs contained in Unit 6, so make sure you have studied Unit 6 before beginning this unit.

Stage A

In this stage you will learn to write conditional sentences to:

- make a personal prediction about a likely event
- describe laws of nature
- give warnings
- give advice

Task 1   Identifying likely events – first conditionals

1.1   **Read the conversation. Think about Rosa's expectations, and answer the questions below.**

Rosa and Said are friends. Rosa has just taken her accountancy examination.

Said: How did it go?

Rosa: Not great. There were quite a lot of questions I know I got wrong.

Said: Do you think you've passed?

Rosa: I don't know. It's the second time I've taken it, and I really need to pass it this time or my company won't keep me.

Said: What will you do if you don't pass?

Rosa: My company will definitely want me to leave. I could go to Paris I suppose – I've always wanted to improve my French. Or I might look for another job in London. Oh, I don't know. Let's hope for the best!

1. Is it likely that Rosa has failed her exam? _____

2. Why does she mention Paris? _____

3. On what condition will she go there? _____

Talking about likely events

Said asked: 'What will you do if you don't pass?'

Rosa replied: 'My company will definitely want me to leave. I could go to Paris I suppose. Or I might look for a job in London.'

Another way for Rosa to express her view is:

'If I don't pass the exam, my company will definitely want me to leave.'

'If I don't pass the exam, I could go to Paris or I might look for a job in London.'

1.2 **Think of something which is likely to happen in your life and write two sentences with conditions, like the examples.**

a. If it's a nice day tomorrow, I'll go swimming.
   (*I'll* is the short form of *I will*, used in spoken language)

b. If I have time later, I might buy a new pair of trousers.

1. If it's a nice day tomorrow, I'll _____.

2. If I have time later, I might _____.

Task 2	**Making a personal prediction about a likely event**

Grammar note: A *likely event* is an event which is really possible.

Rosa said, 'If I don't pass the exam, I could go to Paris or I might look for a job in London.'

It is likely that Rosa has failed her exam. She couldn't answer many of the questions, and she has failed the same exam before. Her prediction is that she might go to London or Paris.

2.1 **Study three more examples of this type of sentence and answer the questions below.**

a. Students who share a house have planned a party for this evening.

   likely situation | prediction

   If the students play loud music tonight at the party, their neighbours will phone the police.

b. It is August in Malaysia (coconut season), and the beach is surrounded by coconut palms.

   likely situation | prediction

   If tourists sit under the coconut palms, the coconuts might fall on their heads.

c. Students are planning a demonstration about government cuts.

   likely situation | prediction

   If the protesters depart from the agreed route, the police could stop the demonstration.

1. Which sentence shows a **certain** prediction? _____

2. Which sentence shows an **uncertain** prediction? _____

3. Which modal verb predicts a **remote possibility**? _____

Grammar note: Use *will* for certain predictions and *might* or *may* for predictions which are uncertain. Use *could* to predict a remote possibility. Do not use *could not* because it means *was/were not able to* (see Unit 6A, 3.2).

2.2 **Imagine your friend is studying at university at the moment, but you are worried about him because he is lazy. Write some sentences to make a personal prediction about likely future problems.**

Use the phrases in the box. Remember to add a comma after the *if* clause.

have to pay a fine	well lack energy	fall behind with the course
~~not understand the topic well enough to write the essays~~		need to take vitamin tablets
easily annoy the teacher	upset his parents	not be able to practise his spoken English

1. He misses lectures.

   <u>If he misses lectures, he may/might not understand the topic well enough to write the essays.</u>

2. He does not return his books to the library on time.

   _____

3. He does not try to make friends with other international students.

   _____

4. He does not play any sport.

   _____

5. He falls asleep in lessons.

   _____

6. He does not do his homework.

   _____

7. He eats junk food.

   _____

8. He never phones home.

   _____

Task 3 Adding supporting detail

Using conditionals to add detail

A writer can use a prediction about a likely event to add supporting detail to academic writing. (For more information about **supporting detail**, look again at Unit 4C.)

For example:

a. *The world economy is changing, and more and more companies are operating internationally. If globalization continues at the current pace, many languages, cultural traditions and local enterprises will disappear.*

b. *Skin cancer is a largely preventable disease, and people can help to protect themselves by adopting the measures discussed above. If these suggestions are followed, the number of sufferers will decrease.*

3.1 When adding supporting details, the writer sometimes puts the *if* clause first, and sometimes they choose to put it second. Study the paragraph pairs below and tick (✔) which ones you think are better.

1. a. A military attack is being planned; the tanks will enter the country via a 'safe road'. If this 'safe route' is attacked, the army will not be able to keep their supply lines open, and the invasion may fail in the long-term. ☐

    b. A military attack is being planned; the tanks will enter the country via a 'safe road'. The army will not be able to keep their supply lines open if this 'safe route' is attacked, and the invasion may fail in the long-term. ☐

2. a. People have lost their homes as a result of the flood, so they are living in a temporary camp. It is certainly not luxurious, but there is a sense of community. Existing 'tent-dwellers' will share their tent if someone new arrives. ☐

    b. People have lost their homes as a result of the flood, so they are living in a temporary camp. It is certainly not luxurious, but there is a sense of community. If someone new arrives without a tent, existing 'tent-dwellers' will let them share theirs. ☐

3. Which paragraphs did you tick? Why? _____

_____

_____

_____

3.2 Study the sentences below. Note which sentence contains a comma. Complete the table below with the correct punctuation.

1. If the flowers do not receive sufficient sunshine, they might not grow properly.
2. The flowers might not grow properly if they do not receive sufficient sunshine.

Conditional clause	Main clause
If the flowers are planted here	they might not grow properly.
Main clause	**Conditional clause**
The flowers might not grow properly	if they are planted here.

Conditional sentence review: predicting the outcome of a likely event	
Conditional clause	**Main clause**
If + subject + main verb (present simple),	subject + *will / may / might / could* + bare infinitive.
OR	
Main clause	**Conditional clause**
Subject + *will / may / might / could* + bare infinitive	*if* + subject + main verb (present simple).

| Task 4 | **Warnings, advice and predictions** |

If you want to give a warning about likely problems in the future in your writing, you can use *unless*.

4.1 **Study the sentences and answer the questions.**

a. Unless pollution levels fall, more and more people will become ill. ☐

b. If pollution levels do not fall, more and more people will become ill. ☐

c. If pollution levels fall, more and more people will become ill. ☐

1. Tick the two sentences which have the same meaning.
2. What does *unless* mean? _____

4.2 **The sentences below all contain warnings. Look at the example answer and rewrite the sentences using *unless*.**

1. If the population in Egypt continues to grow, the River Nile will not be able to support the country's water requirements.

   What is the likely problem?: The population continues to grow.

   What is the opposite?: The population stops growing.

   Complete sentence: Unless the population in Egypt stops growing, the River Nile will not be able to support the country's water requirements.

2. If no more money is given for scientific research, the scientists will fall behind in the race to develop new technology.

   What is the likely problem?: _____

   What is the opposite?: _____

   Complete sentence: _____

3. If the corn crop is not sprayed with pesticide, insects may damage it.

   What is the likely problem?: _____

   What is the opposite?: _____

   Complete sentence: _____

4. If employees continually have to work long hours, they might go on strike.

   What is the likely problem?: _____

   What is the opposite?: _____

   Complete sentence: _____

5. If the hens are not allowed to roam freely, they will produce eggs of inferior quality.

   What is the likely problem?: _____

   What is the opposite?: _____

   Complete sentence: _____

6. If salt is not spread on the roads in icy weather, there might be some accidents.

What is the likely problem?: _____

What is the opposite?: _____

Complete sentence: _____

7. If it does not rain soon, there will be more starvation.

What is the likely problem?: _____

What is the opposite?: _____

Complete sentence: _____

4.3 **When you write a conclusion to an essay, it is common to include a piece of advice, a prediction or a warning. Study the conclusion from a student essay below. It begins by summarizing, then it gives advice and finally it gives a prediction. Use three different colours to highlight the three different sections.**

> In conclusion, although the examination system in Japan is stressful, it has the effect of encouraging students to learn. Acquiring a basic knowledge in many areas of study is useful for life. Students need to adopt good study skills and learn over an extended period of time in order to gradually build on their new knowledge. If they manage to do this, they will feel relaxed and confident in exams, and will undoubtedly improve their grades.

4.4 **Read extracts a, b and c below from conclusions to essays. Match each conditional sentence with its function below.**

> **a.** In conclusion, … in spite of all the efforts that have already been made in the economic and social fields, the problems still exist and unless action is taken within the next few years, the situation will inevitably deteriorate.

> **b.** In conclusion, … if the researchers use statistics properly, they will not mislead their audience.

> **c.** In conclusion, … although the situation is not yet critical, if the strike continues, the government should import supplies of gas from other countries.

1. advice _____

2. prediction _____

3. warning _____

Grammar note:

Use *will* for certain predictions.

Use *might* or *may* for uncertain predictions.

Use *could* to predict remote possibility.

Use *should/ought to* for advice.

Use *must/have to/need* to for duty.

Use *unless* to give a warning.

4.5 **Use the prompts below to give your own predictions, warnings or advice. Link the ideas within an *if* or *unless* clause as appropriate.**

1. wages / not increase / people / remain poor (*warning*)

   Unless wages increase, people will remain poor.

2. class sizes / not remain / small / almost certainly / children / not make progress (*warning*)

   _____

3. parents / not talk to children / they / not learn to speak (*warning*)

   _____

4. factories / continue to burn / fossil fuels / atmosphere / definitely / become hotter (*warning*)

   _____

5. spelling / be / a problem / computer spell check / be used (*advice*)

   _____

6. students / want to / increase their depth of argument / they / read / more widely (*advice*)

   _____

7. price of oil / increase / price of petrol / undoubtedly / go up (*certain prediction*)

   _____

8. people / continue to / eat junk food / they / become / obese (*warning*)

   _____

9. computer / suffer / power cut / work / easily / be lost (*remote possibility*)

   _____

10. there / be / a problem / students / talk to / study skills adviser (*advice*)

    _____

11. there / be / fire / everyone / leave / the building by the nearest exit (*duty*)

    _____

Task 5   Describing laws of nature ('zero' conditionals)

5.1   Read the two sentences below and answer the questions.

a. If a fish is removed from water, it dies.

b. If a fish is removed from water, it will die.

1. Which sentence contains a prediction? ___
2. Which sentence contains a fact? ___
3. Which of the two sentences is more accurate, a or b? ___
4. Does a law of nature require **a personal prediction** or **a fact**? _____

Grammar note: A law of nature is a *fact*, not a personal prediction. Remember to use the present simple form of the verb to show facts which are always true (see Unit 1A).

5.2   Complete the sentences to show predictions and laws of nature. Use the phrases in the box. Add a modal verb where necessary to make a prediction.

> they burn   students' speaking skills improve at a faster rate   they die   ~~be cold~~
>
> people become unhappy   they frighten children   they have hearing difficulties later
>
> people go to prison   ~~oranges do not grow well on trees~~

1. _____ *Oranges do not grow well on trees* _____
   _____ if it is cold. (*law of nature*)

2. If young people listen to too much loud music, _____
   _____. (*uncertain prediction*)

3. _____
   _____ if they commit a crime. (*uncertain prediction*)

4. _____
   _____ if they have a lot of contact with native speakers. (*law of nature*)

5. If plants do not have enough water, _____
   _____. (*law of nature*)

6. If fair-skinned people sunbathe, _____
   _____ . (*law of nature*)

7. _____
   _____if they do not have control over their lives. (*certain prediction*)

8. If dogs are not kept on a leash, _____
   _____. (*remote possibility*)

6.1 Study paragraphs a and b.

a. Statistics do not always tell the truth because they can be falsified. For example, if financial staff change the data on the balance sheet, then any research based on that data will be incorrect, even though the method of calculation is accurate.

b. The countryside is important for relaxation. For example, if people go for a walk in the country at weekends, they feel less stressed and are able to cope better with the working week ahead.

1. Which sentence shows a prediction? _____

2. Which sentence shows a law of nature? _____

3. Which type of supporting detail (see Task 3) has the writer added to the paragraphs above? _____

6.2 Add an example to support the statements below. Use the phrases in the box. For each sentence, decide if you should write a personal prediction or a law of nature.

reduce landfill waste	not have time to give students individual attention
improve their vocabulary	a new product be developed
time be saved	prefer to leave work at 3 p.m.
~~suggest that the teacher should make these lessons more interesting.~~	

1. Statistics about students can be useful to teachers. For example, if the attendance register shows that students never come to lessons on Thursday mornings, but they come at all other times, this *may/might/could suggest that the teacher should make these lessons more interesting*.

2. Sales statistics provide companies with important information. For example, if the figures show that sales are falling, _____ _____.

3. Computers can help students considerably with their studies. For example, _____ _____ if students learn how to compile a bibliography electronically.

4. People can easily improve their English in an enjoyable way. For example, if students regularly watch films, this _____.

5. It may not be a good idea to have big class sizes. For example, if there are 50 students in a lesson, the teacher _____.

6. All employers should offer flexible working patterns. For example, if a parent has young children, he or she _____.

7. Recycling has a beneficial effect on the environment. For example, if carrier bags are reused, this _____.

Stage B

In this stage you will:
- use conditional sentences to evaluate an unlikely event

Task 1 Identifying unlikely events (second conditionals)

1.1 **Read this conversation and answer the questions which follow.**

Anna is a student of agriculture. She is interviewing a farmer about organic methods.

Anna: What type of vegetables do you grow?

Farmer: Well, we get a good price for asparagus and leeks, so we are concentrating on those at the moment.

Anna: How do you make sure they are good quality?

Farmer: We use well-rotted organic horse manure to fertilize the soil. We never use artificial fertilizers.

Anna: Oh I see… but if you decided to use chemicals, what would happen?

Farmer: If we used pesticides and chemical fertilizers, our customers wouldn't trust us and would stop buying vegetables from us. This would have a very damaging effect on our business.

1. Is it likely that the farmer will start using artificial fertilizers?

2. How does Anna ask him to imagine a situation in which he uses them? Underline the sentence where she says this.

3. Why does Anna ask him to imagine this?

Grammar note: An *unlikely event* is an event which is the opposite of the situation now. It is an imaginary event. In this case, the farmer does not use artificial fertilizers.

Task 2 Evaluating an unlikely event

2.1 **The farmer said, 'If we used pesticides and chemical fertilizers, our customers wouldn't trust us and would stop buying vegetables from us.' Think of a situation which is imaginary or unlikely to happen in your life and evaluate it by using an *if* clause.**

1. eat / chips every day

    If I ate chips every day, I would put on weight.

2. speak / Chinese (or another foreign language)

    _____

3. move abroad / permanently

    _____

4. be / a millionaire

    _____

2.2 **Study the sentence again and answer the questions.**

'If we used pesticides and chemical fertilizers, our customers wouldn't trust us and would stop buying vegetables from us.'

1. Which verb tense is used in the *if* clause? _____
2. Which modal verb is used in the main clause? _____
3. Which grammatical form follows the modal verb? _____

Why do we use the past simple to describe an unlikely event?

As you know from Unit 3A, we use the past simple in speaking and writing to communicate facts which happened in the past not connected with 'now'. They are considered to be remote in time, because there is no connection with now.

We can also use the past simple for situations which are remote psychologically. A situation which is remote psychologically is not likely to happen. It could happen, but the speaker or writer feels that it is unlikely. An unlikely event is sometimes called an imaginary or hypothetical event.

2.3 **Study the sentences below. What is the difference in meaning between them?**

a. If I get up early, I eat breakfast at home. I normally manage to do this most days.
b. If I had time, I would eat breakfast at home, but I always wake up too late.

2.4 **Look at the example below. Then write something that you are unhappy about in your everyday life. Imagine the opposite using an *if* clause, and add a result.**

Grammar note: In this type of conditional sentence, we often use *were* instead of *was*. It is good style to write: *If petrol were not expensive …* rather than *If petrol was not expensive …*

1. *What you are unhappy about:* Petrol is expensive. _____
   Now imagine the opposite: If petrol were not expensive, … _____
   Add a result: I would drive to the university every day. _____
   Complete sentence: If petrol were not expensive, I would drive to the university every day.

2. *What you are unhappy about:* _____
   Imagine the opposite: _____
   Add a result: _____
   Complete sentence: _____

3. *What you are unhappy about:* _____
   Imagine the opposite: _____
   Add a result: _____
   Complete sentence: _____

Task 3   Making evaluations in your writing

You can use unlikely conditional sentences in your writing to evaluate present facts, and to persuade the reader of your argument.

For example:

a. *What you are unhappy about:* The town centre is overcrowded.

   Imagine the opposite: If the town centre were not overcrowded, …

   Add a result: More people would do their shopping there.

   More people <u>would do</u> their shopping in the town centre if it <u>were</u> not overcrowded.

b. *What you are unhappy about:* Many people eat junk food.

   Imagine the opposite: If fewer people ate junk food, …

   Add a result: The nation as a whole would stay in better health.

   If fewer people <u>ate</u> junk food, the nation as a whole <u>would stay</u> in better health.

You can even evaluate a situation that you are happy about in order to add detail to your writing.

For example:

c. *What you are happy about:* The halls of residence are quiet at weekends.

   Imagine the opposite: If the halls of residence <u>were not</u> so quiet at weekends, …

   Add a result: Students <u>would not be able to</u> study so easily.

   If the halls of residence <u>were not</u> so quiet at weekends, students <u>would not be able</u> to study so easily.

3.1 **Evaluate the situations below and add detail to persuade the reader of your argument. Write unlikely conditional sentences.**
Remember that you can put the *if* clause first or second in the sentence. Add a comma as appropriate.

1. *What you are unhappy about:* <u>English spelling is not always logical.</u>

   Imagine the opposite: <u>If, … English spelling were logical</u>

   Add a result: (more people / be able / spell) <u>More people would be able to spell.</u>

   Complete sentence: <u>If English spelling were logical, more people would be able to spell</u>
   <u>OR More people would be able to spell if English spelling were logical.</u>

2. *What you are unhappy about:* English grammar is complicated.

   Imagine the opposite: _____

   Add a result: (students / have / less English homework) _____

   Complete sentence: _____

3. *What you are happy about:* The education system set regular examinations.

   Imagine the opposite: _____

   Add a result: (students / not learn / anything) _____

   Complete sentence: _____

4. *What you are unhappy about:* The lorry drivers who supply petrol stations are on strike.

   Imagine the opposite: _____

   Add a result: (there / be / enough petrol for cars) _____

   Complete sentence: _____

5. *What you are happy about:* Water is plentiful in the UK.

   Imagine the opposite: _____

   Add a result: (water rationing / have to / be introduced) _____

   Complete sentence: _____

Task 4 — Using other modal verbs in the main clause

As is the case for likely (first) conditional sentences, we can use a range of modal verbs in unlikely (second) conditional sentences. Before you study the different modal choices for unlikely conditional sentences, revise the modal verbs available for likely conditional sentences (Unit 7A). You can also revise the meaning of modal verbs in general (Unit 6).

4.1 Revision. Think about *likely* conditional sentences (Unit 7A). Match the modal verb on the left with the reason for using it on the right.

1. will	a. to predict (remote possibility)
2. might/may	b. to give advice
3. could	c. to predict (uncertainty)
4. should/ought to	d. to show duty
5. must/have to/need to	e. to predict (certainty)

4.2 Now look at some *unlikely* conditional sentences. Underline three modal verbs and one semi-modal verb. Each one is used twice.

1. **Fact:** Tuition fees are high.
   a. More students might study in the UK if tuition fees were not so high.
   b. If tuition fees were not so high, more students might study in the UK.

2. **Fact:** Powerful nations do not want to cancel the third-world debt.
   a. If powerful nations cancelled the third-world debt, poverty could be eliminated.
   b. Poverty could be eliminated if powerful nations cancelled the third world debt.

3. **Fact:** There are scholarships for studying abroad.
   a. If there were no scholarships, more students would have to study in their own countries.
   b. More students would have to study in their own countries if there were no scholarships.

4.3 **Think about *unlikely* conditional sentences. Match the modal/semi-modal verbs on the left with the reason for their use on the right.**

1. would
2. might
3. could/might possibly
4. would have to/would need to

a. to evaluate (duty)
b. to evaluate (remote possibility)
c. to evaluate (uncertainty)
d. to evaluate (certainty)

4.4 **Look at the example. Then write *unlikely* conditional sentences using the prompts to make evaluations. Remember that you can put the *if* clause first or second in the sentence. Add punctuation as appropriate.**

Grammar note: Be careful when you use *could* to evaluate (remote possibility). *Could* also means *would be able to*. This sentence has two meanings:
*If train travel were not so expensive, more people **would be able to** use it.*
*If train travel were not so expensive, more people **might possibly** use it.*
To avoid confusion, use *might possibly* for remote possibility!

1. *What you are unhappy about:* Train travel is expensive.

   Imagine the opposite: <u>If train travel were not so expensive.</u>

   Add a result (Evaluation: remote possibility): <u>More people might possibly use it.</u>

   Complete sentence: <u>If train travel were not so expensive, more people might possibly use it.</u>

2. *What you are unhappy about:* The swimming pools are dirty.

   Imagine the opposite: _____

   Add a result (Evaluation: certain): (people / swim / more often) _____

   Complete sentence: _____

3. *What you are happy about:* The university has a sports centre on the campus.

   Imagine the opposite: _____

   Add a result (Evaluation: duty): (students / travel a long way to take exercise) _____

   _____

   Complete sentence: _____

4. *What you are unhappy about:* Many health workers do not have sufficient training to work in rural areas. _____

   Imagine the opposite: _____

   Add a result (Evaluation: certain): (fewer people / undoubtedly / die) _____

   _____

   Complete sentence: _____

5. *What you are unhappy about:* Students do not take effective notes.

    Imagine the opposite: _____

    Add a result (Evaluation: uncertain): (they / write / better essays) _____

    Complete sentence: _____

6. *What you are unhappy about:* Food is expensive in the UK.

    Imagine the opposite: _____

    Add a result (Evaluation: remote possibility): (families / have / more holidays) _____

    _____

    Complete sentence: _____

7. *What you are happy about:* Students have their own computers.

    Imagine the opposite: _____

    Add a result (Evaluation: duty): (they / use / computers on the campus) _____

    Complete sentence: _____

8. *What you are unhappy about:* Students do not have access to the Internet.

    Imagine the opposite: _____

    Add a result (Evaluation: certain): (homework / be done / more easily) _____

    _____

    Complete sentence: _____

9. *What you are unhappy about:* Banana growers spray their crops heavily with pesticides several times a year.

    Imagine the opposite: _____

    Add a result (Evaluation: uncertain): (the labourers / be in better health) _____

    _____

    Complete sentence: _____

Stage C

In this stage you will:

■ use conditional sentences to evaluate an impossible event.

Task 1 | Identifying impossible events (third conditionals)

1.1 **Read the conversation below and answer the questions which follow.**

David and his friend Arianna are both teachers. They are talking about the secondary school where they work.

David: I had forty-five pupils in my lesson just now, and there are only forty chairs. Five of them had to sit on the floor!

Arianna: I didn't have enough text books for everyone this morning, and the photocopier's broken, so I couldn't do anything about it.

David: Oh no, that's terrible. It's been out of action for a week now.

Arianna: I know. The school's in a mess, isn't it? We really need more funding and more resources.

David: I know. It's such a shame that President Tully was elected last year. If the Democratic Party had won, they would have invested money in the education system and we wouldn't be in this difficult situation now.

Arianna: Yes. If the Nationalist Party hadn't won, the country would definitely be in a better state.

1. Which party won the election last year? _____
2. Which party does President Tully lead? _____
3. Is it too late for the Democratic Party to win the election? _____
4. Which past situation does David imagine? Why? _____
5. Which past situation does Arianna imagine? Why? _____

Note: An impossible event is a past event that didn't happen. In fact, the opposite happened and it is too late to change it now.
The Democratic Party did <u>not</u> win. President Tully <u>was</u> elected.

Task 2 | Evaluating an *impossible* event (result now)

> You sometimes want to evaluate an event which happened in the past. You may want to show how happy, or how unhappy, you are about its result now. You can show this by imagining that the opposite happened (i.e., an impossible event) and evaluating that.
>
> In the conversation above, David regrets that the Nationalist Party won the election, so he imagines the opposite – he imagines that they didn't win the election, which is impossible. He also imagines the result – the country would be a better place, which is also impossible.

> **For example:**
> a. *Fact in the past:* The Nationalist Party won the election.
>   *Result now:* The country is not a very good place.
>
> b. *Impossible event in the past:* If the Nationalist Party <u>had not won</u> the election.
>   *Impossible result now:* The country <u>would be</u> a better place.

2.1 Think about two situations which happened in the past. Evaluate them by imagining the opposite.

1. *Fact in the past:* The course was not useful.

   Result now: Most students do not have good jobs.

   Impossible situation in the past: If _____

   Impossible result now: _____

2. *Fact in the past:* It rained yesterday.

   Result now: The campus is muddy.

   Impossible situation in the past: If _____

   Impossible result now: _____

2.2 Study this sentence again and answer the questions.

If the Nationalist Party had won, the country would definitely be in a better state.

1. Which verb tense is used in the *if* clause? _____
2. Which modal verb is used in the main clause? _____
3. Which grammatical form follows the modal verb? _____

Grammar note: In the *if clause* of 'impossible' conditional sentences, you use the *past perfect* form (the past simple of the auxiliary verb *have* + the past participle of the main verb). In conditional sentences, the past perfect form has a specific function: it describes an impossible situation in the past.

2.3 Study the example showing how to evaluate an impossible event and its result with an 'impossible' conditional sentence. Then complete the sentences below.

1. *What you are unhappy about:* The students arrived late.
   Imagine the opposite: <u>If the students had not arrived late.</u>
   Imagine the result now: (all of them / have / timetable / now) <u>All of them would have their timetable now.</u>
   Complete sentence: <u>If the students had not arrived late, all of them would have their timetable now.</u>

2. *What you are unhappy about:* There was an air-traffic control strike yesterday.
   Imagine the opposite: _____
   Imagine the result now: (passengers / not / still be at the airport) _____

   _____

   Complete sentence: _____

3. *What you are unhappy about:* House prices increased by 10% last year.

Imagine the opposite: _____

Imagine the result now: (more people / want to buy / their own houses) _____

_____

Complete sentence: _____

4. *What you are happy about:* The government banned this pesticide in the 1980s.

Imagine the opposite: _____

Imagine the result now: (more people / have disabilities / nowadays) _____

_____

Answer: _____

5. *What you are unhappy about:* In the 1960s and 1970s, scientists did not realize that asbestos exposure was harmful.

Imagine the opposite: _____

Imagine the result now: (more people / definitely / be alive / today) _____

_____

Answer: _____

2.4   **As with other conditional sentences, you can use a range of modal verbs in the main clause. Study the table and complete the following sentences as appropriate.**

Modal/semi-modal verbs in 'impossible' conditional sentences (result now)	Reason for use
would	to evaluate (certainty)
might	to evaluate (uncertainty)
could/might possibly	to evaluate (remote possibility)
would have to/would need to	to evaluate (duty)

1. *What you are unhappy about:* The government spent a lot of money on weapons.

Impossible result *(Evaluation: uncertain):* (world / be / a better place / now)

If the government had spent less money on weapons, the world might be a better ___
place now. ___

2. *What you are unhappy about:* The writer destroyed her diary.

Impossible result *(Evaluation: certain):* (people / know more / about her private life / now)

_____

3. *What you are happy about:* The politician studied for his Master's degree in the UK.

Impossible result *(Evaluation: uncertain):* (he / not speak / such good English / now)

_____

4. *What you are happy about:* The students passed their exams.

Impossible result *(Evaluation: duty):* (they / retake their course now) _____

5. *What you are happy about:* The immigrants all had visas.

Impossible result *(Evaluation: remote possibility):* (they / be in prison / now) _____

_____

Task 3 — Evaluating an impossible event (result in the past)

Notice that you can evaluate an impossible event by talking about a result either now or in the past.

Compare the following sentences:

a. *If the Democratic Party had won, the education system would be in a better state now.*

b. *If the Democratic Party had won, they would have invested more money in education last year.*

In a the result is in the present (the situation would be better now); in b the result is in the past (they would have invested money last year). However, both talk about impossible events in the past: the Democratic Party didn't win the election; it is too late to change the situation.

3.1 **Study sentence b in the box above again and answer the questions.**

If the Democratic Party had won, they would have invested more money in education last year.

1. Which verb tense is used in the *if* clause?
2. Which modal verb is used in the main clause?
3. Which grammatical form follows the modal verb?

Grammar note: In both types of 'impossible' conditional sentences, the *if* clause uses the same grammar. However, when talking about an impossible *result in the past*, the form in the main clause changes to: *would* + perfect bare infinitive (*have* + past participle). In other words:

a. an impossible result in the present: *would* + bare infinitive

b. an impossible result in the past: *would* + perfect bare infinitive

Example a is sometimes called a **mixed conditional**. The *if* clause refers to the past (third conditional) but the result clause refers to the present (second conditional).

3.2 **Answer the questions below to show how to refer to an impossible event and imagine the result in the past.**

1. *What you are unhappy about:* The students missed the first day of the course.

   Imagine the opposite: If the students had not missed the first day of the course.

   Imagine a result in the past: (they / meet / the Course Director / at the start) They would have met the Course Director at the start.

   Complete sentence: If the students had not missed the first day of the course, they would have met the Course Director at the start.

2. *What you are unhappy about:* There was a power cut last week.

   Imagine the opposite: _____

   Imagine a result in the past: (the student / might / not / lose / her essay) _____

   _____

   Complete sentence: _____

3. *What you are happy about:* The police arrested some people with knives during the demonstration.

   Imagine the opposite: _____

   Imagine a result in the past: (the situation / might / become / violent) _____

   _____

   Complete sentence: _____

4. *What you are unhappy about:* The government increased tuition fees for international students.

   Imagine the opposite: _____

   Imagine a result in the past: (more students / apply for the course last year) _____

   _____

   Complete sentence: _____

5. *What you are happy about:* The classroom printer was reliable.

   Imagine the opposite: _____

   Imagine a result in the past: (the students / use / the library printer / more often) _____

   _____

   Complete sentence: _____

Task 4 — Order of information in impossible conditionals (text flow)

If you have studied the previous units in this book, you will know that writers can vary the order of information in order to improve text flow. In conditional sentences, you can put the *if* clause first or second in the sentence.

4.1 Study the examples and answer the questions.

a. The local people did not know about the flood warning. <u>If they had known about it</u>, they would have gone to stay with their relatives in other towns.

b. Many local people had relatives in other towns. They would have gone to stay with them <u>if they had known about the flood warning</u>.

1. Why is the *if* clause first in sentence a and second in sentence b?

   _____

   _____

2. What is the difference in punctuation between a and b?

   _____

4.2 **Organize the information to produce the best text flow. For each sentence (1–4), put clauses a and b in the best order to make a conditional sentence that follows the first sentence. Add a comma if necessary.**

1. By January 2004, the fast-growing company was in financial trouble.
   a. if it had not expanded so rapidly
   b. the employees would have avoided redundancies

   If it had not expanded so rapidly, the employees would have avoided redundancies.

2. The UK always insisted on maintaining national control in areas of justice, tax, foreign policy and defence.
   a. the Paris Treaty would have had a greater impact on UK domestic citizens
   b. if this had not been the case

   _____

3. Farmers decided to form a cooperative to sell their crops more widely.
   a. they would have made this decision earlier
   b. if they had known about the new truck

   _____

4. The activity was always carried out by skilled people.
   a. profits would have quickly fallen
   b. if the process had not been performed efficiently

   _____

Task 5	Using other modals in the main clause

5.1 **Study the table and complete the following sentences as appropriate.**

Modal/semi-modal verbs in impossible conditional sentences (result in the past)	Reason for use
would + perfect bare infinitive	to evaluate (certainty)
might + perfect bare infinitive	to evaluate (uncertainty)
could / might possibly + perfect bare infinitive	to evaluate (remote possibility)
would have had to / would have needed to + bare infinitive	to evaluate (duty)

1. If the government hadn't wasted money on unnecessary projects, it would have ___won___ the election. (win)

2. If she had not taken her exam so early, she could have _____ it. (pass)

3. Many people might possibly not have _____ if Oxfam had not organized emergency aid. (survive)

4. She would have had to _____ the course again if she had failed the practical test. (take)

5. If he had not had a heart problem, he would not have needed to _____ weight. (lose)

6. If farmers had not cultivated bananas intensively on this island twenty years ago, prices would have had to _____ higher. (be)

5.2 Look at the sentences. Then imagine the opposite situation and write 'impossible' conditional sentences, using the prompts in brackets.

1. The government allowed the banks to make bad loans.
   (*Evaluation: certain*) (economic crash / not / happen)
   If the government had not allowed the banks to make bad loans, the economic crash would not have happened.

2. The employee leaked secret documents to a national newspaper.
   (*Evaluation: certain*) (he / not lose / his job)

   _____

3. Toyota recalled certain Prius cars to check their brakes in 2010.
   (*Evaluation: remote possibility*) (there / be / more accidents)

   _____

4. The journalists were local people.
   (*Evaluation: duty)* (they / leave the country / before now)

   _____

5. The students all obtained a score of 6.5 or above at the end of the pre-sessional course.
   (*Evaluation: duty*) (they / change study plans)

   _____

6. The employees didn't complete their training on time.
   (*Evaluation: uncertain*) (they / not lose their jobs)

   _____

Task 6	**Putting it all together: review of conditional sentences (Stages A–C)**

6.1 Look at the situations 1–8 below. Then read the conditional sentences below them and correct the bold verb forms. To do this, read the situation carefully, and decide which type of conditional you need:

- predict a likely event (first conditionals: Stage A)
- evaluate an unlikely/imaginary event (second conditionals: Stage B)
- evaluate an impossible event (third conditionals: Stage C)

Note: you need only correct the bold verb form.

1. *Situation*: The waiting lists in hospitals are long.
   If waiting lists **are** not so long, fewer people would be in pain every day.

   Which type of conditional?: _____ Verb form: _____

2. *Situation:* The governors of the Bank of England made some errors in 2008.
   If the governors of the Bank of England **made** fewer errors in 2008, they would **had** avoided causing so many problems for investors.

   Which type of conditional?: _____ Verb form: _____

3. *Situation:* The government intends to increase the price of airline tickets to reduce pollution levels.
   If the government **increased** the price of airline tickets, this **would** not effectively reduce air pollution.

   Which type of conditional?: _____ Verb form: _____

4. *Situation:* The government is going to introduce a smoking ban in public buildings in Dubai.
   If the government **had introduced** a smoking ban in Dubai, bars **would** not be full of smoke.
   Which type of conditional?: _____ Verb form: _____

5. *Situation:* Thousands of young men had to leave their families to fight in the war.
   If thousands of young men **did not have** to leave their families, there would be enough people to work on the land now.
   Which type of conditional?: _____ Verb form: _____

6. *Situation:* Chinese is a difficult language for foreigners to learn.
   If Chinese **is** not so difficult for foreigners to learn, it might be an international language.
   Which type of conditional?: _____ Verb form: _____

7. *Situation:* The hospitals were clean.
   If the hospitals **are not** clean, vulnerable patients **may** have caught infections.
   Which type of conditional?: _____ Verb form: _____

8. *Situation:* People do not always respect each other's religious beliefs
   If people **had always respected** other people's religions, there **would have been** no more wars.
   Which type of conditional?: _____ Verb form: _____

6.2 **In the student essay below, some verbs (1–18) have been removed from the conditional sentences. Read the essay and complete the gaps (1–18) with the correct form of the verb in brackets. Decide which type of *if* sentence (from Stages A–C) is needed.**

> ### Outline the advantages of free-trade agreements
>
> Free-trade agreements are treaties between two or more countries which allow goods to be bought and sold freely across country borders without tariffs or legal obstacles. Such agreements are generally more beneficial for large and stable economies. Eiras (2004) gives five reasons for supporting free trade in the United States.
>
> The first one is that free trade between nations improves the standard of living and quality of life. She points out that trade between countries is like trade between people. If every person **(1)** _____ (*has to*) produce all the goods to be used throughout his or her life, this **(2)** _____ (*be*) an extremely inefficient situation. However, if individuals **(3)** _____ (*focus*) their potential on producing only the goods that they are best at, and then **(4)** _____ (*use*) the profits from this to purchase goods made more efficiently and more effectively by others, they **(5)** _____ (*maximize*) their wealth. This is why the whole society gains from the lower world prices when a country is open to free trade.
>
> The second reason that Eiras (2004) gives is that free trade boosts innovation and the creation of new technologies which increase production efficiency. Producers have an incentive to improve their production methods in order to remain competitive with the rest of the world's producers. At the same time, they can keep prices as low as possible by buying cheap imports from other countries. Introducing new technologies often increases a sector's competitiveness until

its competitors adopt new, more efficient production methods and start gaining from their use. Even if a particular industry **(6)** _____ (*decline*), sooner or later other sectors **(7)** _____ (*emerge*) to do the job more efficiently.

The third reason is that free trade contributes to economic growth. The evidence for this is data presented over a seven-year period between 1995 and 2002, which shows that the economies of countries which opened their markets grew twice as fast as the economies of countries with less open or closed markets. (Eiras, 2004). This happens because if the demand for goods and services **(8)** _____ (*increase*), businesses **(9)** _____ (*start*) to expand at national and international level, which leads to new investments and the creation of new jobs. If China, for example, **(10)** _____ (*not begin*) its process of lifting trade barriers under Deng Xiao Ping in the 1970s, they **(11)** _____ (*not become*) the second largest economy in today's world.

The fourth reason in favour of free trade is that it makes institutions and infrastructure stronger. In order to be able to control all trading contracts, to prevent theft and damage, and to protect its interests adequately, a country has to develop strong legal institutions, police force and an independent, efficient judicial system. Banking and financial institutions are reinforced by international economic activity too, because more credit is demanded, and more money is placed on deposit. Free trade also fosters the expansion and development of infrastructure; if a country **(12)** _____ (*expand*) its imports, more docks with hangars and warehouses **(13)** _____ (*need*), and the road system **(14)** _____ (*need*) to be constantly upgraded. On top of this there is 'the development of all sorts of new businesses to support free trade, including hotels, restaurants, law firms, packaging and delivery services, software development companies, automobile factories, construction businesses, among many others.' (Eiras, 2004)

Preserving peace is the fifth reason for promoting free trade. This is because if two countries **(15)** _____ (*be*) potential trading partners, they **(16)** _____ (*not have*) an incentive to enter into conflict with another one. The empirical evidence for this is that the areas torn by greatest conflict in the world are usually the most economically repressed ones, such as some African countries and some former Soviet republics.

Even though there are many areas of conflict in the world today, if governments **(17)** _____ (*not create*) free-trade agreements, such as the EEC (now the EU), the world **(18)** _____ (*be*) a less peaceful place over the last 50 years. It is important to continue to establish these treaties to ensure peace and economic progress globally in the future.

References

Eiras, A. (2004). Why America Needs to Support Free Trade. The Heritage Foundation. Retrieved 6th December, 2010 from http://www.heritage.org/Research/Reports/2004/05/Why-America-Needs-to-Support-Free-Trade

Unit 7 Self-check

1 **Read the sentence. Which option matches the level of prediction?**

If the sun continues to shine, the apple crop will be excellent.

a. an uncertain prediction

b. a certain prediction

c. a prediction which is only remotely possible

2 **Read the sentence. Which two sentences (a–c) have the same meaning?**

The company will not survive unless the bank agrees to a bank loan.

a. If the bank does not agree to a loan, the company will survive.

b. If the bank does not agree to a loan, the company will not survive.

c. If the bank agrees to a loan, the company will survive.

3 **Choose the correct option to complete the sentence.**

If oil and water are mixed, they _____.

a. will separate

b. may separate

c. separate

4 **Choose the correct options to complete the sentence.**

If the committee _____ the proposal, work on the project _____ immediately.

a. accepted … would begin

b. would accept … would begin

c. accept … would begin

Read sentences 5–10. Choose the option which evaluates the sentence correctly, is grammatically correct and has the best academic style.

5 In some countries, parents have to pay school fees for their children.

a. If parents in these countries do not have to pay school fees, they will have more money to spend on everyday needs.

b. If parents in these countries would not pay school fees, they would have more money to spend on everyday needs.

c. If parents in these countries did not have to pay school fees, they would have more money to spend on everyday needs.

6 Sometimes hospitals are understaffed at weekends.

a. If there were more doctors and nurses in hospitals at weekends, there would be fewer deaths.

b. If there were more doctors and nurses in hospitals at weekends, there might possibly be more deaths.

c. If there are more doctors and nurses in hospitals at weekends, there will be more deaths.

7 The community participation approach is successful for development projects.
   a. If the community participation approach is not successful, the department might not use it for development projects.
   b. If the community participation approach was not successful, the department would not use it for development projects.
   c. If the community participation approach were not successful, the department would not use it for development projects.

8 Gender policy was a barrier to women's empowerment.
   a. If gender policy had been a barrier to women's empowerment, there would be many more female members of parliament.
   b. If gender policy had not been a barrier to women's empowerment, there might have been many more female members of parliament.
   c. If gender policy was not a barrier to women's empowerment, there might be many more female members of parliament.

9 In the late 1980s, China rebuilt its stock market.
   a. If China had not rebuilt its stock market, the Shanghai Index would not have risen so dramatically.
   b. If China did not rebuild its stock market, the Shanghai Index would not rise so dramatically.
   c. If China had rebuilt its stock market, the Shanghai Index would not be so high now.

10 China's security companies are very small and specialized.
   a. If these companies were combined they would be in a good position to widen their investment portfolio.
   b. They would be in a good position to widen their investment portfolio if these companies were combined.
   c. If these companies were combined, they would be in a good position to widen their investment portfolio.

8

Avoiding person-based writing

As you learnt in Unit 1, academic writing is not generally person-based. It is impersonal; it concerns the flow of ideas, facts and concepts.

In this unit you will:
- broaden your ability to create sentences which discuss academic information in a non-personal way

Stage A

In this stage you will:
- use abstract and concrete noun phrases to avoid redundancy and write concisely
- use abstract noun phrases as summary nouns with *this/these* and *such a/such*

Task 1 Review of noun phrases and text flow

In Unit 2, you learnt how simple and complex noun phrases can be used to improve text flow by linking old to new information. Look at the examples below. The subject noun phrases (in bold) link old to new information.

a. Sometimes farmers do not sell <u>their crops</u> to local people. **Their produce** is packaged and flown to other countries within 24 hours of being picked.

b. Sometimes <u>farmers</u> do not sell their crops to local people. **They** package their produce and fly it to other countries within 24 hours of being picked.

c. All the <u>villagers</u> can use common land for their sheep. **People** have followed this tradition for generations.

d. All the villagers <u>can use common land for their sheep</u>. **This widespread tradition** has been followed for generations.

1.1 **Look again at sentences a–d above. Study the subject noun phrases in bold again. Which three noun phrases are simple and which one is complex? (Refer to Unit 2 if you have forgotten the difference between simple and complex noun phrases.)**

1.2 **Look again at the non-personal noun phrases from the examples above. Which headword (in italics) is concrete (C) and which one is abstract (A)?**

Their *produce* _____

This widespread *tradition* _____

Task 2   Concrete and abstract noun phrases

An **abstract noun phrase** describes things you cannot see, such as ideas, actions and concepts, whereas a **concrete noun phrase** describes things you can see and touch. Some examples of abstract noun phrases are: *decision*; *request*; *tradition*; *development*; *burning*. Examples of concrete noun phrases are: *table*; *field*; *produce*; *computer*; *breakfast*.

Grammar note: A gerund (such as *burning*) is a noun formed from a verb. It refers to an action, so it is an **abstract noun phrase**. You have studied gerunds in Unit 1B, 2.5 and Unit 5C, 1.1.

2.1   **Study the words. Write *AN* for an abstract noun, *CN* for a concrete, non-personal noun and *PN* for a concrete, person-based noun. Which three nouns in the list are *gerunds*?**

1.	wheat		11.	produce	
2.	sales		12.	oil	
3.	table		13.	access	
4.	improvement		14.	analyzing	
5.	economists		15.	belief	
6.	government		16.	teenagers	
7.	coal		17.	farmers	
8.	burning		18.	procedure	
9.	decline		19.	lowering	
10.	failure		20.	vehicle	

2.2   **Study the sentences (a–c) and answer the questions.**
   a. **When people burn coal, natural gases and oil,** this alters the composition of the atmosphere.
   b. **When coal, natural gases and oil are burned,** this alters the composition of the atmosphere.
   c. **The burning of coal, natural gases and oil alters the composition of the atmosphere.**

   Which clause in bold …
   1. contains redundant information? _____
   2. contains the passive voice? _____
   3. has a concrete noun phrase as its subject? _____
   4. has an abstract complex noun phrase as its subject? _____
   5. delivers the most concise information? _____

   Grammar note: Abstract noun phrases are particularly common in academic writing because they convey ideas concisely. They can give more detail in fewer words. Notice how sentence c effectively combines two clauses into one concise, simple sentence.

Study how to transform the complex sentence in 2.2a into the more concise sentence in 2.2c, using an *abstract noun phrase*. Follow steps 1–6:

1. Find and highlight the subject (S), verb (V) and object (O) of the first clause of the sentence.
2. Delete the subject.
3. Change the verb into a noun (or a gerund if no corresponding abstract noun exists). The new noun or gerund becomes the subject of a more concise sentence.
4. Place a determiner (such as *a*, *the*, *their*) before the new noun or gerund.
5. Place the prepositional phrase *of* after the new noun or gerund.
6. Delete any words linking the two original clauses (such as *When ... this, Because ...,* *so that*).

       S   V   O

When people burn coal, natural gases and oil, this alters the composition of the atmosphere.

      S (complex abstract noun phrase)

The burning of coal, natural gases and oil alters the composition of the atmosphere.

    S   V   O

They should develop a vaccine so that fewer people die.

S (complex abstract noun phrase)

The development of a vaccine will result in fewer deaths.

2.3 **Now follow steps 1–6 (above) to transform the complex sentence below into a more concise sentence.**

Because the company is producing low-emission vehicles, it will increase sales in Europe.

_____

2.4 **Follow steps 1–5 (above) to transform the compound sentences below into more concise sentences, using abstract noun phrases to replace the underlined clauses.**

1. The student gave a presentation. <u>He described the financial situation</u>, but he confused the audience.

   The student gave a presentation. His <u>description</u> _____ <u>of</u> _____ <u>the</u> _____ <u>financial</u> <u>situation</u> confused the audience.

2. Axxion needs to improve its pricing strategy. In the future, <u>it will sell more mobile phones,</u> so its prices will be more competitive.

   Axxion need to improve their pricing strategy. In the future, increased _____ _____ _____ _____ will result in more competitive prices.

3. The police believed that car theft fell in 2013. However, <u>they reviewed the data</u> and found that this was not true.

   The police believed that car theft fell in 2013. However, a _____ _____ _____ _____ revealed that this was not true.

4. The school suffers from a shortage of resources. For example, <u>it teaches research skills</u> without Internet access, so the pupils are not adequately prepared for the real world.

   The school suffers from a shortage of resources. For example, the _____ _____ _____ _____ without Internet access results in pupils not being prepared for the real world.

5. The milk had an unusual colour. <u>Scientists analyzed its chemical content</u>, and this revealed the addition of melanine.

The milk had an unusual colour. An _____ _____ _____ _____ _____ revealed the addition of melanine.

6. The area needs to be renovated. <u>They could convert the old warehouses</u> into modern apartment blocks, and this could be an interesting option to consider.

The area needs to be renovated. The _____ _____ _____ _____ _____ into modern apartment blocks could be an interesting option to consider.

7. Turkey should join the European Union. If <u>politicians extend the free-trading markets</u>, this will lead to greater stability in Europe.

Turkey may join the European Union. The _____ _____ _____ _____ _____ will lead to greater stability in Europe.

8. Modern ambulances need larger doors and stronger flooring. <u>People have consumed more food over the last decade</u>, and this has resulted in heavier patients.

Modern ambulances need larger doors and stronger flooring. Increased _____ _____ _____ over the last decade has resulted in heavier patients.

Grammar note: You can see how the use of non-person-based noun phrases allows a writer to refer back to concepts, facts or ideas in a previous sentence and achieve a tighter information flow. Of course, this does not mean that person-based noun phrases are **never** used in academic writing. Sometimes they are essential for text flow. Look at the link between the words in bold in the two sentences below:

*There has been a public outcry over the size of bonuses paid to **staff in the finance industry**. **Investment bankers**, for example, received a combined total of £1 billion in 2010, despite the fact that bank losses totalled in excess of £1 billion.*

Task 3   Using abstract noun phrases as summary nouns

You have seen in Unit 2A that a noun phrase is often used at the beginning of a new sentence to introduce old information. Abstract noun phrases are often used to improve text flow by summarizing old information. A summary noun can be used with *this* or *these*, or *such a(n)* or *such* in order to emphasize the closeness of the link.

3.1   **Study the examples of noun phrases with *this* and *these*, and answer the questions.**

a. The burning of coal, oil and natural gases, as well as deforestation and various agricultural and industrial practices are altering the composition of the atmosphere and contributing to climate change. <u>These human activities</u> have led to increased atmospheric concentrations of a number of greenhouse gases.

b. Time is wasted when people travel to and from work, and when goods and important documents are transported from one place to another. <u>These problems</u> cost business time and money, and <u>this inefficiency</u> affects the national economy as a whole.

1. What do these *human activities* refer to?

_____

2. What do *these problems* refer to?

_____

3. What does *this inefficiency* refer to?

_____

3.2 **Look at the summary nouns (1–7). Match each noun with its meaning (a–g).**

	Summary noun		Meaning
1.	procedure _____	a.	a sequence of events which repeatedly happen in the same order
2.	view _____	b.	the correct way of doing something
3.	issue _____	c.	a serious situation of great difficulty or danger
4.	cycle _____	d.	a result or consequence
5.	action _____	e.	an important, often controversial, topic for discussion
6.	effect _____	f.	an opinion or belief
7.	crisis _____	g.	an activity or behaviour

3.3 **Choose the correct summary noun from 3.2 to complete each sentence. Use each summary noun only once. Decide if the noun should be singular or plural, and add either *this* or *these* as appropriate.**

1. When Germany invaded Poland in 1939, Hitler knew that _____*this action*_____ would lead to a major war in Europe.

2. Many thousands of people were killed or made homeless by the tsunami in Asia. As well as having nowhere to live, the survivors also had no food or any way of earning a living. _____ touched the hearts of many people, who then donated money to help rebuild the devastated communities.

3. The new law against drugs has led to further crime and violence, although the government did not intend it to have _____.

4. Some people think that the number of immigrants allowed into Britain should be reduced. However, there are others who disagree with _____.

5. Farmers in the jungle cut down trees in order to plant crops. However, the soil there is not very rich or fertile, so they soon have to move on to clear new areas for cultivation. _____ is causing serious deforestation in the Amazon rainforest.

6. There has been a mixed reaction to the idea that the debts owed by poor African countries should be cancelled. It is important to consider _____ carefully before any action is taken by the World Bank or the IMF.

7. Chilling human tissue allows it to be preserved. _____, which involves allowing the body temperature to drop to 18°C, is routinely practised in open heart surgery.

3.4 **Look at some more common summary nouns. Check the meanings in a dictionary if necessary. Complete each sentence with the correct noun. Decide if it should be singular or plural, and add either *this* or *these*.**

condition	situation	improvement	theory	~~research (U)~~	result	problem

(*U* indicates that a noun is uncountable. You have studied uncountable nouns in Unit 1B.)

1. Smith has been investigating the theory for the last ten years. _*This research*_ has been very important for the future of the energy industry.

2. The calculations made about black holes were correct. _____ show the importance of quantum mechanics in this field.

3. Figures have been published which show that the number of illegal immigrants in Britain is rising. People have widely differing reactions to _____.

4. Overpopulation can lead to overcrowding in cities and to a shortage of housing. The government finds _____ difficult to solve.

5. Scientist George Basalla believes that the ongoing search of the universe for intelligent life is inspired by religious fervour. _____ is, however, rejected by most astronomers.

6. In 2009, California's legal emission levels were cut, and vehicles began to emit significantly lower levels of greenhouse gases. _____ in air quality led to a fall in hospital admission numbers.

7. Naturalists have found a new type of caterpillar in the Amazon which can release poison if its hairs pierce human skin. The treatment for _____ is to pull off the hairs with sticky tape, and then go to hospital.

3.5 **Study the paragraphs with *such* or *such a(n)* and answer the questions that follow. *Such/such a(n)* with a summary noun means *like this* or *of that type*.**

> Studies that aim to identify human influences on climate attempt to separate human-caused climate change from the background noise of natural climate variability. Such investigations usually consist of two parts.
>
> **Source:** UNEP/WMO (1997). Common questions about climate change. Geneva: United Nations Environmental Programme/World Meteorological Organisation. Retrieved July 21st, 2011, from www.gcrio.org/ipcc/qa/index.htm

1. What does *such investigations* refer to?

_____

> Just as families once combined into tribes and tribes into nations, so nations are combining into regional power blocks, and thence perhaps into a single world political community. Such an outcome is a very long way off.

2. What does *such an outcome* refer to?

_____

> Tourism has made the retention of traditional cultures more difficult while giving it new economic value – thus local festivals and dances are staged not as part of regional tradition but as a show for foreign visitors. Such developments appear to reinforce the view that the world is being reshaped according to Western values.

3. What does *such developments* refer to?

_____

3.6 Complete sentences 1–7 with *such* or *such a(n)* followed by one of the summary nouns from the box. Use a singular or plural noun as appropriate.

| behaviour | reform | ~~scheme~~ | solution | symptom | information | decision |

Grammar note: If you study sociology or psychology, you may sometimes see *behaviour* used as a countable word to mean 'types of behaviour'. For example: *Sufferers from schizophrenia or ADHD may display different <u>behaviours</u>.*

1. Sweden was one of the first countries to allow both parents to have paid holiday for the birth of a child. <u>   Such schemes   </u> help workers to find a better balance between their family and their job.
2. We need to find a way of improving the situation which is both cheap and effective. It may not be easy to find _____.
3. There is a relaxed, friendly atmosphere, and students refer to their teachers by their first names. However, _____ is not always the norm in other departments.
4. After the explosion at the chemical factory, many local people went to hospital complaining of headaches, vomiting and diarrhoea. _____ are often the result of chemical poisoning.
5. Because of the increasing cost of pensions, the government would like to raise the age of retirement. However, many people, in particular those who are middle-aged, would be very unwilling to agree to _____.
6. The need to successfully skim-read large amounts of data is well accepted in today's fast-moving world. The ability to understand and use _____ is a desirable skill.
7. The decision-making process can be traced by using the History function. Internet sites can be bookmarked, shared and restored to understand how _____ are made.

Task 4   Review of summary nouns

4.1   Read the following paragraph written by a student.

Many young people are spending in excess of 20 hours a week online using sites such as Facebook and Bebo. **(1) The fact that young people spend many hours using online communication tools** <u>has</u> prompted universities to carry out research to find out more information. For example, a study done by Liverpool University in 2009 discovered that one young adult spent 15 hours in a stretch on the Internet. He missed meals and did not sleep. **(2) The fact that some people spend up to 15 hours on the Internet without eating** <u>is</u> becoming more common, and addiction clinics have been set up to deal with people who are addicted to the Internet.

Another study shows that the majority of young adults believe that the time they spend on the Internet is not excessive and is as useful as studying or reading novels. **(3) The fact that young people believe this** <u>is</u> not shared by many educators or parents who have tried to monitor Internet usage and encourage a more responsible attitude to it. However, **(4) the fact that parents and educators have tried to reduce the use of the Internet and its communication tools** <u>has</u> not necessarily proved successful. The amount of time spent on the Internet continues to rise and **(5) the fact that the time spent on the Internet is increasing** <u>is</u> likely to have a serious impact on young people and their families.

The bold sentences are repetitious and do not create a good flow of information. Improve the text flow by rewriting the phrases in bold. Use *this/these* or *such/such a(n)* and a suitable summary noun. Change the form of the underlined verb following each phrase if necessary. Write your phrases in the spaces below.

1. _____

2. _____

3. _____

4. _____

5. _____

Note: When reading academic texts, look for the abstract noun phrases. As you become more familiar with **reading** them, you will gradually gain confidence using them in your **writing**.

Stage B

In this stage you will use impersonal sentence structures to:

- discuss opinions and beliefs
- refer to and comment on data

Task 1   Using impersonal verbs to discuss opinions and beliefs

When reporting opinions or beliefs, students often use phrases like *people believe that* or *many people think that*.

However, more sophisticated academic writers find alternatives to using the noun phrase *people*. They might write *it is thought that* or *it is widely believed that*. In these cases, the noun phrase *it* is an **impersonal pronoun**.

Study the examples below to understand more about how to avoid person-based noun phrases:

a. People believe that elephants have good memories.

Sentence a is a complex sentence. It has two clauses connected with the subordinator *that*. It can be depersonalized in two different ways.

Type 1
The first way to depersonalize the sentence involves changing the subject of the first clause.
1. Highlight the subject and the verb in clause 1.
2. Change the subject to *it*.
3. Transform the verb to the passive voice.

| clause 1 | clause 2 |

a. *People* believe *that elephants have good memories.*

S   V

b. *It is believed that elephants have good memories.*

Type 2

Alternatively, the subject of the **second** clause in sentence **a** can become the subject of a new, simple sentence. An infinitive then follows the verb.

1. Highlight the subject and the verb in clause 2.
2. Change the subject of clause 2 into the subject of clause 1.
3. Transform the verb to the passive voice in clause 1.
4. Change the verb of clause 2 to an infinitive, to make just one clause.

```
            clause 1              clause 2
       ┌─────────────┐┌──────────────────────┐
              V         S        V
a. People believe that elephants have good memories.

       S            V      infinitive
b. Elephants are believed to have good memories.
```

1.1 **Depersonalize the sentences below. Write two versions of each sentence, following Types 1 and 2 above.**

1. People estimate that fewer than 4,000 pandas exist in the wild.

   Type 1 _____

   Type 2 _____

2. Environmentalists say that fewer than 1,000 blue whales survive in the southern hemisphere.

   Type 1 _____

   Type 2 _____

1.2 **Read the *Grammar note* and then depersonalize the sentences below.**

Grammar note: If the second clause contains a verb in the present continuous, Type 2 sentence use a **continuous** infinitive.

Study the example:
People believe that thousands of birds <u>are dying</u> because of the oil spill.

Type 1
It is believed that thousands of birds <u>are dying</u> because of the oil spill.

Type 2
Thousands of birds are believed <u>to be dying</u> because of the oil spill.

1. People think that global warming is increasing.

   Type 1 _____

   Type 2 _____

2. People consider that one in three bathing beaches is suffering from pollution.

   Type 1 _____

   Type 2 _____

1.3   **Read the examples, and then depersonalize the sentences below.**

Grammar note: If the second clause contains a verb in the present perfect aspect, Type 2 sentence uses a **perfect** infinitive.

Study the example:

Scientists report that the number of butterflies in Britain <u>has fallen</u> over the last few years.

Type 1

It is reported that the number of butterflies in Britain <u>has fallen</u> over the last few years.

Type 2

The number of butterflies in Britain is reported <u>to have fallen</u> over the last few years.

1. People think that 1,500 sea otters have died because of oil pollution.

    Type 1 _____

    Type 2 _____

2. People say that computer games have encouraged children to be more aggressive.

    Type 1 _____

    Type 2 _____

1.4   **Depersonalize the following sentences, using appropriate verb forms. Add the word *widely* if you want to emphasize the large number of people who hold these beliefs.**

1. Many employers in the UK believe that educational standards are lower than 30 years ago.

    Type 1 <u>In the UK it is widely believed that educational standards are lower than 30 years ago.</u>

    Type 2 <u>In the UK educational standards are widely believed to be lower than 30 years ago.</u>

2. Meteorologists think that the temperature of the Gulf Stream is gradually falling.

    Type 1 _____

    Type 2 _____

3. People think that wearing masks in public places protects against infectious diseases.

    Type 1 _____

    Type 2 _____

4. Historians believe that policies of the colonial era in Zimbabwe have helped to shape current agricultural policies (Johns and Waite, 2007).

    Type 1 _____

    Type 2 _____

5. Many researchers consider that the Health Belief Model is the best theoretical model of decision-making in the health sector.

    Type 1 _____

    Type 2 _____

When describing data in graphs and charts, we often write in a depersonalized way.

2.1   **Study the bar chart, which gives information about one-person households in the UK. Then answer the question below.**

Why do you think that the numbers of people living alone in the UK has increased? Give at least *two* reasons, and then check your answers by reading the text below.

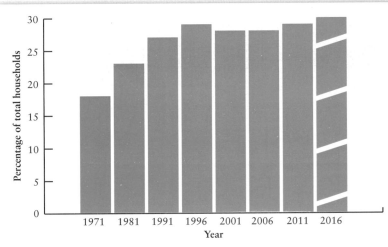

Figure 1: One-person households in the UK (2014)

The number of one-person households in the UK has gradually increased. As can be seen from Figure 1, in 1971 18% of all households had only one person in them. This figure rose to 29% in 1996, and since that date the figure has remained about the same. It is predicted that the number of people who live alone will increase slightly to 30% in 2016. It is clear that the 'singleton' lifestyle has become more common in Britain in the last 40 years. This increase may be the result of more people getting divorced, or living longer and therefore outliving their partners, or choosing to live alone to concentrate on their studies or work.

2.2   **Using different colours, divide the paragraph into four different sections.**

1. topic sentence (paragraph leader)
2. statistical evidence
3. writer's interpretation of statistics
4. discussion of reasons

2.3   **Underline a phrase used to:**

1. refer the reader to the bar chart
2. introduce the statisticians' prediction
3. introduce the writer's interpretation of statistics
4. introduce reasons

2.4 **Study the bar chart below and complete the text. Use one phrase in each category from the box.**

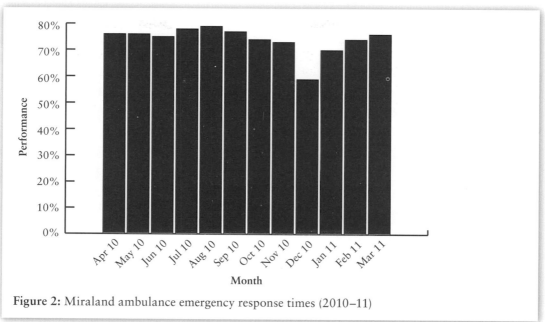

Figure 2: Miraland ambulance emergency response times (2010–11)

Study the phrases below:

Referring to data
As can be seen from Figure X, + clause
As is shown in Figure X, + clause

Introducing predictions
It is predicted that + clause

Interpreting statistics
It is clear/surprising/interesting that + clause

Discussing reasons
This (increase/decrease/situation) may be the result of + noun phrase

(1) _____ ambulance performance in Miraland in the financial year 2010–11 remained stable. At the beginning and end of the year, approximately 76% of ambulances reached the patient within eight minutes of receiving an emergency 999 call. There was a sharp decline in meeting response times in December; only 58.5% of ambulances arrived within seven minutes of the emergency call in this particular month. (2) _____ bad weather, snow and ice made the roads impassable in some parts of the town, particularly near the river. (3) _____ response times could be better; 100% of ambulances reaching patients within eight minutes should be the government's aim. (4) _____ response times will improve in the next decade due to extra government funding to cope with seasonal weather problems.

Stage C

In this stage you will:
- review the use of abstract noun phrases and impersonal language in academic writing
- study extracts from a research project proposal on autism

Task 1 Abstract complex noun phrases

The text below shows extracts from a Psychology student's research project proposal. The topic of the proposed research project is autism, which is a developmental condition affecting children's ability to make sense of the world around them. Many children with autism have learning difficulties and problems with social interaction.

1.1 **You have studied in Unit 8A how abstract noun phrases are predominantly used to convey ideas and concepts in academic writing. Compare the two paragraphs a and b below.**

> **a.** One question that experts do not agree about in the field of autism research is how far children with autism can imitate other people. Experts are very interested in the theory that children with autism do not imitate well, because non-autistic children imitate at an early age. The reason why autistic children do not tend to imitate may be that they are not aware of their social environment. This may be why such youngsters find it difficult to interact with others as they grow up.

> **b.** One question that remains contentious in the field of autism research is whether children with autism demonstrate impaired imitative abilities. Imitation deficits in autism are of considerable theoretical interest because imitation occurs very early in non-autistic children. The lack of imitative behaviour in autistic children may be due to a lack of awareness of their social environment and may explain why such youngsters find it difficult to interact with others as they grow up. (Meltzoff and Gopnik, 1993).

1. Which paragraph makes greater use of person-based noun phrases? _____

2. Which paragraph flows better from 'old' information to 'new'. _____

3. Which paragraph is more academic? _____

1.2 **Part of the key to using abstract language in academic writing lies in using an abstract noun phrase to summarize previous information. Study the noun phrases in bold and draw an arrow back to show where the previous information lies.**

> One question that remains contentious in the field of autism research is whether children with autism demonstrate impaired imitative abilities. **Imitation deficits in autism** are of considerable theoretical interest because imitation occurs very early in non-autistic children. **This lack of imitative behaviour in autistic children** may be due to a lack of awareness of their social environment and may explain why such youngsters find it difficult to interact with others as they grow up. (Meltzoff and Gopnik, 1993.)

1.3 **Read the following paragraphs. Try to fill in the gaps with complex abstract noun phrases that summarize or rephrase information that has been previously expressed. For each numbered gap, refer back to the previous information in bold. Each separate line represents one missing word.**

Grammar note: Remember that noun phrases are used to give synonyms and to repeat a previous word or phrase in order to achieve good text flow. You studied this in Unit 2A.

> One question that remains contentious in the field of autism research is whether **(1) autistic children demonstrate impaired imitative abilities. (▶ 1)** _These imitative abilities_ are of considerable theoretical interest because imitation occurs very early in non-autistic children. This lack of **(▶ 1)** _____ _____ in _____ _____ may be due to **(2) a lack of awareness of their social environment** and may explain why such youngsters find it difficult to interact with others as they grow up. (Meltzoff and Gopnik, 1993.)
>
> If this study indeed provides support to the theory that children with autism have imitation deficit, there will be a need for contributory research to explore the reasons for this. Baron-Cohen (1988) suggests that such children's **(▶ 2)** _____ of _____ of the link between thoughts and behaviour accounts for their difficulties in understanding **(3) the reason for other people's gestures**; if the **(▶ 3)** _____ for a _____ is not understood, no attempt to copy it is made.
>
> Aims: This study will consider both whether autistic children **(4) are able to match body postures**, and whether they can **(5) understand the meanings behind gestures**. It is hypothesized that a non-autistic group will give a better performance on matching **(▶ 4)** _____ _____ trials. It is also predicted that non-autistic children will demonstrate better performance on **(▶ 5)** _____ the _____ _____ _____.

1.4 **Look again at the text above. Which expressions does the writer use instead of 'I hypothesize that …' and 'I also predict that …'?**

_____

2.1 Read an extract from the literature review section of a research proposal. The person-based language is in bold. Why are there so many person-based noun phrases in this short extract?

_____

_____

> **Rogers and Pennington** (1991) argue that a motor-imitation deficit is a core deficit in autism and the existence of this deficit has been reported consistently by many researchers (e.g. **Bartak, Rutter and Cox**, 1975; **Hammes and Langdell**, 1981). However, **other researchers** have found no evidence to suggest that specific impairments in imitation exist in autistic children (**Nadel**, 2003; **Charman and Baron-Cohen, 1994**).

2.2 Read an extract from the methodology section of the proposal. How does the writer ensure impersonality in this section?

_____

> Ten children aged 6–8 will be seated at a table across from the experimenters in a quiet room. The participants will first be presented with a training picture card with a body posture on it. They will be asked to find a matching picture. If they point to the incorrect picture, they will be given accurate feedback. After the training, they will be presented with 20 new test cards, each showing a different body posture. The order of presentation will be randomized. The participants' responses will be recorded and positive feedback will be given after they have pointed to a matching image, whether it was the correct choice or not, in order to minimize experimenter anxiety.

2.3 Draw a line linking the noun phrases on the left to their verbs on the right. Check your answers with the extract in 2.2.

1. they		a. will be randomized
2. the participants		b. will be asked + infinitive
3. the participants' responses		c. will be seated at + NP
4. ten children aged 6–8		d. will be given
5. the order of presentation		e. will first be presented with + NP
6. positive feedback		f. will be recorded

2.4 **Read the extract below from the methodology section of another student's research project proposal. Correct the errors underlined, using the information you have gained from 2.3 as a guide.**

> I will ask some people who are engaged in the real-estate industry in China for interviews. I will give interviews to those who agree. I will first present them with a questionnaire via email and I will then record the conversations. I will use Excel to analyze the data and figures from my research exercise.
>
> From these responses, I will review and discuss prospects for the development of China's real-estate industry and future targets.

Task 3   Referring to data in a research project

You are now going to read extracts from the *Findings* and *Recommendations* sections of the research project.

3.1 **Complete the sentences below using the language in Stage B of this unit to help you.**

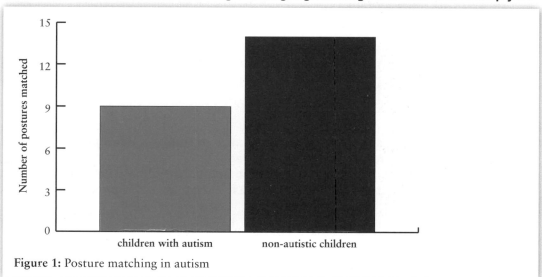

Figure 1: Posture matching in autism

> As **(1)** _____, non-autistic children aged between 6–8 were able to match body postures on 14 out of 20 picture cards (70%), whereas children with autism accurately matched 9 out of 20 cards (45%). **(2)** _____ children with autism are not as able as non-autistic children to imitate body posture. However, this task was not performed accurately by all non-autistic children, indicating that it may not have been simply the presence of autism which prevented accuracy of matching. The training period for the task may not have been sufficient.

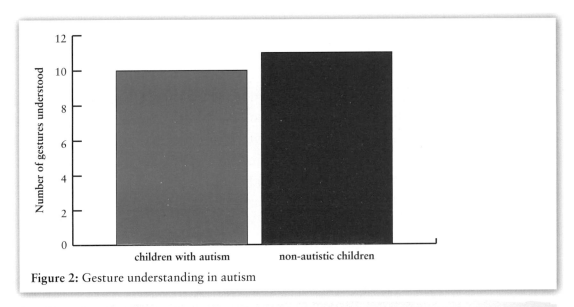

Figure 2: Gesture understanding in autism

Since it appeared that children with autism displayed some posture-matching impairment, the second experimental task was conducted to discover whether children with autism could understand the meaning behind gestures. **(3)** _____, children with autism were able to accurately interpret the meaning of 10 out of 20 gestures (50%), compared to 11 out of 20 for non-autistic children (55%). **(4)** _____ non-autistic children had similar levels of difficulty to the children with autism when matching gestures to tasks because it is well known that children with autism find social interaction challenging.

3.2 **The following task shows you the importance of complex noun phrases in academic texts. Read the extract from the *Recommendations* section of the research project. All the complex noun phrases have been deleted. Notice how it is impossible to understand the writer's message without the complex noun phrases.**

This study has supported **(1)** _____, but found that **(2)** _____ may not be connected with **(3)** _____. It is possible that **(4)** _____ impairs **(5)** _____. It is recommended that **(6)** _____ should be repeated with **(7)** _____, and that **(8)** _____ should be improved.

Now complete the sentences with the missing noun phrases (a–h) in the box. Write the correct letter in each gap.

a. the training session for the posture-matching tasks
b. a broader representative sample of children
c. difficulties in understanding the reasons behind gesture
d. the hypothesis that children with autism find it more difficult to imitate body posture
e. the experimental task
f. the ability to harness motor skills for accuracy of movement
g. cognitive deficit
h. the reason for this

Noticing complex noun phrases

Start to notice complex noun phrases in your reading. Underline them, if possible, and find the headword. This will help you to understand the text better. Notice whether such noun phrases link back to a previous idea, fact or concept. Think about how you can use them in your writing, too.

1 **Underline two nouns below that are not abstract nouns. What type of nouns are they?**

determination	investigation	farm
aspect	analysis	situation
researchers	understanding	identification

Rewrite the sentences in 2 and 3 below, reducing them to one simple clause to give them a more academic style.

2 He set up the experiment. This took longer than she expected.

_____

3 He could not understand the main points of the lecture. This was because he had a low level of English.

_____

4 **Choose the correct summary noun to complete the sentence.**
Teachers should always encourage students in the classroom. This is an important _____ in the process of teaching and learning.
a. situation
b. factor
c. crisis

5 **Read the paragraph. Complete the gap with a suitable summary noun.**
Some developing countries experience difficulties when small-scale local innovation is not valued by outside consultants. This _____ can occur when there is excessive interest in promoting the use of technology.

6 **Rewrite this sentence in two ways to give it a more academic style.**
Some historians think that the first Europeans landed in North America in the year 1000 CE.

a. _____ that the first Europeans landed in North America in the year 1000 CE.

b. The first Europeans _____ have landed in North America in the year 1000 CE.

7 **Rewrite this sentence in two ways to give it a more academic style. Use the present simple passive.**
Some people believe that killing badgers stops the spread of tuberculosis to cattle.

a. It _____

b. The _____

8 Complete the paragraph, using words from the box. There is one word for each gap.

is	improvement	probable	in	it	was	due	survival

In 1956, one in 50 babies died in the UK in their first year of life, compared to one in six in 1900. _____ _____ _____ that this _____ _____ _____ rates _____ _____ to better housing and improved medical care.

9 Rewrite the following essay outline, using the passive voice to replace the active voice expressions in bold.

> **The development of the real-estate market in China**
>
> **I will describe** the background to the real-estate industry in China **in this essay**. First, **I will delineate** the policies in the real estate market before 1990; then **I will divide** the later policies into the 1990–2001 period and the post-2001 period when China joined the WTO. **I will then analyze** the policies of the early 21st century. Finally, **I will examine** the future development of the Chinese real estate industry, as well as several factors constraining its development.

_____

_____

_____

_____

_____

_____

10 Complete the following paragraph with the missing abstract noun phrases (a–e).
a. an emotional perception
b. these initiatives
c. adequately maintained housing with modern facilities for the older generation
d. emotional needs and preferences
e. society's understanding of what constitutes a 'home' rather than just a house

> The Decent Homes programme links housing with physical health and well-being and seeks to provide _____ _____ (DCLG, 2006). However, _____ _____ only address physical needs; they neither consider _____, nor do they address _____. The terms 'house' and 'home' are inextricably linked; the latter being _____ of the former physical structure. (Clough et al., 2004; Rapaport, 2002).

9 Using relative clauses

In this unit you will:
- learn to expand a subject noun phrase by using an embedded relative clause
- learn to reduce a relative clause
- learn to expand an object noun phrase by using a linear set of clauses
- use *whose* as a possessive relative pronoun
- use relative adverbs – *where, when* and *why*
- learn to recognize the difference between defining and non-defining relative clauses
- use a relative clause to refer back to a previous idea

Stage A

In this stage you will:
- learn to expand a subject noun phrase by using an embedded relative clause
- learn to reduce a relative clause

Task 1   Review

Grammar note: The structure of embedded relative clauses is explained in Unit 2B, 2.1.

A **relative clause** is a new clause beginning with a **relative pronoun**, such as *who* or *which*. Relative clauses are sometimes called **adjectival clauses**, because, like adjectives, they add information about a noun phrase. A relative clause comes immediately after the noun it qualifies. In this way, it expands the noun phrase, making it into a complex noun phrase.

For example:
a. The *solution which seems easiest* is not always the best.
b. *Students who find a subject difficult* often form study groups.
c. *Children who read books* are better at Maths.

In a **defining relative clause**, the relative clause identifies the noun. Look at sentence c:

Which children are better at Maths? Answer: *The ones who read books.*

1.1   **Since the words *which* and *who* are subordinators, what is the name of the type of sentence structure in examples a–c? (Check back to Unit 5A, 1 if necessary.)**

1.2 **Relative clauses which combine with a main clause in the following way are called** *embedded clauses*. **Why? What does** *embedded* **mean?**

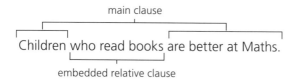

main clause

Children who read books are better at Maths.

embedded relative clause

Grammar note: In academic writing, you should use *who* for people and *which* or *that* for things, concepts and ideas. There is an exception when that is preferred to which in academic English, and this is explained below.

It is sometimes possible for the relative clause to give more information about a prepositional phrase that comes *after* the headword of a noun phrase.

noun phrase

headword + prepositional phrase   relative clause

The loans in the **scheme** *that was set up by the government* attract a low interest rate.

The relative clause gives more information about the *scheme* not about the *loans*: the *scheme* was set up by the government; the *loans* were *not* set up by the government.

1.3 **Combine two sentences 1–8 below into one complex sentence. Use the information in the first sentence to make a relative clause that expands the subject noun phrase. Check whether the information qualifies the** *headword* **or the** *noun in the prepositional phrase*. **Underline the words in the relative clause. Label subject and verb.**

1. The students work hard. They achieve academic success.

   The students who work hard achieve academic success.

2. The lecturer received the best student feedback. She is on a temporary contract.

   who

3. The computers in the classroom will be replaced. The classroom is being modernized.

4. The money came from a research grant. It was used to employ a new assistant.

   which

5. The people live in East Street. They have signed a petition about the traffic.

   who

6. The laboratory was used for animal experiments. It is now closed.

   which   has

7. The Credit Scheme provided smallholder farmers with loans. It proved very successful.

   which

8. The eggs from the farm are cheap. The farm is close to the housing estate.

CW 29 Aug

Task 2 — Reducing the relative clause

2.1 Study the following sentence pairs and answer the questions below. Notice the words which are different in each pair.

a. Decisions **which are made** without enough evidence often have to be changed.

b. Decisions **made** without enough evidence often have to be changed.

c. The sector **which is showing** the best signs of recovery at the moment is agriculture.

d. The sector **showing** the best signs of recovery at the moment is agriculture.

e. The experimental task **which involved** autistic children was not easy to organize.

f. The experimental task **involving** autistic children was not easy to organize.

1. For each sentence pair, which sentence has the better academic style, first or second? _____

2. For each sentence pair, which sentence is more concise? _____

> Relative clauses can be reduced in the following way:
> 1. Delete the relative pronoun (*who*, *which* or *that*).
> 2. For a verb form in the active voice, change the verb to the **present participle** (*~ing* form):
>
> | involve | *involving* |
> | is showing | *showing* |
>
> 3. For verb form in the passive voice, delete the auxiliary *be* and keep the past participle:
>
> | are based on | *based on* |
> | was provided by | *provided by* |

2.2 Reduce the relative clauses according to the instructions above.

1. The course which most closely relates to the job is finance.

   The course most closely relating to the job is finance.

2. The countries which were required to reduce the quantity of their exports were defiant.

   _____

3. The policy which was introduced last year was successful.

   _____

4. The progress that has been made in the last three months is minimal.

   _____

5. The issue which requires immediate attention is class sizes.

   _____

6. The agreement that was reached at last month's conference involved trade restrictions.

   _____

7. Farmers who use ~~harmful~~ insecticides should be encouraged to change to organic pest control methods.

(handwritten: ing)

_____

8. Some regions that face serious food shortages have appealed for help.

(handwritten: facing)

_____

2.3 **When you are reading, you need to look out for reduced relative clauses. You need to _mentally add in_ the full relative clause to be sure that you understand the meaning of the text.**

Study paragraphs a and b, and answer the questions below.

a. There is no simple answer to the question of whether the world should promote free or fair trade. They can both bring benefits and disadvantages to countries, according to their specific economic conditions. Countries should consider carefully their own economic structure and that of their trading partners in order to establish a trading agreement which will maximize benefits and minimize negative effects on both societies. In most cases, free-trade agreements are beneficial for economically developed countries whereas agreements based on fair trade are generally more advantageous to poorer and smaller countries.

(handwritten margin note: which are based on)

b. The increasing number of countries in the European Union and the growth of free-trade agreements, such as the North American Free Trade Agreement, show today's global tendency to open countries' borders. At the same time, the World Fair Trade Organization seeks to protect producers in economically underdeveloped countries by pointing out that many of the world's economies need support and protection and are not suitable for free trade. Both free- and fair-trade policies have their supporters and adversaries. The world should continue its process of opening up to trade because the benefits of international trading are many, but policies and fair-trade agreements protecting the poor and more vulnerable groups of society should always be adopted.

(handwritten: which protect)

1. Underline the two places where a relative clause has been reduced after a subject noun phrase.

2. It is good practice to reduce relative clauses where possible after a subject noun phrase. However, in this case, can you expand the two noun phrases into relative clauses, in order to practise the pattern?

_____

_____

2.4 **Return to the reduced relative clauses you have identified in 2.3. Underline the complex subject noun phrases. Draw an arrow to show which previous information these noun phrases refer back to.**

| Task 3 | The relative pronoun as object of a relative clause |

You have so far studied the relative pronoun as the **subject** of a relative clause.

For example:

relative clause

| S | V | O |

a. *The speaker who attracted the most interest at the conference was David Smith.*

However, the relative pronoun can also be the **object** of a relative clause.

relative clause

| O | S | V |

b. *The sample which the research team used was taken from the Pacific Ocean.*

3.1 **Study the sentences. Underline the *subject* of the verb in the relative clause. Circle the *object* of the verb in the relative clause.**

1. The law <u>which</u> reduces (the speed limit) is sensible.

2. The politician whom Margaret Thatcher admired most was Churchill.

3. The trade agreement which the United States and Canada signed in 1988 was favourable to both countries.

4. The crop that earns the highest foreign currency in Zimbabwe is tobacco.

3.2 **Complete the sentences with a suitable relative clause from the list below. Decide whether the relative pronoun is the subject or object of the relative clause.**

that the team adopted	who became President
whom the border police deported	~~which was written by their professor~~
which was on climate change	that the pupils preferred

1. The book <u>*which was written by their professor*</u> was also the most interesting.

2. The experimental techniques _____ were designed by Frank and Fischer (1994).

3. The lecture _____ was outdated.

4. The style of teaching _____ was interactive.

5. The asylum seeker _____ was from Bandonia.

6. The politician _____ was originally from the Mindan States.

Grammar note: If a relative clause contains the verb *be* + noun phrase or prepositional phrase you can reduce it. For example:
The lecture ~~which was~~ on climate change was outdated.

3.3   Underline the relative pronouns in 3.2 and complete the box below.

	Person	Thing/fact concept/idea
Subject of relative clause	_____	_____
Object of relative clause	_____	_____

3.4   **Complete the following sentences with an appropriate relative pronoun. State whether the pronoun is used as subject or object in the relative clause.**

1. The most industrious researcher _____*whom (O)*_____ they have ever employed was Imran Al-Harthi.

2. The speaker _____ the students enjoyed most was a doctor from Istanbul.

3. The model _____ the students were studying was difficult to understand.

4. The pollution _____ is emitted from the chemical factory can be captured and treated.

5. The airline _____ seems to be the most efficient is Airfast.

6. People _____ live in low-lying coastal regions are most at risk from the effects of climate change.

7. The book _____ the lecturer recommended is very good.

3.5   **Study 3.4 again. Which sentences can be reworded in spoken English without the relative pronoun?**

_____

3.6   **Study the sentences in 3.4 again. Two sentences with the relative pronoun as a *subject* can be reduced, as has been explained in Task 2. Which two? Rewrite them in their reduced forms.**

Stage B

In this stage you will:

- learn to expand an object noun phrase by using a linear set of clauses
- use *whose* as a possessive relative pronoun
- use relative adverbs *where*, *when* and *why*

Task 1 — Expanding object noun phrases

Defining relative clauses are not only used to describe the **subject** of a main clause, but they are also used to describe the noun phrase which is the **object** in a main clause. In this case, the relative clause is not embedded inside the main clause (as you have studied in Stage A). It is instead a **linear sentence**, with the relative clause directly following the main clause. (The relative pronoun gives information about the headword at the end of clause 1.)

For example:

```
              main clause                              relative clause
    ┌─────────────────────────────┐          ┌─────────────────────────────┐
        S        V         O                    S        V         O
                         headword
a.  Producers are receiving a reduced price which doesn't cover their costs.
```

1.1 **Study the sentence below and answer the questions.**

```
              main clause                   relative clause
    ┌─────────────────────────┐   ┌─────────────────────────────────┐
a.  The workers are guaranteed a wage which will ensure food for their families.
```

1. Label the subject (*S*), verb (*V*) and object (*O*) of both clauses.
2. Which headword does the relative pronoun describe?

1.2 **Join the two sentences using a relative clause to expand the object noun phrase of the main clause. Answer the following questions for each of the sentences below.**

- a. Identify the subject (*S*), verb (*V*) and object (*O*) of the main clause.
- b. Change the second sentence into a relative clause, to make a complex noun phrase object for the main clause. Decide whether the relative pronoun will be the subject or object of the relative clause.
- c. Label the subject (*S*), verb (*V*) and object (*O*) (if applicable) of the new relative clause.
- d. Underline the new complex object noun phrase.

1. The student borrowed the book. She needed it for her essay.

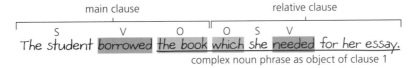

```
              main clause                   relative clause
    ┌─────────────────────────┐   ┌───────────────────────────┐
        S        V         O         O    S    V
    The student borrowed the book which she needed for her essay.
                         └──────────────────────────────────────┘
                    complex noun phrase as object of clause 1
```

2. The lecturer referred to the computer model. It predicted an increase in global warming.

_____

3. Governments do not understand the urgency of the problems. Communities face them every day.

_____

4. The government introduced a new health care programme. It lasted until 2000.

_____

5. The hospital lost the file. It contained the patients' medical records.

_____

6. The local cooperative group paints the furniture. Their agent sells it abroad.

_____

7. Professor Smith has a colleague. She went to work in France last month.

_____

8. The research assistant conducted the experiment. It led to the department's prize-winning discovery.

_____

1.3 **You have learnt that in academic writing we normally use *which* as a relative pronoun to describe things, fact, concepts and ideas. However, only *that* can be used in the two sentences below. Why?**

   a. When a country opens up to free trade, it introduces lower market prices for goods <u>that</u> are purchased from foreign countries.

   b. Free trade can bring inefficiencies causing unemployment and a lowering of workers' wages in industries <u>that</u> are competing with ones in other countries.

   _____

   _____

1.4 **Sometimes writers use more than one relative clause in the same sentence. Read the long sentence below and answer the questions.**

   According to Dunkley (2004), free trade can lead to lower wages in industries competing with similar ones that are located in other countries which use very cheap or even exploited labour.

   1. How many relative clauses are there in the sentence? _____

   2. What is the main clause of the complete sentence? Label the subject (*S*), verb (*V*), object (*O*) of the main clause.

   _____

   3. Remember that you studied reduced relative clauses in Stage A, 2.1. Rewrite the sentence below as a complex sentence with a *full* relative clause.
   Free trade can lead to lower wages in industries competing with similar ones in other countries.

   _____

   4. Label the subject (*S*), verb (*V*) and object (*O*) of the relative clause which you have written in 3 above.

5. Which word does the relative pronoun *that* describe in the complete sentence? _____

6. Which headword does the relative pronoun *which* describe in the complete sentence?

   _____

Task 2 *whose* – possessive relative pronoun

2.1 Study the examples and answer the questions.

a. Dr John's team is researching into proteins. Their structures change with a rise in temperature.

b. Dr John's team is researching into proteins whose structures change with a rise in temperature.

c. Solar panels and small wind turbines are given to people. Their homes do not have electricity.

d. Solar panels and small wind turbines are given to people whose homes do not have electricity.

1. Is *whose* + noun phrase the subject or object of the relative clause? _____

2. Does *whose* refer to a person or to a thing? _____

Grammar note: It is not common to find *whose* + noun phrase used as an **object** in a defining relative clause because the sentence would have two noun phrases side by side, and might be difficult for the reader to understand:

*Solar panels are given to people **whose homes the council identify** as suitable.*

This sentence would be more commonly written using the passive voice:

*Solar panels are given to people **whose homes are identified** as suitable **by the council**.*

2.2 Re-read the sentence and answer the questions.

> If a developing country which produces tea starts selling its product internationally, the unit cost may be higher than that of global producers whose price would be set at a lower rate because of more efficient production methods.

1. Is *whose* the subject or object of the relative clause? _____

2. Does *whose* refer to a person or to a thing? _____

3. What does *whose* refer to? _____

4. Why is the relative clause in the passive voice? _____

2.3 **Match the sentences 1–6 with a sentence from the box. Combine them using** *whose*, **following the pattern in 2.1.**

their principles are still highly regarded   their IELTS score is 7.0
their lives are threatened by ill health
~~its main area of expertise involves analyzing sedimentary rocks~~
his books were on the reading list   their parents were in a safe house

1. The course participants work for an engineering company *whose main area of expertise involves analyzing sedimentary rocks.*

2. The clinic works with clients _____

3. The course is for students _____

4. Keynes is still studied for his economic theories _____

5. After the earthquake, the rescuers found some children _____

6. The students had seminars with a lecturer _____

Task 3	Relative adverbs – *where, when* and *why*

A relative adverb is most commonly used when the relative clause expresses:
■ reason   ■ place   ■ time

3.1 **Match the use of the relative adverb to the correct meaning from the list above:**

1. He returned to Manchester, where he had studied in the 1970s. _____

2. The syllabus focused on the Renaissance period, when art and literature gained importance in society. _____

3. There were many reasons why the government was not re-elected. _____

3.2 **Study the following sentences. Make a single complex sentence for each of them, using a relative adverb. Use each one once only.**

1. A new economic and social policy is emerging in the USA. The new president is attempting to make changes.

2. Important decisions should be taken. Everyone is present.

3. There are many reasons. The economy of China has developed quickly.

3.3   **Expand the final noun in the clauses below by adding a relative clause. Use the appropriate relative adverb (*where*, *why* or *when*). Choose a sentence ending from the box below.**

it is traditional to have parties   the production methods are less efficient and flexible the experiment did not work   internals are popular there were many strikes in the UK   ~~Byron lived~~

1. She has found the house in Rome *where Byron lived.* _____

2. They lived abroad during the period _____

3. The samples were contaminated; this is the reason _____

4. New Year's Eve is a time _____

5. It is difficult for young people to secure a job in today's economic climate; this is the main reason _____

6. However, this is not the case for poor countries _____

Task 4	**Using *there is/there are* with a relative pronoun or relative adverb**

You learnt in Unit 1A, 5, that *there is/there are* is a useful construction for presenting new information. You also know from Unit 1C, 4, that *there is/there are* is followed by a complement. You can expand a complement noun phrase by adding a relative clause, in the same way that you can expand an object noun phrase.

complement noun phrase

There are many reasons why people should learn English.

4.1   **Look at the sentence below and complete the gaps in the table.**

Main clause			Relative clause			
Subject	**Verb**	**Complement**	_____	_____	_____	_____
There	are	many reasons	why	people	should learn	English.

Grammar note: After the noun phrases *little* and *nothing*, use *that* **not** *which*. (*Little* as a noun phrase means *not much*. It is quite common in academic writing).

4.2   **Expand the final noun in the clauses on the next page by adding a relative clause. Use the appropriate relative adverb (*where*, *why* or *when*), or a relative pronoun. Choose a sentence ending from the box below.**

could interest the farmers	can be done	~~had total control over all the beef exports~~
operate on a non-profit basis		the country needed to improve its export figures
the government should lower taxes		women did not have the right to vote
help the poorest people		the rescuers could do to help the survivors

1. There were four marketing boards *which/that had total control over all the beef exports.*

2. There was a time in Britain _____

3. There are three main reasons _____

4. There are no policies _____

5. There is little _____

6. There are few companies _____

7. There was nothing _____

8. There were periods of economic difficulty _____

Stage C

In academic writing, there are two different types of relative clauses. The most common type is called a **defining relative clause**, which you have studied in Stages A and B of this unit. The second type, a **non-defining relative clause**, is used less frequently. It is important that you understand the difference between these two different types of relative clauses so that you can use them accurately in your writing.

In this stage you will:
- learn to recognize the difference between defining and non-defining relative clauses
- learn to use a relative clause to refer back to a previous idea

Task 1 — Recognizing the difference between defining and non-defining relative clauses

1.1 Study the embedded relative clauses in examples a and b. Then match the definitions below with the examples.

a. There are many islands in this region. The islands which lie off the coast of Sangam are wildlife sanctuaries.

b. Tourism is banned in the Xing islands. These islands, which lie off the coast of Sangam, are wildlife sanctuaries.

1. **Defining** relative clause: The relative clause identifies **which exact islands** the writer means. Example _____

2. **Non-defining** relative clause: The relative clause does **not define which** islands the writer means. Example _____

1.2 **Study examples a and b below, which both include linear relative clauses. Then match the definitions below with the examples.**

   a. The workers receive <u>a wage which will ensure food for their families</u>.

   b. The workers receive <u>a good wage, which will ensure food for their families</u>.

   1. The relative clause identifies **which type of wage** the writer means. _____

   2. The relative clause **does not define** the type of wage the writer means. _____

   3. Delete the relative clause in both sentences. Which one still makes sense even without the relative clause? Why?

   _____

   _____

   4. Which relative clause is **defining**? Example _____

   5. Which one is **non-defining**? Example _____

1.3 **What difference in punctuation do you notice between defining and non-defining relative clauses? What is the reason for the difference?**

Task 2   Non-defining relative clauses

2.1 **The following sentences all contain non-defining relative clauses. Label each one *E* or *L* to indicate whether it is embedded or linear.**

   1. Dr Jones is a lecturer at Oxford University, which is one of the oldest universities in the UK. _____

   2. The student's personal tutor is Dr Smith, who is famous for his research into string theory. _____

   3. Dr Barratt, who leads a dynamic research team, is the new Chair of Physics. _____

   4. Dr Bogle, who has written many journal articles, is supervising the art project in India. _____

   5. The professor's main area of interest is soil fertility, which has become an important concern for agriculturalists. _____

2.2 **Add non-defining relative clauses to the sentences below. Follow the instructions.**

   a. Match sentences 1–9 on the page opposite with the correct phrases from the box below.

   b. Decide if the new sentence requires an *embedded* or *linear* relative clause structure.

   c. Add the appropriate relative pronoun (*who*, *which* or *whom*).

   d. Add a comma before the relative clause. Add another comma after the relative clause if it is embedded.

Grammar note: you cannot use *that* as a relative pronoun in non-defining relative clauses.

It is a beautiful country with many historical sites.   It is increasingly changeable.
The students liked him.   ~~The president respected him.~~
It makes the land useless for production.   It has 90 participants.
The Queen opened it recently.   Everyone thought he was lazy   It was well received.

1. The president praised the efforts of the education minister.

   The president praised the efforts of the education minister, whom he respected. (linear)

2. The pre-sessional course started in July.

   _____

3. Dr Paolo Rossi now teaches English to international students in London.

   _____

4. Higher rates of deforestation sometimes result in desertification.

   _____

5. The current weather pattern is a result of the high pressure over the Atlantic Ocean.

   _____

6. The President delivered a fierce anti-war speech.

   _____

7. They decided to visit Argentina.

   _____

8. The new library holds over one million books.

   _____

9. The staff were surprised by the good results of one student, John.

   _____

Task 3	**Possessive relative pronoun *whose* in non-defining relative clauses**

3.1 **You have already studied the use of *whose* in defining relative clauses in Stage C, 2.1. Study the sentences below. Underline the relative clauses and label them *D* (defining) or *ND* (non-defining).**

1. Dr James is a psychologist <u>whose work involves researching the effect of television violence on children</u>. __D__

2. The director of the company, whose administrative assistant has moved to a different town, had to carry out all the administration tasks himself. _____

3. Policies whose aims are to redistribute wealth more equally are popular with many people. _____

4. Dr Johnson's team is researching into proteins whose structures change with a rise in temperature. _____

5. Professor Sylvia Campbell, whose research was highly praised by her colleagues, received an award from the government. _____

Grammar note: The passive form is often used to link back to a previous idea. The subject of the passive verb is often an abstract noun. In many passive sentences, the person who does the action (the 'agent') is not expressed:

Her research was highly praised. (= We do not know who praised her research.) However, it is possible to include the agent in a passive sentence, using *by:*

Her research was praised by her colleagues.

3.2 **Add relative clauses with *whose* to the sentences below. Follow the instructions.**

a. Match sentences 1–6 with the correct phrases from the box.

b. Decide if the new sentence requires an embedded or linear relative clause structure.

c. Add *whose*.

d. Decide if the relative clause is defining or non-defining. Add commas to separate the clauses if it is non-defining.

~~Their jobs involve working in hospitals~~   Their taxes have been raised by the council

Their policies were introduced too quickly   Its interior was designed by the occupants

His main interest is in soil aggregates.   Their examinations are next summer

---

1. The course participants were most interested in the presentation about the future of the National Health Service.

   The course participants, whose jobs involve working in hospitals, were most interested in the presentation about the future of the National Health Service.

2. The students still have plenty of time to study.

   _____

3. Single people have less disposable income.

   _____

4. The geologist Howard Fontaine has discovered a very interesting fact.

   _____

5. The problem can be traced back to the UK government.

   _____

6. The building failed to comply with regulations.

   _____

Task 4   Relative adverbs in non-defining relative clauses

In Stage B3 of this unit, you have learnt how to use *where*, *when* and *why* in relative clauses. In non-defining relative clauses it is only possible to use *when* and *where* (not *why*).

4.1 **Study the underlined sentences in texts a and b. Decide which relative clause is defining and which is non-defining, and add a comma in the correct place.**

a. In an economically developed country, companies can more easily adapt to changes by altering their product to suit market forces. <u>However, this is not the case in countries where the production methods are less efficient and flexible.</u>

b. In an economically developed country, companies can more easily adapt to changes by altering their product to suit market forces. <u>However, this is not the case in Bamania where the production methods are less efficient and flexible.</u>

4.2 **Add relative clauses with *relative adverbs* to the sentences below. Follow the instructions.**

a. Match sentences 1–6 with the correct phrases from the box.

b. Decide if the new sentence requires an embedded or linear relative clause structure.

c. Add the correct relative adverb (*when* or *where*).

d. Decide if the relative clause is defining or non-defining. Add commas to separate the clauses if necessary.

> McGill University has a training school.   The *Pickwick Papers* was published.
>
> They have studied for two hours.   The fire broke out.
>
> ~~The natural environment is under threat.~~   A wide variety of commercial activities occur.

1. The Amazon basin is one of the regions *where the natural environment is under threat. D*

2. The company's head office is in London _____

3. Students are advised to take a break _____

4. Accident investigators tried to locate the place _____

5. The physics conference is held every year in Barbados _____

6. Dickens' first success came in 1837 _____

Task 5	Using a relative clause to refer back to a previous idea

In a non-defining relative clause, *which* can also be used to refer back to a complete idea in the previous clause.

For example:

a. *The trial was very successful, which encouraged them to launch the project nationally.*

b. *The level of liquid solution is falling, which indicates that there is a fault in the apparatus.*

5.1 **Study sentences a and b below. In order to use *which* to refer back to an idea in a previous clause, you need to delete the same two words in each sentence. Add a relative clause using *which* in the correct place, then add the comma.**

a. Sanctions meant the government had to increase import support and this eventually happened in 1980, when Zimbabwe gained its independence.

_____

_____

b. The policies introduced during the first 10 years after independence were funded solely by the government and this increased the government's expenditure.

_____

_____

Task 6   Review

6.1   Place the following words into the appropriate column according to whether they are relative pronouns or relative adverbs.

| which | when | where | whose | that | whom | who | why |

Relative pronouns	Relative adverbs

6.2   Correct the errors relating to relative clauses in the following sentences.

1. There are many problems need to be solved before the policy can be implemented.

   _____

2. Developing countries depend on developed countries to extract the natural resources lie deep underground.

   _____

3. The first problem relates to population growth is that cities are overcrowded.

   _____

4. China has a policy of one child per family, it has slowed the speed of population growth dramatically.

   _____

5. The second problem faces the world is food shortage.

   _____

6. Population growth is one of the main challenges governments and communities face.

   _____

7. There are several issues are not easy to resolve.

   _____

8. The majority of these people live on the poverty line. Which means an uncomfortable life.

   _____

6.3 **Read the introduction to a student essay about agricultural policies in Zimbabwe. Replace the missing relative pronouns in the gaps. Add commas as appropriate.**

It is believed that the reasons for current agricultural policies in Zimbabwe can be traced back to the colonial era (1890–1979) (Johns and Waite, 2007), so this essay will first examine this historical period. It will then delineate the domestic agricultural policies (1) _____ have been introduced in Zimbabwe since the colonial era. These policies will be divided into two categories, the first being the colonial age (2) _____ covers the period 1890–1979, the second being the period of independence from 1980 onwards. The colonial period will focus in greatest depth on the events of the 1920s and beyond. The post-independence period will be further divided into two phases, the first covering the period 1980–1995 and the second covering the period 1995–2005. An analysis will then be made of the changes (3) _____ have occurred to the domestic agricultural policies since Zimbabwe joined the WTO in March 1995 (WTO 2008).

6.4 **Study an extract from the section of the essay which concerns the early colonial period. Replace the missing relative pronouns in the gaps. Add commas as appropriate. Choose from the list below, using each word once, except where indicated otherwise.**

that	who	which (x5)	whose	when

Prior to the 1920s, the bulk of the food in Zimbabwe (then known as Southern Rhodesia) was produced by Africans. When the Europeans' mining activities failed, they embarked upon agricultural production. African farmers (1) _____ maize production systems were more cost-effective than those of the European farmers were then perceived to be a threat. The government of the day then decided to put measures in place (2) _____ would ensure that the European farmers were protected from such a challenge. In addition, pressure from organized farmer lobbies at a time (3) _____ the export price of white maize dropped in the 1930s induced the government to take action. The government set up the Maize Control Act of 1930 (4) _____ led to the creation of a dual marketing system. Under this system, European farmers sold their grain to state marketing boards (5) _____ were established in their areas (6) _____ ensured that they received prices (7) _____ were 30% to 60% higher than those Africans received by selling to private traders (8) _____ were agents of the marketing boards. A restriction was imposed on grain movement (9) _____ forced the Africans to sell through the private traders.

6.5 **Study an extract from the section of the essay which concerns 1980–1995. There are two reduced relative clauses.**

a. Underline them.

b. Replace them with a full relative clause.

c. Add commas if necessary.

> The policies introduced by the government during the first ten years after independence were funded solely by the government and this increased government's expenditure. As the government borrowed the funds to finance development, its fiscal deficit increased and the International Monetary Fund (IMF) and the World Bank (WB) began to put pressure on the government to adopt other measures not based upon government intervention, but on market reform.

Unit 9 Self-check summary

1 **Combine the two clauses into one complex sentence. Is the relative pronoun the subject or object of the relative clause?**

Respondents installed the Document Management System. They were generally positive and welcomed its benefits.

2 **Underline the subject in this sentence.**

Factors which affect the oxidization activity can come from the environment or from the food-processing techniques used.

Reduce the relative clause in sentences 3–8.

3 The library which is in the town centre now has a bookable computer room.

4 The schools which need financial support are mostly in rural areas.

5 **Combine the two clauses into one complex sentence. Is the relative pronoun the subject or object of the relative clause?**

The candidate comes from New York. The company interviewed him yesterday.

6 **Combine the two clauses into one complex sentence. Does the relative pronoun expand the subject or object of the main clause?**

British tourists buy high-grade Japanese green tea. They cannot purchase it in their own country.

7 **Read the sentences. Write *L* next to the one which is linear and *E* next to the one which is embedded. Label the subject, verb and object of each of the clauses.**
a. The students identified the words which showed the author's attitude. _____
b. Developing countries which have adopted trade liberalization report a 5% increase in trade _____

8 **Choose the correct word to fill the gap: *where/whose/when/why*.**

Henry Ford, _____ ideas for a moving factory assembly line were based on Taylor's system of production efficiency, developed the technique of mass production.

Is the relative clause defining (*D*) or non-defining (*ND*)? Add a comma if necessary.

9 A low-carbon economy is essential for reducing CO_2 emissions which pollute the atmosphere. _____

10 Some female publishers who wanted to give women a stronger voice set up a publishing house, Virago, in the 1970s. _____

Appendix A: Using *a*, *an*, *the* or no article

1A

When mentioning something for the first time in your work		
Use *a* or *an**	**Use *the***	**Use no article**
Their study showed **a loss of vitamin C** in onions. There was **a demonstration** against animal experimentation.		Their study examined **spiders**. The team carries out **research** into economic growth.

*See *Grammar note* on page 223

1B

When writing about one or more of many		
Use *a* or *an**	**Use *the***	**Use no article**
Unemployment is **a big problem**. (There are many big problems.) poor healthcare crime unemployment homelessness		Unemployment and homelessness are **big problems**. (There are many big problems.)
To write about jobs		
Use *a* or *an**	**Use *the***	**Use no article**
He was **an artist and a philosopher**. (There are many artists and philosophers.) She became **a successful politician**. (There are many successful politicians.)		Englert and Higgs are **successful scientists**.

*See *Grammar note* on page 223

1C

To refer back to something you have already mentioned.		
Use *a* or *an**	**Use *the***	**Use no article**
	Note: You can repeat the noun directly or you can use a synonym or an associated noun.	
	Their study showed a loss of vitamin C in onions. However, **the vitamin** C loss was less than 10%.	
	A research project has investigated why ambulances do not always arrive within eight minutes. **The results** are communicated in their report.	
	There is a difference between the two sets of results. **The discrepancy** must be investigated.	

*See *Grammar note* on page 223

1D

To indicate things in general		
Use *a* or *an**	**Use *the***	**Use no article**
		▪ Plural with no article if countable ▪ Singular with no article if uncountable **Students** normally submit **assignments** online. **Research** requires **determination**. **Prisoners** do not have **freedom**.
To talk about all things of a type: *the* + singular countable noun		
Use *a* or *an**	**Use *the***	**Use no article**
	The computer was invented by Alan Turing in 1936. **The mobile phone** allows easy bank transfers.	

*See *Grammar note* on page 223

To indicate when there is only one		
Use *a* or *an**	Use *the*	Use no article
	The Sun will burn itself out in five billion years.	
	The big problem is cost. (There are no other big problems.)	

To specify the exact person(s) or thing(s) you are talking about		
Use *a* or *an**	Use *the*	Use no article
	A researcher found **the information that was needed** to complete the project.	
	She is **the lecturer whose talk we went to** last week.	
	He wrote down **the main points from the Astronomy lecture**.	
	The employment market is related to the supply of labour. (There are many types of market; this sentence is about the *employment* market).	

With superlatives		
Use *a* or *an**	Use *the*	Use no article
	The three largest banks comprise 83% of the market share in Hong Kong.	
	The best solution is to use SMS to remind patients about their appointments.	

*See *Grammar note* on page 223

1F

With some geographical categories		
Use *a* or *an**	Use *the*	Use no article
	▪ seas; oceans; rivers; straits; canals; gulfs	▪ countries; continents; lakes
	the Mediterranean Sea	The population of **France** is approximately 60 million.
	the Atlantic Ocean	
	the River Thames	**North** and **South America** are separate continents.
	the Straits of Hormuz	
	the Suez Canal	**Lake Superior** is the largest lake in **North America**.
	the Gulf of Mexico	
	▪ mountain ranges; groups of islands; countries with names such as: 'Kingdom' 'States' 'Republic'	
	the Yorkshire Dales	
	the Cayman Islands	
	the United Kingdom	
	the United States of America	
	the Republic of Ireland	

With names of buildings/organizations		
Use *a* or *an**	Use *the*	Use no article
	the University of Reading	▪ If the first word is a place name:
	the Natural History Museum	**Reading** University
		Amsterdam Airport
		Windsor Castle

*See *Grammar note* below

Grammar note:

* When to use *a*? When to use *an*?

Use *a* in front of a noun phrase beginning with a **consonant** sound.

   a plan; **a busy** area; **a university**

Use *an* in front of a noun phrase beginning with a **vowel** sound.

   an office; **an unusual** result

Task 1

1.1 **Read the following sentences, and add *a*, *an*, *the* or no article in the gaps. Which reason from the list which starts on page 220 supports your answer?**

1. Krauss was ___a___ modernist sculptor.

2. _____ literature search will be conducted in order to establish the research context.

3. Stiglitz began _____ new country-level study in 2006. _____ study showed that the effects on export growth were positive.

4. Learner drivers need to pass _____ theory test before they are allowed to drive. _____ test is taken online.

5. _____ water is essential to support _____ life.

6. _____ domestic refrigerator was invented in 1913.

7. The community made good use of _____ equipment which the Red Crescent had donated.

8. The students could not choose their essay title. They had to write about _____ economic situation in their country.

9. _____ most common gas in _____ Earth's atmosphere is nitrogen.

10. Khalifa Tower in Dubai is _____ tallest man-made structure in the world.

11. _____ Yellow River is _____ second longest river in China.

Task 2

2.1 **Read the following sentences, and add *a*, *an*, *the* or no article in the gaps. Which reason from the list above supports your answer?**

Note: in some sentences, you may have to add a capital letter to the first word.

1. The students could choose their essay title. They had to write about _____ problem in their country.

2. _____ gender roles in Japan are different from those in _____ UK.

3. _____ government should pay more attention to problems in _____ education system.

4. Burglary is _____ criminal offence.

5. Congestion is _____ problem in big cities.

6. Parikh (2007) examined _____ relationship between growth and trade liberalization.

7. _____ Second World War lasted from 1939 to 1945.

8. _____ donkeys need 15 litres of water per day.

9. Manufacturing industries should not pollute _____ environment.

10. This essay will discuss _____ government policies

11. _____ education is important.

12. _____ love is fundamental for a happy life, but _____ love of money can lead to selfishness and greed.

13. _____ researcher was appointed to collect data

14. Dr Jones is _____ expert in marine biology

15. _____ exposure of food to light and oxygen leads to a breakdown of antioxidants.

16. There are many exhibitions in the British Museum. _____ British Neo-Romantics exhibition is the focus of this paper.

17. Zimbabwe is _____ developing country.

18. Cleano is a company which makes _____ baby products

19. Rural to urban migration and hunger are _____ consequences of poverty.

20. This essay will discuss _____ government policies of the Thatcher era.

2.2 Read the longer extracts below, and add *a, an, the* or no article in the gaps.

1. _____ government introduced some financial reforms in 2008. _____ foreign-owned organizations in China now have the same corporate tax responsibilities as _____ local companies. This means that _____ level of competition is fairer than before.

2. _____ Reading San Francisco Libre Association is _____ town-twinning organization which encourages _____ towns of Reading and San Francisco Libre to work together . It promotes _____ links and _____ exchange programs between these towns. _____ money is raised in Reading to sponsor _____ projects in San Francisco Libre and _____ University of Reading sends volunteer students to work in this area of Latin America in the summer.

Appendix B: Describing data

Task 1   Selecting statistical evidence

1.1   **Read the paragraph which accompanies the bar chart. What is the problem with it?**

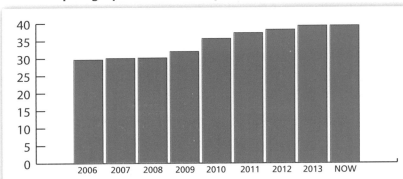

Figure 1: Taiwan GDP per capita (US$1,000)

As Figure 1 shows, the GDP of Taiwan has increased steadily over the last decade. It is clear that the government strategy of transferring to technology has been a critical factor in the promotion of industrial development and economic growth in Taiwan.

1.2   **Which sentence below best describes the information in Figure 1?**

a. Between 2006 and 2008, GDP remained steady at approximately $30,000. By 2013, Taiwan's GDP had reached its highest point of approximately $39,000. ☐

b. Between 2006 and 2008, GDP remained steady at approximately $30,000, but by 2012, this figure had risen to just over $38,000. One year later, Taiwan's GDP reached its highest point of approximately $39,000. ☐

c. In 2006, GDP was approximately $30,000, and by 2013 it had risen to approximately $39,000. ☐

Task 2   Verb forms for describing data

2.1   **Underline the verbs in a–c below and name the verb forms used. Explain the reasons for their use.**

a. The GDP of Taiwan has increased steadily over the last decade.

b. By 2013, this figure had risen to approximately $39,000.

c. Between 2006 and 2008, GDP remained steady at approximately $30,000.

Past perfect aspect

You use the past perfect aspect when you want to show that one activity finished *in the past* before another event started *in the past*.

*By 2013 GDP **had risen** to $39,000.* (*By 2013* means 'before the beginning of 2013'.)

this event started and finished   before this event started

= *GDP had already risen to $39,000* when 2013 began.

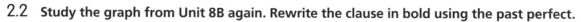

2.2 **Study the graph from Unit 8B again. Rewrite the clause in bold using the past perfect.**

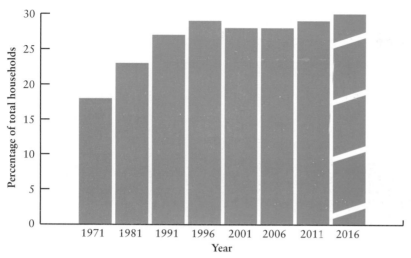

In 1971, only 18% of all households had one person in them. **This figure rose to 29% in 1996**.

By _____

2.3 **The present perfect continuous verb form is sometimes useful when describing a trend. You have studied the continuous form of the present tense verb in Unit 1B, Task 2. When is the continuous form of the present tense used?**

> **Study the differences between sentences a and b:**
>
> present perfect of auxiliary *to be* + ~ing form of main verb
>
> **a.** *Computer sales have been rising over the last few years.*
>
> You can use the **present perfect continuous** form of the verb when there is *no result now* because the situation is still continuing. The situation began at some point in the past and is still continuing now, but it is considered to be *temporary*.
>
> present tense of auxiliary *to have* + past participle of main verb
>
> **b.** *Computer sales have risen over the last few years.*
>
> You can use the **present perfect simple** form of the verb when there *is* a result now ('sales are high') and the situation has finished ('the period of increase has stopped'). There is, therefore, a *permanent* result. (Even if the writer is wrong, and sales continue to increase in the future, the important point is that *today* there is a result which *the writer considers* to be permanent.)

2.4 **Study Figure 2 below. Tick the sentence which best describes the trend in book sales.**

a. The number of printed books sold **has been steadily declining**. ☐

b. The number of printed books sold **has steadily declined**. ☐

c. The number of printed books sold **is steadily declining**. ☐

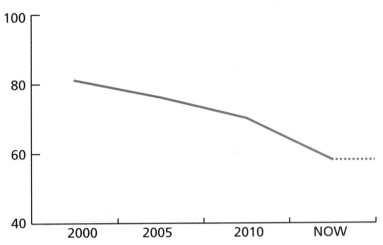

Figure 2: Sales of printed (non-electronic) books in UK (millions)

2.5 **Study Figure 3 below. Tick the sentence which best describes the trend in car sales.**

a. The number of electric cars sold **has been steadily increasing**. ☐

b. The number of electric cars sold **has steadily increased**. ☐

c. The number of electric cars sold **is steadily increasing**. ☐

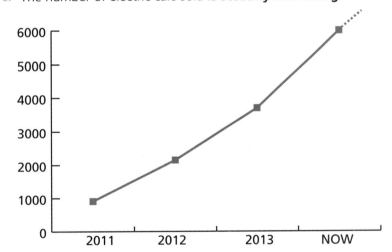

Figure 3: Sales of electric cars in UK

Describing graphs

Subject	Verb	Adverbial phrase
Oil production	increase / grow / rise / recover / improve ↗	sharply steadily gradually slowly slightly rapidly
	decrease / fall / decline ↘	sharply steadily gradually slowly slightly rapidly
	plunge ↓	rapidly
	fluctuate ∿	slightly greatly
	peak ∧	at (e.g., 74%)

Subject	Verb	Complex noun phrase		Headword	
There	is / was has been	a	sharp / steady / gradual / slight	increase	in oil production.
			strong / steady / slight	growth	
			sharp / steady / gradual / slight	decrease / decline	
			sharp / steady / slight	fall	

Grammar note: To discuss the amount of change, use *by*. For example:
Between 1965 and 1970, oil production in Saudi Arabia increased by about 60%.
Verbs which describe changes are usually used in the active form.

2.6 Study Figure 4 below and read the paragraph. Fill in the gaps in the text, choosing from the tables on page 229. (There are more words in the tables than you will need and you may need to change the form of the verbs.)

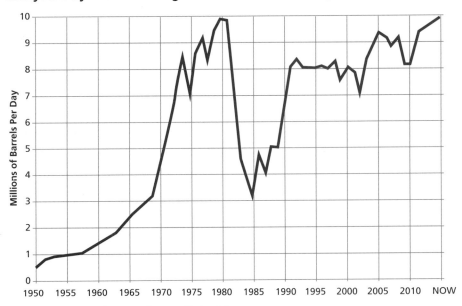

Figure 4: Oil production in Saudi Arabia

Saudi Arabia has not always been a rich country. In 1932, when King Abdul Aziz unified most of the country, the main trade was in dates and milk, and Saudis were poor. The King decided to invest in the country, which gave the American company, Aramco, the opportunity to conduct oil explorations. As Figure 4 shows, oil production changed the fortunes of Saudi Arabia's economy in the second half of the 20th century; it is clear that _____ _____ _____ _____ in oil production between 1950 and 2010, and it _____ _____ _____ ever since that date. Between 1959 and 1974, Saudi Arabian oil production _____ _____ _____ 8.5 million barrels. Between 1974 and 1980, oil production _____ between 7 million and 10 million barrels. Between 1980 and 1985, _____ _____ _____ _____ _____ the production of oil from 10 million barrels to 3 million barrels; this was a deliberate policy to try and keep world oil prices high. After this period, production _____ again; it _____ _____ 8 million barrels by 1992. Since 2002, it _____ _____ _____, currently reaching approximately 10 million barrels.

Task 3   Review

3.1 **Study the extract and figure from an essay about the history of China's stock market. It gives data as evidence, but only one figure accompanies it (Figure 5).**

1. Highlight the sentences to which the writer should have added data as evidence.

2. Fill in the gaps. Sometimes the verb is supplied after the gap to help you. For other gaps, you may find the words in boxes on page 229 helpful.

After the foundation of the People's Republic of China in 1949, the Chinese government shut down the stock market, mainly because it was considered to be a feature of a capitalist economy. In December 1978, China initiated economic reforms in an attempt to establish a 'socialist market economy', but it was not until the late 1980s and early 1990s that China rebuilt its stock market. Although the stock market in China does not have a long history, it _____ rapidly _____ the 1990s and 2004.

By 2005, the government _____ _____ (*relax*) the rules which separated different categories of investors, and the free market economy _____ _____ (*become*) more highly developed; this situation _____ (*signal*) a turning point in China's stock market. Encouraged by additional factors, such as the appreciation of RMB, excess liquidity and public companies' good performance, the stock market _____ _____ _____ 2005 _____ 2007, as shown in Figure 5. The Shanghai Stock Exchange (SSE) Composite Index _____ _____ 6400 points in October 2007.

Faced with such a rapidly rising stock market, economists expected the Shanghai Index to reach 10,000 points. Unfortunately, this boom time ended with the sudden levy of stamp duty tax and the unexpected global subprime mortgage crisis. The index _____ to less than 2,000 points _____ December 2007 and December 2008, with a _____ of 65%. (Leijonhufvud, 2007).

Year (data correct on December 31ˢᵗ)

Figure 5: SSE Composite Index

Appendix C: Referring to academic sources

As you become a more advanced writer, you will need to support your ideas with factual details and examples from other sources. If you do not provide evidence from written sources, your reader will not know whether your ideas are rooted in academic research, and will not therefore be able to trust what you write. Accurate referencing is essential if you want to achieve success in your academic writing.

Task 1	Sentence types for citing sources

There are three main ways of citing sources.

1. Paraphrase or summarize the source text. Put a full stop. Add the author name and date in brackets. Add a comma between the name and date.
    a. *Workers' opinions about their bosses give useful information about their management style. (Knights and Wilmot, 2007).*

2. Put the citation at the beginning of the sentence, followed by a comma.
    a. *According to Jones (2009), older residents' attitudes towards living spaces must be taken into account.*

    subordinator   reporting verb

    b. *As Kellaher (2001) asserts, older people do not want residences which look different from other people's homes.*
    Note: *As* here means *'in the way that'*

3. Use a reporting verb + *that* clause:

    reporting verb   verb clause

    a. *Li (2007) states that the government should increase the corporate tax rate.*

    or verb + noun phrase

    reporting verb   noun phrase

    b. *Allen (2006) highlights the wide variety of Chinese economic indicators.*

1.1 Read the sentence. Rewrite it as sentence Types 2a, 2b, 3a above.
Workers' opinions about their bosses give useful information about their management style. (Knights and Wilmot, 2007).

1. According to _____. (Type 2a)
2. As _____. (Type 2b)
3. Knights and Wilmot (2007) _____. (Type 3a)

1.2. Read the sentence. Rewrite it as sentence Type 3b above.
There are two competing teaching approaches: the 'empty vessel' and the 'progressive'.
Jones (2010) _____

1.3 **Read the sentences and rewrite them as sentence Types 2a, 2b, 3a or 3b, according to the prompts.**

1. People transform their house into a home by the way they use, decorate and adapt it. (Clough, 2004). (Type 2b)

   _____

2. Residents do not have a sense of home, because of the inappropriate design of their housing. (Clough, 2004). (Type 3a)

   _____

3. There is a direct link between the design of a building and older residents' attitudes towards it (Wilmot, 2009). (Type 3b)

   _____

4. Older people focus on the personal and social meaning of home rather than aspects of design. (Peace, 2006). (Type 2a)

   _____

Task 2	Reporting verbs

Reporting verbs allow you to show how you interpret the sources which you have read. There are many different reporting verbs which express different meanings.

The present simple tense is used even if the source cited was published some years ago. This shows that the views of the author are still valid and have not been disproved by subsequent research. As you learnt in Unit 3B, it is also possible to use the present perfect to report the result _now_ of an activity in the past.

2.1 **Read the sentences. Match the reporting verbs in bold with the correct definitions from the table below. Then tick the correct column ('+ _that_' or '+ noun phrase').**

1. The global Climate Research Council (2004) **states** that the amount of carbon dioxide has increased by approximately 25% since the Industrial Revolution.
2. Research by Tribal et al. (2006) **shows** that elderly people would rather stay in the home in which they brought up their children.
3. Kendig (1999) **suggests** that the current provision and design of age-specific housing fails to meet the emotional and physical needs of older people.
4. Tagore (2006) **reports** that farmers in southern Ghana are constantly developing new ways of coping with difficulties.
5. Fathman and Whalley's (1990) research **confirms** that the correction of errors by re-drafting texts is an important technique for improving writing skills.
6. Zamel (1985) **highlights** the need for praise and encouragement rather than negative student feedback.

You think that the original author ...	Reporting verb	+ _that_	+ noun phrase
... makes an idea more prominent			
... expresses something clearly and strongly			
... tentatively puts forward an idea			
... gives a clear, written account of a situation			
... provides facts or information to prove that something is true			
... states that something is definitely true, possibly by providing further evidence			

Grammar note: It is common in academic writing to use an abstract or concrete noun phrase as the **subject** of a reporting verb: for example, ***This essay*** suggests that …; Smith's (2009) ***findings*** reveal that …

2.2 **Match more reporting verbs in bold with the correct definitions in the table below. Then tick the correct column ('+ *that*' or '+ noun phrase').**

1. Hyland and Hyland (2006, p. 4) sensibly **conclude** that the consideration of form and content as separate entities in the research is of 'dubious theoretical value', not accurately reflecting what happens in real practice.
2. Ferris (2004) **argues** that learner preferences for error correction, as identified by Radecki and Swales (1988), should not easily be dismissed.
3. Kellaher (2001, p. 15) **has found** that people do not want age-specific dwellings 'which loudly declare their special nature'.
4. Tekere et al. (2003) **investigate** the reasons why expenditure on general support measures fell from $13,471 in 1995 to $10,610 in 1999.
5. Popper (2002) **believes** that academic knowledge in scientific disciplines results from observation and analysis.
6. Boody (2011) **discusses** the effectiveness of management practices within certain multinational companies.

You think that the original author …	Reporting verb	+ *that*	+ noun phrase
… has discovered something			
… states that something is true, giving clear reasons, even though others may not agree			
… writes about a subject in depth			
… decides that something is true (after considering all the information)			
… is sure that something is true			
… tries to discover the truth about something			

Task 3 — Present simple or past simple

In some situations, a writer can use the past simple with a reporting verb:
- to focus on the chronological stages of the research process; to tell a story or narrative.
- to show that the original author's ideas are now considered to be outdated and old-fashioned, and have been superseded by more modern research.

3.1 **Study the pairs of sentences and choose the correct reporting verb to complete each one. Use the correct tense of the reporting verb: present simple or past simple.**

1. calculate / estimate
   a. Brown (2004, p. 56) _____ that the number of storm days per month during the winter increased from 7 to 14 in 2003.
   b. Predictions are often inaccurate, but the IPCC (2003) _____ that the increase in the Earth's average surface temperature relative to 1991 will be within the range of 1–3.5°C by the year 2100.

2. mention / emphasize
   a. Seacott's research (2008) _____ that the three main indicators of global warming are temperature, precipitation and sea level.
   b. In his introduction to the subject, Brown (2003) only briefly _____ that the local innovation projects in Uganda had not been successful.

3. agree / disagree
   a. Smith (2001) states that there is strong evidence that global warming is increasing, and Jones (2002) clearly _____ that this is highly likely.
   b. Smith (2001) stated that there was strong evidence for criminal activity, but Sutton (2002) strongly _____ that this is the case.

4. claim / maintain
   a. According to Maslin (2004), the climate change expert, sceptics falsely _____ that every data set showing global warming has been corrected or adjusted to achieve a desired result.
   b. Maslin (2005) impressively _____ that this fact is itself part of the scientific process, whereby knowledge and understanding moves forward incrementally.

5. hypothesize / explain
   a. In the 1890s, early scientists such as Arrhenius and Chamberlin _____ that 'human activity could substantially warm the Earth by adding carbon dioxide to the atmosphere' (Faulkner, 2000: 197). However, it was only in the 1940s and 1950s that modern technology was able to show that this was indeed the case.
   b. Smith (1997) _____ the importance of local people's participation in community projects.

6. assert / deny
   a. De Witt (2010) rightly _____ that one of the major obstacles to dealing with the problem of climate change is cost, or more importantly perception of cost. Indeed, it may cost as much as 2% of world GDP.
   b. Salvesen (2011) _____ that the experiment had been a failure.

3.2 **Look at the adverbs below and find them in the sentences in 3.1. Why has the writer used these adverbs?**

briefly	clearly	strongly	falsely	impressively	rightly

Appendix D: Sample student essay

Essay A
This is a student essay, with errors which have been marked by a teacher. See page 238 for a key to the 'error correction' symbols.

> **Discuss the benefits of adopting a low-carbon economy.**
>
> R PV PL AR PL
> The government exposes many country to/risk of energy security and global warming. They
> M CL
> urgently/move to a low-carbon economy. In general,/three main reasons for adopting a low-
> P
> carbon economy: economic development, fighting global warming, and energy security.
> S/V
> A low-carbon economy not only help to fight against global warming but it creates
> WO AR AR VOC
> opportunities also for the employment and strengthens the national competitiveness. Such as,
> AR
> /results of a green economic recovery program show that/United States create two
> AR T
> T
> million jobs since it adopt a lower-carbon economy (Pollin, R.,et al. 2008). A low-carbon
> M WF AR LW IF M AR
> economy/stimulus/employment market./A low-carbon economy/help to protect/environment,
> VOC
> especially in reducing carbon dioxide (CO_2) emissions, they cause serious global warming
> PL T INF
> problem. In recent years, CO_2 emissions increased dramatically. As you can see in Figure 1,
> T VOC
> in pre-industrial times, CO_2 is relatively stable at under 300 ppm. But, over the last 250
> T T VOC
> years, CO_2 levels rose dramatically by nearly 100 parts per million (ppm). They peak by
> IF/CL
> 390ppm in the year 2000. There are two causes should be responsible for this increase in
> CO_2 emissions: human activities and the high population numbers.
>
>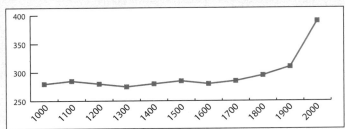
>
> **Figure 1: CO_2 levels (parts per million) 1000–2000 CE**
>
> R/IF
> The third reason for adopting a low-carbon economy is that the government should
> PV IF LW
> guarantee energy security. Energy security is of great importance,/it directly affects the
> LW
> sustainability of the development of the national economy./Most countries rely on fossil
> VOC IF
> fuels. They are non-renewable. In the long term, most countries are exposed to great risks.
> P R/IF PV PL
> Renewable energy is an irreversible trend and the government should promote it in business
> PL
> and household.
> VOC R/IF PV S/V T
> For summary, the government needs to rebuild old-style economies because it was heavily
> reliant on non-renewable natural resources, especially on a narrow range of carbon-intensive
> M VF
> sources. The need for a low-carbon economy/encourages renewable energy research and
> IF IF T VOC
> promotion. The future will be different if/research was carried out. So, adopting a low-
> carbon economy is necessary for most countries.

Essay B

This is a corrected and rewritten version of the essay. The changes have been highlighted and, in addition, there are references to the relevant units from the book, so that the grammar point can be revised if necessary.

Discuss the benefits of adopting a low-carbon economy.

Many countries are exposed to the risks of energy security and global warming. They urgently need to move to a low-carbon economy. In general, there are three main reasons for adopting a low-carbon economy: economic development, fighting global warming and energy security.

A low-carbon economy not only helps to fight against global warming but it also creates opportunities for employment and strengthens national competitiveness. For example, the results of a green economic recovery program show that the United States has created two million jobs since it adopted a lower-carbon economy (Pollin, R., et al. 2008). A low-carbon economy can stimulate the employment market. Furthermore, such an economy might help to protect the environment, especially in reducing carbon dioxide (CO_2) emissions, which cause serious global warming problems. In recent years, CO_2 emissions have increased dramatically. As can be seen in Figure 1, in pre-industrial times, CO_2 was relatively stable at under 300 ppm. However, over the last 250 years, CO_2 levels have risen dramatically by nearly 100 parts per million (ppm). They peaked at 390ppm in the year 2000. This increase in CO_2 emissions is caused by human activities and the high population numbers.

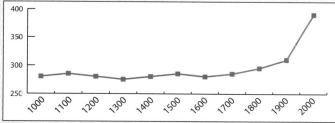

Figure 1: CO_2 levels (parts per million) 1000–2000 CE

The third reason for adopting a low-carbon economy is that energy security should be guaranteed. This issue is of great importance since it directly affects the sustainability of the development of the national economy. However, most countries rely on fossil fuels, which are non-renewable. In the long term, these nations are exposed to great risks. Renewable energy is an irreversible trend; therefore, it should be promoted in businesses and households.

In summary, old-style economies need to be rebuilt because they are heavily reliant on non-renewable natural resources, especially on a narrow range of carbon-intensive sources. The need for a low-carbon economy will encourage renewable energy research and promotion. If this research is carried out, the future will be different. Therefore, adopting a low-carbon economy is necessary for most countries.

Error correction symbols

?	meaning unclear
Λ	missing word(s)
AR	article
AV	use active voice
C	noun is countable
CL	clause construction
IF	information flow
INF	language too informal
IR	irrelevant information
LW	linking word
M	modal verb
P	punctuation

PR	preposition
PV	use passive voice
R	redundant word(s)
S/PL	singular or plural change needed
S/V	subject–verb agreement
SP	spelling mistake
T	tense
U	noun is uncountable
VF	verb form
VOC	vocabulary choice
WF	word form
WO	word order

Index

Page numbers in **bold** refer to entries in the *Glossary of grammatical terms*.

a / an (indefinite article) 220, 223
abstract nouns **7**, 181–7, 192–3
academic citations 232–5
active voice **7**
adjectival clauses (relative clauses) **9**, 48, 200–18
  defining vs. non-defining clauses 211–15
  embedding and reduction 200–3, 205, 215
adjectives **7**, 46–7, 222
adverbs **7**, 13, 69–70, 72, 131, 133, 147–8, 209–11, 214–15, 235
agreement **9**, 13, 20–3, 26, 30
although / even though 109–11
always 72
argument, development of 145–51, 165–6, 191, 233–4
articles **7**, 220–5
as 105–7
as a result of 119–20
aspect. *see* tense and aspect
auxiliary verbs **7**, 13–14, 90, 91–2, 95
  modal verbs **8**, 130–7, 145–52, 155, 166–8, 171, 174–5
bar charts, description of 190–1, 195–7
bare infinitive ('zero' infinitive) **8**, 15, 60, 136, 172
bare nouns ('no article' nouns) 220–3
be 16, 62, 136
because 105–7
because of 121
beliefs, discussion of 187–9
besides 89
both … and 89–91
can 135–6, 155, 167
change, description of 26–7, 227–30
citing academic sources 232–5
clauses **7**. *see also* linking words
  embedding and reduction 48, 200–3, 205, 215
  order of information 173–4, 192–3
  relative clauses **9**, 48, 200–18
  simple clauses **9**, 29–34
  subordinate clauses **9**, 104–16
commas 112, 212
complement **7**, 34
complex noun phrases **7**, 31, 40, 45–50, 180, 192–3, 195–7

complex sentences **7**, 29, 104–26. *see also* simple sentences
compound sentences **7**, 29, 84–9, 116–17
conclusions 144, 159
concrete nouns **7**, 181
conditional sentences **7**, 154–77
connected vocabulary 44–5, 180, 193
continuous infinitive 188
could 155, 167
countable nouns **7**, 23–5, 184–6, 221
critical thinking 83
data, describing 190–1, 195–7, 226–31
defining relative clauses 211–12
deletion 51, 95, 205, 215
despite 118–19
determiners **8**, 41
do (auxiliary) 13–14, 16, 139, 140
due to 121
either … or 92–3
embedded relative clauses 48, 200–1, 211
emphasis 21, 89–95, 109–11
'empty' words 51, 95
essay structure 81–100, 103–27
  citations 232–5
  conclusions 144, 159
  describing data 190–1, 195–7, 226–31
  introductions 75–8, 146, 150
  order of information 40–58, 173–4, 192–3
  paragraphs 96–8, 147–8
  planning and preparation 145–8, 165–6
  thesis statements 146, 150
even though 109–11
eventually 89
few / a few 21
finally 89
first conditionals 154–60
first-person pronouns **8**
formal style 11–13, 87, 95, 180–97
generalizations 17, 135–6, 221
geographical terms 223
gerund 28, 118
have to 137–42, 144
headwords 31, 33
how long …? (duration) 71–4
if clauses (conditionals) **7**, 154–77
impersonal sentence structure **8**, 11–13, 17–18, 180–97

impersonal verbs 187–9
impossible events 169–75
in order that / in order to 113–14
in spite of 118–19
infinitive **8**, 15, 60, 114, 134, 136, 172, 188
information flow 40–58, 173–4. *see also* essay structure
  adding emphasis 21, 89–95, 109–11
  citing academic sources 232–5
  connected vocabulary 44–5, 180, 193
  describing changes and transitions 26–7, 227–30
  describing data 190–1, 195–7, 226–31
  describing duration 71–4
  describing permanent / regular events 13–17, 27
  describing purpose 113–16
  describing simultaneous events 107–9
  generalizations 17, 135–6, 221
  giving advice and recommendations 141–4, 158–60
  giving reasons for situations 68–71, 112, 115–16, 119–21
  giving supporting evidence 96–8, 122, 156–7
  introducing new information 18–20, 40–5, 210–11, 220
  prediction and evaluation 154–7, 163–75, 191
  reporting opinions and beliefs 187–9
  stance and argument 145–51, 165–6, 233–4
  summarizing old information 172–3, 192–3
~ing 27, 28, 118, 188
intensifiers 131, 148–9
introductions 75–8, 146, 150
irregular verbs **8**, 62, 65
likely events 154–62
linking words 81–100, 103–27
  paired linking words 89–95, 112–13
  sentence-connecting words 86–9
  short linking words 83–6
  subordinators 104–16
little 210

meaning 130–51
  advice and recommendations 141–4
  conditional sentences **7**, 154–77
  developing arguments 145–51, 165–6, 191, 233–4
  generalizations 17, 135–6, 221
  intensifying meaning 131, 148–9
  necessity, importance and obligation 137–41, 142
  opinions and beliefs 187–9
  possibility and uncertainty 132–4, 154–75
modal verbs **8**, 130–7, 145–52, 155, 166–8, 171, 174–5
much / many / a lot of 23
must 139–40, 142

need to 137–41, 142, 144
negative sentences 13–14, 21, 60, 61, 139–40
  linking words 93–5
neither … nor 93–5
new information, presentation of 18–20, 210–11, 220
'no article' nouns ('bare' nouns) 220–3
non-defining relative clauses 211–15
not only … but also 91–2
nouns **8**, 40–50, 180–7, 192–5
  abstract nouns **7**, 181–7, 192–3
  complex noun phrases **7**, 31, 45–50, 180, 192–3, 195–7
  countable nouns **7**, 23–5, 184–6, 221
  geographical terms 223
  linking words 118–22
  person-based nouns **8**, 20–2, 181, 194–5
  simple noun phrases 40–5
  uncountable nouns **10**, 23–6, 184–6

objects **8**, 23, 32–3, 204–9
obligation 142
opinions, discussion of 187–9
ought to 137–9, 141–2

paired linking words 89–95, 112–13
paragraphs 96–8, 147–8
passive voice **8**, 51–6, 136–7
past perfect 170, 226–7
past simple 59–61, 63–7, 164, 234–5
perfect bare infinitive 134, 172
permanent events 13–17, 27
person-based nouns **8**, 20–2, 181, 194–5
plurals **8**, 17
possessive relative pronoun 208–9, 213–14
possibility 132–4, 154–68

prepositional phrases **9**, 47
prepositions **8**
present continuous 26–9, 188, 227
present perfect 59, 61–4, 68–78, 227
present simple 13–17, 51–6, 227, 234–5
probability and possibility 132–4, 154–68
pronouns **9**, 42
  first-person pronouns **8**
  possessive 208–9, 213–14
  relative pronouns 200, 204–5, 208–9, 212
  second-person pronouns **9**
  third-person pronouns **10**, 12
punctuation **9**, 100–1, 112, 117–18, 212
purpose linking words 113–16

quantity expressions **9**, 20–3, 25
questions 13–14, 32, 60, 61, 131, 138, 140

relative adverbs 209–11
relative clauses **9**, 48, 200–18
  defining vs. non-defining clauses 211–15
  embedding and reduction 200–3, 205, 215
relative pronouns 200, 204–5, 208–9, 212
reporting verbs 71, 233–5
results, presentation of 112, 115–16, 119–20, 226–31

second conditionals 163–8
second-person pronouns **9**
semi-colons 100–1, 117–18
semi-modal verbs **9**, 137–52, 166–8, 174–5
sentence-connecting words 86–9
short linking words 83–6
simple noun phrases 40–5
simple sentences **9**, 29–34. *see also* clauses; complex sentences
simultaneous events 107–9
since 105–7
singular nouns **9**
so that / so as to 113–14
so … that / such … that 112–13
stance and argument 145–51, 165–6, 233–4
statistical evidence, presentation and interpretation 190–1, 195–7, 226–31
style, formal vs. informal 11–13, 87, 95, 180–97
subject–verb agreement **9**, 13, 20–3, 26, 30
subjects **9**, 30–2, 34, 95
subordinate clauses 9, 104–16
subordinators 9, 104–16, 121
such as 122

summary nouns 183–7, 192–3
superlatives 222
supporting evidence 96–8, 122, 156–7

tense and aspect
  continuous infinitive 188
  modal verbs 134, 136–7
  past perfect 170, 226–7
  past simple 59–61, 63–7, 164, 234–5
  perfect bare infinitive 134, 172
  present continuous 26–9, 188, 227
  present perfect 59, 61–4, 68–78, 227
  present simple 13–17, 51–6, 227, 234–5
that 207, 210, 212
the (definite article) 221–3
there is / there are 18–20, 210–11
thesis statements 146, 150
third conditionals 169–75
third-person pronouns **10**, 12
time 66–7
  describing changes and transitions 26–7, 227–30
  describing duration 71–4
  describing past events 134, 170, 172–3, 174–5
  describing permanent / regular events 13–17, 27
  describing simultaneous events 107–9

uncertainty 132–4, 155
uncountable nouns **10**, 23–6, 184–6
unless 158–60
unlikely events 163–8

verbs **10**, 114. see *also* tense and aspect
  auxiliary verbs **7**, 13–14, 90, 91–2, 95
  impersonal verbs 187–9
  irregular verbs **8**, 16, 62, 65
  modal verbs **8**, 130–7, 145–52, 155, 166–8, 171, 174–5
  reporting verbs 71, 233–5
  semi-modal verbs **9**, 137–52, 166–8, 174–5

warnings 158–60
whereas / while 107–9
word order 34, 70, 72
  conditionals 157
  linking words 89–92
  modal and semi-modal verbs 131–2, 137–8
  questions 13–14, 60, 61, 131, 138

zero article 220–3
zero conditionals 161
zero infinitive **8**, 15, 60, 136, 172